RECENT PHILOSOPHIES
OF
EDUCATION IN INDIA

By the same author

1. Western Educational Thinkers (with *Akhilesh Chaube*)
2. Psychology of Adolescents in India
3. आधुनिक सामाजिक मनोविज्ञान के मूल तत्व (Fundamentals of Modern Social Psychology)
4. किशोर मनोविज्ञान के मूल तत्व
5. कुछ पश्चिमी देशों और भारत में शिक्षा : उद्देश्य, महत्व और विषय-विस्तार
6. बाल विकास मनोविज्ञान के मूल तत्व
7. सामान्य मनोविज्ञान के मूल तत्व (Fundamentals of General Psychology)
8. सामान्य मनोविज्ञान के मूल तत्व

About the Author

Prof. S.P. Chaube (*b.* 1919) retired as a Professor of Education and Dean, Faculty of Education, University of Gorakhpur in 1979. After doing his M.A. from Banaras Hindu University and M.Ed. from Allahabad University, he earned his Ph.D. in Education from the University of Indiana, USA. Lucknow University conferred on him the degree of D.Litt. in 1965. Also Prof. Chaube received the G.J. Watumull Memorial Award and the Banerji Research Prize in 1963 and 1965 respectively.

Dr. Chaube has more than 50 books to his credit in the fields of Education and Psychology, both in Hindi and English. Many of his books are taught as textbooks in several universities in the country.

RECENT PHILOSOPHIES OF EDUCATION IN INDIA

S.P. Chaube
Retired Professor of Education and Dean,
Education Faculty, University of Gorakhpur, U.P.

CONCEPT PUBLISHING COMPANY, NEW DELHI-110059

Cataloging in Publication Data—DK
Courtesy: D.K. Agencies (P) Ltd. <docinfo@dkagencies.com>

Chaube, S. P. (Sarayu Prasad), 1919-
Recent philosophies of education in India / S.P. Chaube.
p. cm.
Includes bibliographical references (p.)
Includes index.
ISBN 8180692167

1. Education—India—Philosophy. 2. Educators—India—Biography.
3. Philosophers—India—Biography. I. Title.

DDC 370.109 54 21

ISBN : 81-8069-217-5 (P.B.)

First Published 2005

Published and Printed by
Ashok Kumar Mittal
Concept Publishing Company
A/15-16, Commercial Block, Mohan Garden
New Delhi-110059 (India)

Phones : 25351460, 25351794
Fax : +91-11-25357103
Email : publishing@conceptpub.com

PREFACE

Many of the points that should have been discussed here in this preface have been purposely given in the first chapter entitled "Scope and Objective" of this book. So we are necessarily being very brief here. In this volume we have described the major educational ideas of some great personalities of our country who have been the makers of modern India by consistently endeavouring all through their lives to bring India to its own in the comity of nations. These great souls had very rightly realised that in spite of vicissitudes of historical event and centuries of foreign domination India has succeeded in maintaining its own culture and essentials of its basic spirit. What is that culture and what are those essentials? The educational philosophers chosen herein for discussion have very clearly highlighted these essentials and the spirit, and accordingly have suggested inspiring and constructive ideas on which education in our country should be patterned. It is very much hoped that a perusal of this volume will inspire our leaders and planners of education to adopt the much needed course for rejuvenating the youths of the day to make India stronger and stronger day by day according to our accepted democratic set-up.

It has been really a pity that a study of our educational philosophers has long been neglected in the universities of our country. But happily, now the idea has dawned upon the framers of the courses in education that a study of our own educational philosophers will provide the much needed light for finding the path towards the coveted direction for the proper growth of our young men and women. It is hoped that a study of this work will be helpful in understanding what our educational philosophers have to offer for strengthening the roots of educational edifice in terms of the essentials and the basic spirit of our culture which will always be colouring our personalities.

It is difficult to claim any originality in a work of this nature. But some of the interpretations and evaluations of the educational ideas of the thinkers herein chosen for study have been the author's own. So some marks of originality may be perceptible in these alone. Perhaps, the same will arrest the attention of the reader.

The author expresses his gratitude to the writers and publishers of the sources from where he has freely drawn in the preparation of this work. These have been listed in the bibliography appended at the end of the book.

Karma Bhumi,
B-955, Sector A,
Near New Railway Crossing,
Mahanagar,
Lucknow-226006 (India)

S.P. Chaube

CONTENTS

1

THE OBJECTIVE AND SCOPE INTRODUCTORY

With the dawn of the nineteenth century we step into the modern period in India, during which the Marathas, the Sikhs and the Nawabs were subjugated and the British supremacy was established throughout the whole length and breadth of the country. During this period the government was transferred from the East India Company to the Crown after the revolt of 1857. Law and order was established in 1858. A uniform system of administration, law and coinage was gradually developed. Under the British rule, India realised a political unity which it had lost for many centuries. It was also brought into contact with European civilization and culture.

From about the middle of the eighteenth century, a darkness prevailed over the spiritual horizon of India, and for about a century her own civilization and culture remained at the lowest ebb. During this dark period, because of lack of patronage, all indigenous arts died, many old works of arts languished due to ignorance and neglect, and in no language literature of first rate importance was produced. The ushering in of a completely different civilization in the form of British influence gave a set back to all creative work for a time. Hence, the Indian mind began to feel enamoured by all things Western. This was an uncritical admiration of the Western on the part of the Indian mind which became contemptuous of things of native origin. Consequently, the Indian mind was thrown out of balance. Even the devastating foreign invasions, the destructions and the forceful conversions made by conquerors in the medieval era could not produce a result of this nature.

However, there were already certain hidden forces which were working towards a great renaissance which was revealed in its full vigour during the first quarter of the present century. Of course, the most important of these forces was English education which brought the Indian youth in contact with Western science, literature and history. Thus the intellectual isolation of the Indian youth was broken. Consequently, there took place a great mental expansion in India in the same manner in which the revival of classical learning during the fifteenth and sixteenth centuries infused a new spirit in all walks of life of the European nations. The Indian students in schools and colleges were dazzled by a world of new ideas. So far the majority of the Indian students studied extravagant mythical geography, pseudo-science and legendary history. Now the Indian students came face to face with the sober and correct facts about the shape of the earth, unalterable laws of nature and the rise and fall of nations. As a result of this new knowledge, many of the Indian ideas and customs which were regarded as a decree of God appeared as the folly of man. Some of the social evils, such as, the caste system, child marriage, enforced widowhood, untouchability, infanticide, *Sati, Devadasi,*[1] *Purdah* (veil system) and the prohibition on travel abroad began to lose their tyrannical grip on the minds of the people. Happily, reformers came forward who were determined to remove these evils from the society.

Along with the new knowledge, the influence of Christianity has also been a great factor in the ushering in of a new era in our country. The early Christian missionaries made fierce attacks on Indian religions and ways of life. However, it may be noted that the zealous Christian missionaries who unfailingly pointed towards the faults and evils of some Indian social institutions were both crusaders and educators. These missionaries opened schools and colleges where they imparted the new secular knowledge and taught that Christianity was the only religion which could bring salvation. These two forces worked together to produce in the minds of the educated classes either a complete scepticism or a partial leaning towards Christianity. They also served as whips to awaken Indian culture and civilization from its prolonged slumber. Consequently, the innate vitality of the nation asserted itself with full vigour and the people became conscious of their glorious past.

At first in this revival there appeared to be an inclination of compromise but gradually this tendency was transformed into a feeling of defence. The feeling that Indian culture and religion had been very powerful civilizing influences throughout the ages, grew stronger in the minds of the Indians and it restored their self-respect and self-confidence. This feeling was further strengthened by the labours of such orientalists as Sir Charles Wilkins, Sir William Jones, Monier Williams, Colebrooke, Muir, Wilson and Max Muller who brought to light the treasures of Indian wisdom and civilization to the educated people of Europe and India through their translations of ancient Sanskrit literature. Later the work of archaeologists, epigraphists and art-critics like James Fergusson, Dr. Buhler, Dr. Fleet, Havell and Dr. Ananda Coomaraswamy revealed the glory of the ancient monuments in the country. These works filled the Indian people with pride about their past.

But it will be a mistake to think that the above external forces alone were responsible for bringing in a period of Renaissance in our land. It must be remembered that these forces were coupled with our own inherent vitality of a long spiritual tradition. So there appeared a number of reformer saints, scholars and educators who tried to purify some of the social customs and traditions by condemning the evils existing in our society. We may particularly mention the names of Raja Ram Mohun Roy, Justice Ranade, Swami Dayananda, Mrs. Annie Besant, Pandit Madan Mohan Malviya, Sir Syed Ahmad Khan, Ramkrishna Paramhamsa, Swami Vivekananda, Sri Aurobindo, Rabindranath Tagore, Mahatma Gandhi and a host of others. These great personalities made an analysis of our various problems and focused the attention of the people on the essentials, urging them to ignore the non-essentials. Many of them confirmed the efficacy of the ancient truth by their own personal experiences and placed them before the people with a force which could never be ignored. Moreover, some of these great personages even carried the unique message of India to Europe and America. Consequently, our culture today is undoubtedly, as fresh as in any other period of its history. Now we do not harbour the fear that it will be engulfed by Christianity or Western civilization. It has outlived the invaders' oppression of the medieval period and the Christian propaganda of the modern period. Now it is alive to stand with any other force of the world as a friend and ally in a common cause of guaranteeing peace to humanity.

It will be interesting here to touch some of the other important forces that caused the emergence of such personalities as Mahatma Gandhi, Tagore, Sri Aurobindo and others included in this study.

The impact of British domination and Western civilization began, to be clearly realized in India by the beginning of the present century. The Indian youths brought up under the discipline of British education in the country and abroad experienced for the first time a compelling urge for political freedom and economic emancipation. When they came in contact with Westerners they felt greatly indignant at the treatment meted out to them. The national humiliation that they had thus to face abroad and also at the hands of the alien rulers at home made them think of their own nation, their own language, culture and spiritual heritage. The establishment of the Indian National Congress towards the close of the preceding century gave an added impetus to these reactions in an organised form which resulted in an unconquerable tide of the *Swadeshi* movement. In fact it was in the wake of this movement that the organised voice of the nation against political suppression and economic exploitation became louder and more effective. Hence, the leaders in the country became alive to the burning national problems and interests, and they thought to strive for the revival of those traditional spiritual values which had distinguished India throughout the ages. It was this atmosphere generated by the *Swadeshi* movement which may be regarded as generally responsible for creating a love for everything Indian, may it be culture, educational system, philosophy, arts or crafts, etc.

Another powerful factor that gave rise to the educational thinkers like Vivekananda, Tagore, Mahatma Gandhi and others has been the sense of frustration born out of the imperialistic exploitation of the economic resources of the country and a consequent underdevelopment of Indian industries and agriculture. The educational philosophers chosen in this study well recognised that the educational system in the country should be geared to generate forces for affecting a rapid economic growth and solving the problem of unemployment and underemployment. Above all, they also wanted that this new educational system should enable the Indian youth to imbibe his own cultural heritage and not to be led away by those forces of the modern, materialistic civilization which are prone to create spiritual bankruptcy. Towards the fulfilment of this purpose, they thought to base education in the cultural roots of the country and make it, at the same time, more technical and vocational so that the cottage and agro-industries in the country might be better rehabilitated. Mahatma Gandhi's Basic Education has largely been focused to these objectives. Almost all the educational philosophers have tried to draw the attention of the nation towards these aspects of the educational system. They have, therefore, emphasised the introduction of a system of education which, while providing adequate opportunities for a harmonious development of the pupil's personality may also give proper place to an education which ensures subsistence and economic independence.

Besides, the Indian people were becoming averse to the existing system and content of education which aimed at producing office assistants and clerks for running the mighty British government machinery. It was mainly as a revolt against this pattern of education that some of the leading social thinkers of the period raised their voice. The modern renaissance in education in India may largely be ascribed to these feelings of revolt against the ills of the existing system.

Lastly, we may, also, mention some of the sociological forces that were militating against each other. Some of the age-old traditional social evils, such as caste system and untouchability, etc., were ruthlessly criticised by national leaders like Swami Dayananda and Mahatma Gandhi. It was for the eradication of these evils, amongst others, that some of them chose to reform the system of education by making it more suitable to the changing social aspirations of all the castes and classes of Indian community. Hence, they tried to re-orient it towards the establishment of an egalitarian society.

The above forces culminated into a kind of revivalism and adjustment between the East and the West which touched almost all the aspects of our national life. There have been new developments in the areas of art, literature, science[2], social arrangement and manners, politics, education and many others. In all these spheres our country has produced great personalities who could be valued by any progressive nation in the world. But our aim in this study is to give a short account only of those great men and women who developed a philosophy of education for bringing India to its own. It is true that the thinkers chosen herein for discussion have ennobled other spheres of our life as well by their monumental efforts, but here our scope is limited to the educational sphere alone.

The Objective

The present study has been conceived because of the envisaged need of exploring the educational philosophies of some of India's recent thinkers who have influenced, not only India's educational thoughts and practices, but also the life of Indian people in various respects and who have contributed immensely to the regeneration of the country. The necessity of exploring this aspect is borne out of the conviction that the prevailing system of education in India can be put on a more satisfactory and sounder foundation if we build the superstructure of Indian education on the basis of India's cultural and spiritual heritage, wherein lie the roots of the present generation. The spirit of Indian civilization and culture which has been evolved through the ages, has largely found its expression in the life-works of some of the modern Indian thinkers and reformers, such as Dayananda, Vivekananda, Mrs. Annie Besant, Sri Aurobindo, Tagore, Mahatma Gandhi and others.

For the purposes of the present study we have chosen only these six prominent thinkers who have left indelible imprints on the educational trends of the country. It may be made clear at the very outset that the object of the present study is not so much to emphasis the inadequacies and omissions of the above philosophers as to analyse and evaluate their positive contributions and to throw light on the impact they made on the educational thought in India. It may, however, be mentioned here that the extent to which these various ideologies have been implemented and given shape by their followers has not been taken into consideration as it would have involved an examination of the values and stands of their followers who have tried to put them into practice as they thought best. For instance, we have not examined the different aspects of the various institutions brought into existence in the wake of their orientation, such as, the *Gurukula*, Viswa Bharati, Basic Education Scheme, Pondicherry Ashram Schools, Institutions run by Sri Ramkrishna Mission and Theosophical Society Schools etc., which profess to follow respectively the educational ideologies of Dayananda, Tagore, Mahatma Gandhi, Sri Aurobindo, Vivekananda and Annie Besant. Undoubtedly, a probe into their workings would have been a very interesting study, but this would have diverted us from our major purpose.

In this study we have tried to see how far the basic teachings of these philosophers can help us to wipe out the malaise that exists in our present system of education. It appears that mankind is running an incessant race towards the goal of materialistic prosperity in utter disregard of spiritual values which sustain life on a superior plane. In fact, this imbalance between the ephemeral matter and eternal spirit has been, to some extent, responsible in the modern times for many an ill in the world. These great thinkers have tried to awaken mankind towards the inherent dangers of over-emphasising mundane occupations and have drawn attention to the need to inculcate higher spiritual values in the very system of education so as to lead the would-be generations on the path of permanent peace. It is with the object of bringing out clearly the magnitude of this impact made by these thinkers in the sphere of education in general, and in particular, in India, that the ninth chapter entitled "What we can Imbibe" has been envisaged. An attempt has been made in this chapter to show the extent to which the ideologies and teachings of these philosophers can be incorporated in order to establish a better system of education which may provide more adequate opportunities to the future generation for the growth of well-balanced personalities. It, indeed, has not been our purpose to provide a critique of the current system of education in the country and to suggest any new pattern of education re-organised on the basis of their teachings.

The Scope

In the second chapter we have concentrated upon the ideals of education that should be adopted in India so as to ensure an unhampered growth of the individual and society. In fact, it has unmistakably been these ideals which have inspired our educational thinkers.

From the third chapter we start the discussion of the various philosophies of education as propounded by the different thinkers. For instance, we have taken up for our discussion Swami Dayananda who is supposed to be one of the pioneer social reformers in India during recent times. Swami Dayananda expounded, in his own unique way, the fundamentals of Vedic civilization and gave a new interpretation to the ancient spiritual values for the regeneration of modern India. He stood for re-orientation of Indian education on the basis of Vedic culture and civilization.

The fourth chapter pertains to Swami Vivekananda who was moved by the sad plight of the teeming millions in the country, suffering from the want of bare necessities of life. As a great protagonist of the Vedanta (a philosophy of life based on the major Upanishads) he declared that the Vedanta in India must be able to feed its starving people. He was grossly disappointed at the lethargy and incapacity of his people and tried to create in them a sense of self-confidence and self-reliance. He also spoke of the spirit that should guide the system of education in India, for he believed that education was the basis of regeneration of any society.

In the fifth chapter we have taken up Mrs. Annie Besant. Though an Irish by birth, she regarded India as her motherland and hence sacrificed herself for its emancipation. Consequently, she developed a penetrating insight into the various needs of India. It is towards the fulfilment of these needs that she thought of an educational system suited to our national requirements. Throughout her whole life she struggled to establish national institutions for educating the Indian youth on the basis of her cherished Indian traditions. She advocated a system of education based on the fundamental principles of religion, Indian culture, history and ancient literature. She aimed at infusing in the students a spirit of patriotism through her national scheme of education. We have analysed her educational philosophy and the methods suggested by her to reform the Indian educational system.

In the sixth chapter we study Sri Aurobindo who devoted the forty years of his life for regeneration of spiritual India. Through his various writings, he tried to give a new orientation to Indian philosophy and culture, and by his unique re-interpretations of the same he struggled to give new hopes to mankind. In consonance with his conviction about Supermind and Integrated Yoga he developed a new method of education.

The seventh chapter pertains to Mahatma Gandhi. There has hardly been any one of modern times who has done more than what Mahatma Gandhi did for the regeneration and emancipation of India. He identified himself so much with the soul of India that he could feel the pulse of the nation. Very truly, he is regarded as the Father of the Indian nation. He wanted to make India great so that it might give to the world the message of peace, non-violence and truth. Accordingly, he developed a philosophy of life and believed that it would help him realise his cherished goal for the benefit of all mankind. In consistence with his philosophy of life he thought of a philosophy of education which could serve as a basis for education in this country. He was convinced that education in India had become purely theoretical, bereft of practical and vocational bias necessary to solve some of the burning socio-economic problems of the country. He, therefore, wanted to give a new bias to education by relating it to activity. Mahatma Gandhi has given to the nation the idea of reorganising Indian education on the basis of what he called as Basic Education.

In the eighth chapter we study Rabindranath Tagore who endeavoured towards the renaissance of India mainly through his literary writings both in Bengali and English.

Tagore had grown disillusioned with the sophistications and artificial values of the so called modern civilization. He wanted to go back to nature and guide the youth of the country in the manner in which the ancient *Gurus* (preceptors) did in their *Ashramas* (forest-schools). In the modern age when man is being gradually relegated to oblivion in the face of a scientific civilization based on materialistic values, Tagore raised his voice and established the superiority of man over everything else—so much so that he held that even God needs the assistance of man for His Full Realisation. Such is the unique humanism of Tagore. It is in the context of this supreme humanism that he wanted to guide the youth so that the latter may reach his own destiny.

It is believed that the outstanding features of educational

philosophies of Indian thinkers can make valuable contributions to the various aspects of our educational system. So, in the ninth chapter entitled "What we can Imbibe", we have undertaken to analyse what we can basically learn from reorienting education, particularly in India, from the philosophies of education as advocated by the thinkers herein chosen for discussion.

NOTES

1. The custom of maintaining a dancing girl in the temple on the plea of her being dedicated to the deity. This custom specially prevailed in some parts of Southern India.
2. "In the great forward movement of India in our day, which is so universally acclaimed, there is nothing more outstanding than the part her sons are taking in science and scientific research, and some of the most notable advances in physics, mathematics and the biological sciences have come from Indian Workers. Among them the names of our Indian F.R.Ss—Raman, Saha, Sahni, Krishnan, Bhaba, Bhatnagar—are known over the world of science and have added luster to India even outside the domain of science"—Field Marshal Smuts (in his message to the special meeting of the Royal Society held in New Delhi on January 3,1944).

2

IDEALS OF EDUCATION IN INDIA

For more than a century powerful forces have been operating resulting into changes of far-reaching significance in various countries of the world. Though the pace of these changes has been rather slow in the underdeveloped countries like India, yet we cannot fail to observe a large number of developments that have taken place in modern times even in these countries. The underdeveloped regions of the world are passing through a transition in their traditionally rigid social, economic and cultural institutions under the impact of modern science and technology. Consequently, there is a move towards reorganisation of the outmoded socio-economic institutions in the light of modern national requirements. A happy tendency has also been noticed in older countries, like India, to come out of the abyss of traditional seclusion. However, it cannot be said that all that is ancient or traditional is worthless. In fact, howsoever, a country may progress in the material sense, it cannot progress in the real sense, bereft of its past wherein lie its roots. One of the main and dominating characteristics of Indian philosophy of life and therefore of education has been the all pervading spirit of higher values of life transcending the very concept of mundane opulence or grossly materialistic acquisitions. The flame of these spiritual values has been kept alive through the course of history even amidst devastating storms that swept the country. It is, indeed the radiance of the flame of spiritualism that has illumined and glorified the life and actions of the people of this land through the ages. Hence, in any development of the country, in any direction, this fundamental truth has got to be inevitably kept in mind. In brief, we may say that the modern edifice of Indian economic prosperity, social reorientation and cultural renaissance has got to be built on the bed-rock of Indian spiritualism which have stood many a tide of political vicissitudes and destructive upheavals caused by the marauding conquerors during the darkest days of its history.

Our Constitution showed the path to a new orientation, but it has still to be put into practice in many aspects of our social, moral and intellectual life. At present we are inclined towards the achievements of modern science and technology and are gradually using scientific methods of productions in order to achieve an accelerated economic growth, yet we should not lose sight of the limitations of science in solving all human problems. Along with its achievements and powers to conquer and unravel the mysteries of nature, science has also placed incredible powers in the hands of man, which, if not properly used, might annihilate all that is known as human civilization from the face of the earth. It is, therefore, an imperative need of the hour that humanity should be saved from total destruction and the vast store of knowledge which man has accumulated since times immemorial should be preserved for the benefit of the posterity. This could only be accomplished through the right type of education. The role of education cannot be over-emphasised in bringing about this reorientation so essential for the welfare of mankind. This naturally brings us to the question of the personality of the educator and the role he should play as a leader of the society. The personality of the educator should be shaped in accordance with the educational requirements of society and the aspirations and ideals of the nation so that he may play his role of social leadership more effectively. So long he is capable and worthy of playing this role effectively and is actively engaged in discharging his duty towards posterity, we can always look towards future with faith and with a sense of security of our fundamentally essential values and requirements. The difficulty arises only when the educator is either incapable of or reluctant to play his full role and leaves the posterity to its doom like a rudderless boat. So education must accept the moral responsibility of nurturing the young in such a way as to make them capable of living in a world marked by global interdependence. For furthering the development of the emerging democracy in India, the young must be taught a new concept of social welfare in terms of rights, responsibilities, and loyalties befitting an ideal democracy. We must be prepared to recognise and organize bold institutional adjustments if democracy is to be developed without any hindrance in the country. We have already established in India the rule of law, and a democratic system of Government based on the sanctity of human personality and the fundamental rights of the individual. Happily, all these principles have been enshrined in the Indian Constitution.

India is a democratic republic and stands for justice, liberty, equality and fraternity. Hence we have to produce in our country citizens inspired with the spirit of liberty and justice, having complete faith in the values of equality and fraternity. In fact, it is being increasingly realised that education can play a most significant role in the national integration and unity and in the development of a society free from the distinctions of caste, creed, sex and regionalism. So our children are to be nurtured on a philosophy of life which enables them to imbibe the true spirit of democracy and inspires them to work towards the promotion of international peace which is one of the Directive Principles of our Constitution. From these we should derive our faith and ideal working philosophy of life.

Evidently, for achieving the above aims we must consider education as a creative process. Education should not be considered merely a method for adjusting to all environments. It must be an agency to bring about a desirable social change—as Dewey says:

> *"The school cannot immediately escape from the ideals set by prior social conditions. But it should contribute, through the type of intellectual and emotional disposition which it forms, to the improvement of those conditions."*[1]

Our educational institutions must undertake this responsibility. The whole background of Indian philosophy of life suggests that this world is a perpetual procession of events in which men continue to march on the journey of life. Education has to enable us to prepare ourselves for that march and enthuse us with the dynamism necessary for our progress. In fact, education has to raise the standard of the people in all the walks of life and enable them to reach the lofty heights of advancement.

Since the advent of independence, our educational problems have taken new shapes; we are now required to consider the wider responsibilities of education at all the stages, primary, secondary and university. Leaders in education are now supposed to give guidance in the rights and duties of citizenship, democratic living and behaviour, and vocational preparation.

Education, must be of all kinds—general, literary, scientific, technical and vocational. All these aspects of education are to be fitted into a specific kind of social order which has been in broad terms contained in the preamble to our Constitution. To teach the specific meanings and to provide concrete educational situations where these means can grow in the lives of our young are the major goals still to be achieved.

The very conception of democracy implies that education should mean the growth of the individual. What type of growth do we want for our democracy? We want the individual to be a good citizen:

> *"Who will have sense enough to judge of public affairs, discernment enough to choose the right officers, self-control enough to accept the decisions of the majority; honesty enough to seek the general welfare rather than his own at the expense of the community; public spirit enough to face trouble or even danger for the good of the community".*[2]

Hence our ideal of education is to realise the potentialities of the individual in the above context. Here we must remember that the individual is not to be treated as a means because, in fact:

> *"The individual, the particular, is the end; society, the universal, is the means. The supreme aim of education is the enrichment of the life of the individual, and the social inheritance is only a means to that end."*[3]

Thus our educational ideal should be that of treating the individual as an end, as was the case with our ancient system of education in which a student was considered as an end and education aimed entirely at the fullest development of the individual. The society served as a means to enable the individual student to achieve his educational objectives. In the modern times also we should keep this basic fact before us while shaping our present educational system. In the succeeding chapters we shall see that our recent educational philosophers in India have always insisted on adherence to this ideal.

One of the most important educational problems today is to resolve the conflict between science and humanism. The homogeneous union of science and culture is the condition of human survival today. Students of arts and sciences today do not find a common ground for anchorage and inspiration. They do not appreciate each other's point of view. Many of our educated youths are ignorant of a large section of the world's common cultural heritage. If world peace is to be preserved, we must be able to produce young men who are imbued with great human values and do not suffer from want of faith in man. "The faith in man" is one of the greatest lessons that Indian culture is capable of giving. We have to promote this ideal in our youth. Our philosophy of education must help us to resolve the conflict between science and humanism.

We shall see in this study how Indian educational reformers have tried to resolve this conflict. Our educational institutions from now on must be able to infuse in the students the ideas of constant progress, because life is dynamic and ever changing. The danger of dogmatism, isolation, and stagnation is writ large in the sufferings of the Indian people and in the pages of Indian history. Now we are to endeavour to rise above this narrow seclusion. Education in our country, as indeed anywhere else, should help in this great endeavour. In India this is possible only if our ideals of education are made consistent with the essentials of Indian philosophy of life. Then alone we can hold our own in the face of the possible dangers of the modern civilisation.

In the present work we see that the educational reformers in our country during the recent times have always tried to put the ideals of education at par with our Indian philosophy in such a way as to meet the demands of the day. Speaking on aims of education, Maritain says:

> *"It is to guide man in the evolving dynamism through which he shapes himself as human person—armed with knowledge, strength of judgement, and moral virtues while at the same*

time conveying to him the spiritual heritage of the nation and the civilisation in which he is involved, and preserving in this way the century-old achievements of generations."[4]

The ideal of education in India must fall in line with this concept of education. In order to convey to the future generations the full meaning and implications of the spiritual heritage of the nation and of the ancient civilisation, we must enable them to see an integrated picture of the whole universe. This means that the pupil must be able to see unity in diversity. He must understand that there is an essential unity in all human endeavours.

> "*In a democratic society authority and leadership in education, as in Government, are not supposed to be lodged in the hands of any ruling group—hereditary, military, ecclesiastical, or economic. It is the very essence of democratic theory that authority and ultimate control in all public affairs should be transferred from all such limited groups to the people as a whole.*"[5]

Our Constitution recognizes that education is the obligation of the state until the child is 14 years of age. But this should not be confused with the authoritarian governmental control of educational policies and practices. Speaking of democratic education, Kallen says that it is:

> "*A continuing process from birth to death; subordinates transmitting the past to creating a future different from the past; makes precept a function of practice; exalts variations over repetition and encourages the free co-operation of differences to displace the regimented reproduction of identicals; prefers the doubt, the enquiry, the experiment of competitive co-operation competition of the sciences, the obedient credulity and unrequesting rehearsals of dogmatic faith.*"[6]

Here is a true picture of democratic education which may be adopted for India as one of the ideals of education. Evidently, educational institutions should not become mere agencies of the government. In a democratic State the teacher should be as free to believe in and write on controversial matters as any other citizen. To refuse to consider teachers at par with other citizens in such matters will amount to abusing democracy and maintaining a group of dogmatists who will poison the minds of the younger generation. Happily this situation does not exist in our country.

Education of the child in democratic India should be rooted in the cultural heritages of the land in terms of both the past and present with the main aim of making a new and great future. The present is not always the same. So the school begins to die both emotionally and intellectually when it ignores the needs of the present community.

> *"Man and society are conceived, as interrelated. It is this concept which reinforces the belief that the curriculum of the schools should he developed in relation to the nature of the community, and that education is not preparation for living but life itself. It is this concept which stresses the continuity of education and the belief that education goes on through life."*[7]

Thus it is with this conviction that we should conduct our education so that the people and the country may ever be on the path of progress according to the demands of democracy.

In the subsequent chapters we shall see how the educational philosophers in our country have strived to strengthen the roots of education in order that the people may work towards progress in terms of perfect individual growth which is nonetheless the real demand of democracy.

NOTES

1. Dewey, J., *Democracy and Education,* p. 160.
2. Bryce, J., *Promoting Good Citizenship*, p. 3.
3. Childs, J.L., *Education and the Philosophy of Experimentalism,* p. 88.
4. Maritain, J., *Education at the Crossroads,* p. 10.
5. Childs, *op. cit.*, p. 27.
6. Sidney Hook quoted in *Education in Modern Man*, p. 112.
7. Progressive Education Association : *Progressive Education Advances,* p. 11.

3

SWAMI DAYANANDA (1824—1883)

His Life

Swami Dayananda was born in the native state of Morvi in Kathiawar, Gujarat in 1824. His first name was Mulaji or Mul Samkar. His father's name was Amba Samkar, an orthodox Brahman and a devotee of Lord Siva. Mul Samkar's sacred thread ceremony was held when he was eight. His education in Sanskrit began when he was only five. He had an extraordinary memory and could memorise several parts of the Vedas and Panini's Sanskrit Grammar when he was only fourteen. During the fourteenth year the first crisis in his life occurred when he watched a rat crawling over the idol of Lord Siva in a temple. He doubted whether that idol could be the great Deity. He urged his father to clear his doubts but was not satisfied with his father's explanation. This incident was a turning point in the life of Mul Samkar and consequently he decided to fight against idol-worship. Thus at the age of fourteen Mul Samkar became determined to make a all out attack on idol-worship in his later life, and the Arya Samaj founded by him disregarded the experiences and feelings of millions of Hindus by this attack. In fact, this feature of the Arya Samaj has been both its strength and weakness.

During his boyhood, occurred the death of his sister and uncle whom he loved most. These incidents were most painful to him and he decided to attain salvation through *Yoga* and thus conquer death. He continued his studies with redoubled zeal. His parents, after knowing his mind, decided to get him married but Mul Samkar ran away from home and later became a *Sanyasi*[1] and changed his name to Swami Dayananda.

After renouncing the world, Swami Dayananda wandered from place to place for over fifteen years in search of truth and knowledge. During these years he came in contact with people of all ranks and castes, rich and poor, princes and priests. He was very unhappy to see that, the so called custodians of the Hindu traditions, learning and religion had degenerated to a deplorable degree. He found Hindu society torn into numerous factions and castes. Dogmas, superstitions and inventions of the selfish priesthood had tarnished the fair name of the Hindu religion. So he took upon himself to bring to his people the noble traditions and beliefs of the ancient times. He decided to prepare himself to accomplish this task, and for this he practised *Yoga* and studied the Vedanta philosophy. Moreover, he became most restless to find a real *Guru* after his own heart. In Virajananda of Mathura he found a *Guru* of his aspirations in 1862. Virajananda made clear to him his (Dayananda's) mission in life. He taught him to dedicate his life to the dissemination of truth and to wage a war against the falsehood of Pauranic[2] Hinduism and to bring back the true teaching of the Vedas.

Swami Dayananda left his *Guru* in 1863 and devoted his next twelve years to the preparation for the arduous task before him. During this period he visited various places in Northern India; and in Bengal he met the leaders of the Brahmo Samaj—Maharshi Debendranath Tagore and Keshab Chandra Sen. He could not be converted to the Brahmo Samaj beliefs and parted company with them and proceeded to Bombay. He, however, accepted a suggestion, from the Brahmo Samaj leader Keshab Chandra Sen, to deliver his lectures in Hindi and not in Sanskrit. This enabled him to come in direct contact with people amongst whom he gradually became more popular. By establishing the Arya Samaj on April 10, 1875 in Bombay, he gave a definite shape to his movement. He declared the official creed of the Arya Samaj as :

1. All true knowledge comes from God. He is the cause of everything. Everything should be regarded as His.
2. To God alone worship is due, because He is All-Knowledge, All-Truth, All-Beautitude, Incorporeal Just, Unbegotten, Almighty, Merciful, Unchangeable,

Infinite, Immortal, Without a Beginning (*Anadi*), Incomparable, Omniscient, Eternal (*Sanatana*), Imperishable, Holy, Supreme, Exempt from Fear, Lord of All.

3. It is the duty of every Arya, to learn, teach and preach the Vedas.
4. One should not be afraid of declaring untruth as untruth and truth as truth. The truth should be accepted and untruth renounced.
5. It is only after a thorough consideration of right and wrong that all actions should be performed, i.e., actions must conform to virtues.
6. The Arya Samaj wants to improve the physical, social and spiritual condition of mankind.
7. Love and justice should guide one's conduct. Due regard should be paid to one's merits.
8. Ignorance should be eradicated and knowledge disseminated.
9. One can be happy only when others are happy, so one's prosperity should be considered as included into that of others.
10. In personal matters one may enjoy freedom to act but in matters which concern the general social well-being, one should discard all differences.

Thus Swami Dayananda tried to base his creed on universally accepted axioms. However, he went still further. He, being deeply versed in the Vedic learnings, regarded the Vedas as the divine revelation. He, therefore, accepted them as the source of all knowledge and tried to prove that even some of the modern inventions were mentioned in them. Sri Aurobindo Ghose has defended Dayananda's contentions by asserting that :

> *"There is nothing fantastic in Dayananda's idea that Veda contains, truth of science as well as truth of religion. I will add even my own conviction that Veda contains other truths of a science the modern world does not at all possess, and in that case Dayananda has rather understated than overstated the depth and range of the Vedic wisdom."*[3]

It should be noted that Dayananda was not a Hindu fanatic. He fully realised the value of studies in comparative religions. So he did not want his supporters to follow him blindly. He did not attack Hinduism alone. He resisted and attacked evils wherever he found them. The Christian missionaries and his Mohammedan friends, unfortunately, could not understand that Dayananda was not a reformer of Hindu religion alone, but a lover of mankind and world redeemer. Dayananda says :

> *"Though I was born in Aryavarta (India) and live in it, yet just as I do not defend the falsehoods of the faiths and religions of this country, but expose them fully; in like manner, I deal with the religions of other countries. I treat the foreigners in the same way as my own countrymen, so far as the elevation of the human race is concerned."*[4]

Thus he wanted to eradicate the evils which existed in Hinduism and other faiths that were prevalent in India at that time. He was not intolerant to those who followed other faiths. The Swami himself declared :

> *"The Arya Samaj was meant to be, and is an essentially Hindu organisation. Yet it is open to everyone regardless of caste, colour or nationality, who subscribes to its principles and desires to be enrolled as a member. Once a member, he has all rights and privileges of a member whether he is a Hindu or not."*[5]

He rightly realised that the cause of Indian's sufferings was disunity. So national, social and religious integration of India became an ideal—very dear to his heart. For this purpose he, wanted to abolish the foreign rule, eliminate the caste and class distinctions, and integrate India on the basis of religion by substituting the Vedic religion in place of the various sects and beliefs that had disintegrated the people into a number of splintered groups. For fulfilling this purpose he dedicated his whole life. After the establishment of Arya Samaj in Bombay he devoted his time mainly in organizing its branches in various places in the country and in translating the Vedas into Hindi and writing a Hindi commentary of *Rig Veda.*

In 1878, Colonel Alcott and Madame Blavatsky proposed a union of the Theosophical Society and the Arya Samaj; Swami Dayananda consented. The leaders of the two movements had many meetings and exchange of views, but differences arose and in 1881 the two groups decided to remain separate. Swami Dayananda died in Ajmer at the age of fifty-nine on October 30, 1883. The tribute paid by the Theosophist, the official organ of the Theosophical Society on the premature death of the Swami, is worth quoting here as it highlights the profound impression that the Swami created on the minds of the Theosophists and it also hints at his life work:

> *"We bear in mind but his life-long devotion to the cause of the Aryan regeneration, his ardent love for the philosophy of his forefathers; his relentless, untiring zeal in the work of the projected social and religious reforms ... He threw, as it were a bombshell in the midst of the stagnant masses of degenerated Hinduism and fired, with love.for the teachings of Rishis and Vedic learnings, the hearts of all who were drawn within the influence of his eloquent oratory..."*[6]

Dayananda considered superstitions of dogmas as impediments to the forces of progress. So he decided to bring about a social regeneration on the basis of *Vedas*. A deep study of the *Vedas* had convinced him that it was wrong to believe that English education and Western ideas alone could give a person progressive ideals. So he raised the voice "Back to the *Vedas*". By giving a call to the nation to go back to *Vedas,* he, in fact, wanted to check the growing tendency of materialism and a kind of blind imitation of the Western civilisation which was increasingly catching the fancy of our younger generation. Swami Dayananda, therefore, emphasised the study of the *Vedas*, the *Upanishads*, the *Gita,* the tenets of Manu and other ancient literature so as to imbibe the spirit of true Indian civilisation.

Swami Dayananda condemned idol-worship and priestcraft, which in his opinion, had led to the degeneration of Hinduism. He wanted to re-establish the Vedic religion for social reconstruction in the country. But reconstruction of the Indian society was not possible without studying the prevailing conditions in the country. The British rule had brought into existence certain new forces, which had to be studied, and only then rejected or accepted on merits. So the educated Hindus began to study critically the environment in which they were placed. The problem before them was how to achieve a synthesis between old and new and a fusion of the best ideas of the East and the West so that a regeneration of India might be effected. This was the problem which Dayananda and the Arya Samaj took to their hearts to solve. Towards the attainment of this ideal the Arya Samaj made an all-round attack on the prevailing evils of Hindu society, viz. caste-system, untouchability, child marriage, the enforced widowhood system, and degenerating bondage of the womenfolk. The Arya Samaj regarded education as one of the means for regenerating India and it wanted to base this education on the Vedic traditions. For this the Samaj adopted various methods such as lecturing, discussing, intelligent persuading, widow remarriage, eradicating untouchability and social distinctions based on caste and sex, etc. We are not dealing with all these measures except the educational philosophy that the Samaj adopted for the regeneration of India. Therefore, we shall restrict our discussion only to this feature of Dayananda's work. His educational philosophy, very naturally, originates from his Vedic Philosophy. So, in order to understand his educational ideas, we must first understand his Vedic philosophy.

Dayananda's Vedic Philosophy

To Swami Dayananda the four *Vedas* are the words of God. He regarded them as flawless and an authority in themselves. He thought that the *Samhita* alone comprises the *Vedas*. The Brahmanas, the six *Vedangas*, the six *Upangas*, the four *Upavedas* and the eleven hundred and twenty-seven *Sakhas* offer only expositions of the Vedic texts. Hence, he regards these as secondary sources. These should be considered reliable insofar as they agree with the teachings of the *Vedas*. Therefore, he considers the *Vedas* as a determinant of right conduct. According to him the *Vedas* are not to be studied for the sake of study alone, but because they help in determining the right conduct.

"Those who are desirous of knowing righteousness should ascertain it from the Vedas. What is righteous and what is not cannot be rightly determined without the help of the Vedas ..."[7]

The *Vedas* form one and the main of the four determinants of right conduct :

"First the Vedas; second the Smritis made by master minds and in agreement with the Vedas such as Manusmritis; third the conduct of the righteous person which has come to us as traditions from the beginning of the Universe, i.e., conduct enjoined by God through the Vedas; fourth, that which conforms with our conscience, e.g. truthfulness..."[8]

It is noteworthy that much against the practices of the orthodox group of people, Swami Dayananda wanted to make the *Vedas* available to all. He considered every one worthy of studying them. In his opinion:

"... All persons should read and hear the Vedas, increase their knowledge, accept good things, quit bad habits, and be happy ... Does not God want to do good to the Sudras? Is God so partial that he permits the reading of the Vedas only to the twice born and not to the Sudras? Had God designed to prohibit teaching in the case of the Sudras, he should not have endowed them with tongues and ears. Just as God has made the earth, water, fire and air, the moon, the sun, and other objects for all, similarly he has revealed the Vedas, too, for all..."[9]

Swami Dayananda holds that God permeates the whole universe. He is a personification of *Sat, Cit,* and *Ananda* (Existence, Knowledge and Bliss). He is Formless, Infinite, and Almighty. He creates, sustains, and dissolves the universe. He gives to all souls the fruits of their deeds according to absolute justice.

Swami Dayananda holds that the soul is immortal and eternal. Its capacity for knowledge is limited. It has consciousness and feelings of pleasure and pain.

God and the Soul are two distinct entities. They have both similar and dissimilar attributes and characteristics. They cannot be separated from each other, because they are related to each other as the pervader and the pervades. *Prakriti* (Nature) is the material cause of the universe. According to the Yoga system of philosophy, Swami Dayananda believes that God, the Soul and *Prakriti* are *Anadi* (beginningless). They and their attributes are eternal. The creation of the universe is the natural exercise of the creative energy of God. Due to ignorance the soul is in bondage in this world. This ignorance is the cause of sin. Out of ignorance man is deviated from the truth and he does so many things which he should not do, *e.g.* he worships material objects instead of God. Salvation lies in the emancipation of the soul from pain and suffering and in the employment of extreme happiness. According to Swami Dayananda the enjoyment of extreme happiness is *Svarga* (Heaven); and *Naraka* (Hell) is the undergoing of sufferings. He believes that Heaven and Hell are here on this earth, and they are not separate *Lokas* (worlds) as conceived by *Puranas* (Hindu mythologies).

To Swami Dayananda, religion (*Dharma*) means bringing into practice equitable justice in terms of truthfulness in thought, word and deed (*Mansa, Vacha* and *Karmana*). He feels that *Artḥa* or wealth should be righteously acquired. The wealth that is obtained by foul means is *Anartha* (sin), *Kama* is the enjoyment of legitimate desires by means of the wealth honestly obtained. Merits alone should determine one's class and order, *i.e. Varna* and *Ashrama*. The wise and the learned are *Devas* (righteous people). Therefore, Devapuja (honour and devotioṇ) should be offered to the wise and the learned, to one's mother and father, to the teacher, to a ruler showing justice and righteous conduct, to those who lead honest lives, to women who are faithful to their husbands, and to the men who are faithful to their wives. The foolish and the ignorant should be regarded as *Asuras*,[10] the wicked and the sinful as *Raksasas*[11] and filthy in habits as *Pisachas*.[12]

Swami Dayananda regards marriage as a union between a man and a woman through mutual agreement according to the laws specified in the *Vedas* and *Sastras*. He, however, mentions that *Niyoga* is a temporary union between a man and a woman for the raising of issue to be accepted only in unavoidable circumstances.

Swami Dayananda believes that one may attain salvation through the worship of God, the performance of righteous deeds, the acquisition of true knowledge, by practising *Brahmacharya* (celibacy), and by keeping the society of the wise, the learned and the virtuous. He recognizes three stages in the worship of God—*Stuti* (glorification), *Prarthana* (prayer) and *Upasana* (communion, meditation). *Stuti* means praising the attributes and powers of God in order to develop love for God. *Prarthana* stands for praying to God so as to obtain the highest knowledge and other boons. *Upasana* is directed towards having a direct cognition of God. In this process one has to conform to the Divine Spirit in holiness and purity and in feeling His presence in one's heart through the practice of *Yoga*. Each of these three stages of worship are classified into either *Saguna* and the *Nirguna*. In the *Saguna Upasana* one resigns oneself to God and His will, and finds Him as having attributes that are in harmony with His nature. In the *Nirguna Upasana* one resigns oneself to God and His will and regards Him as devoid of attributes that are not akin to His nature.

Swami Dayananda says that there are sixteen *Samskaras* (sacred ceremonies) in a man's life. These are those rites which contribute to the physical, mental and spiritual development of man. Hence everyone must observe these rites. But nothing should be done for those who are dead.

Swami Dayananda commends *Agnihotra* (fire-offering) because it acts towards the purification of air and vegetation and helps the well-being of all sentient beings. He places *Yajna* (worshipping) and *Tirtha Yatras* (visiting sacred places) on a moral basis and does not regard them as belonging to the realm of rituals. He recommended that *Yajna* should include showing due respect to the learned and wise people and in the application of the principles of chemistry and physical sciences to the various domains of life and in the spread of culture and knowledge. He thinks that *Tirtha Yatras* should not be regarded as going to sacred places of land or water. In fact, *Tirth-Yatras* are the means by which the ocean of misery may be crossed. They comprise of acquiring true knowledge, to practise of truthfulness in speech, living in the society of the wise, spreading of knowledge, performing of various kinds of good deeds and following the principles of *Yamas*.[13-24]

It may be mentioned here that Swami Dayananda is not original in propounding a Vedic philosophy, which in fact, originates from the existing *Vedas*. He has simply tried, according to his own understanding and convictions, to bring out a truer interpretation of the *Vedas* in order to regenerate the modern Indian society. In this context he speaks also of the kind of education which should be given to the children in this country so that the foundation of society may be laid on a stronger ground as the ancient Aryan forefathers in India envisaged. The ideals and the processes of education as laid down by him are really based on his Vedic philosophy as we shall study shortly. Hence what he says about education is not fundamentally different from the type of education which generally existed in the ancient *Gurukula* or the forest school of India. However, he does give a reorientation to the same in the light of the needs of the modern society as he could see them. Here we analyse the ideas and processes of education as have been advocated by Swami Dayananda. This account is based on his book *Satyartha Prakash,* first published in 1882, an epitome of all he stands, for as a reformer of the modern society.

Education According to Swami Dayananda—Swami Dayananda's Major Stands in Education

Before we begin to study Swami Dayananda's views on education in detail, it will be helpful to mention here in brief the points that he specially emphasises in the education of boys and girls. In their education, amongst other things, he has laid stress on parents' role, religious and moral training, chastity and *Brahmacharya* (celibacy), personal hygiene, the study of *Vedas, Upavedas, Vedant, Shastras* and *Upanishads*, fatherly relations between the teacher and the student, abandonment of foreign language in favour of the mother tongue as the medium of education. State responsibility for education from the primary to the highest stage, location of schools and colleges amidst natural surroundings away from the allurements of city life. We shall study how Swami Dayananda has advocated the cause of education according to his line of thinking. For obvious reasons we may not agree with some of his views, but it will be difficult to discard all of them. There can be no denying that he, as a true emancipator, looks at all the aspects of human life and has considered education as a true remedy for many social evils. We have to appreciate the way in which he struggled for the regeneration of India and should imbibe the spirit he evinced.

Parents, the First Educators

Swami Dayananda has laid stress on the 'education' of the individual even at the time of a child's growth in the mother's womb. He believes that:

> " ... *the character of the mother influences the character of the child in the womb. Therefore, the upbringing of the child begins not at its birth but at the conception.*"[25]

Quite naturally then, Swami Dayananda believes that the hereditary influence on the child can be controlled by controlling the food taken at, during and after the time of conception, because the food taken by the mother may affect the physical and mental development of the child. He wrote in his *Satyartha Prakasha* thus:

> *"It is very essential for the mother and the father that before, during and after the conception they should avoid the use of intoxicants, liquor, foul-smelling, dry and such substances as are injurious to mental development and should take only such things as contribute towards calmness, health, strength, wisdom, energy, civility and gentleness, e.g., clarified butter, milk, sweets, and other useful substances of food and drink, so that the generative juices of the mother and the father be healthy and free from disease."*[26]

Swami Dayananda recommends that the first education of the child should be given by his mother. The mother has to see that child does not pick up any bad habit. When he begins to speak, the mother should see that he pronounces the letters distinctly with the right amount of effort and in the right place. The child should be guided to cultivate a sweet voice. When he begins to talk, he should be taught how to address his elders and how to conduct himself in the presence of others so that he may be always treated with respect. From the very beginning the parents should try to develop in children an intense love of knowledge, elevating company, and control of the senses.

Swami Dayananda has stressed on the duty of parents as regards education of their children in the following manner:

> *"To give their children the highest education possible, to instruct them in the ways of truth, to make them refined in character and manners, in short, to devote all their wealth, body and mind to accomplish this object is the paramount duty, the highest virtue, and the glory of parents."*[27]

Thus Swami Dayananda acknowledges the great role of parents in the education of the child.

The Child in the School

Swami Dayananda advises that at the age of eight children should be sent to school where persons of good character and adequate knowledge are appointed as teachers.

As long as the children are students they should abstain from the following eight types of intercourses, with the opposite sex:

1. Indulging in lascivious thoughts.[28]
2. Intimately talking about them.
3. Playing with them.
4. Looking up on them with lustful eyes.
5. Associating with them.
6. Reading or talking of libidinous subjects.
7. Embracing them.
8. Having sexual intercourse with them.

The teachers should also try to keep themselves aloof from the acts, and only then they can cultivate knowledge and good character in order to be ideal teachers. All students should be treated alike in matters of food, drink and dress, etc., and all of them should practise physical and mental discipline. Simple living and high thinking should be their motto. They should not covet bodily comforts. Their sole purpose should be to devote themselves entirely to the acquisition of knowledge and culture.

Swami Dayananda recommends that the first *Upanayana*[29] ceremony should be performed at home, and the second in the school. Parents and the teachers should teach the children the *Gayatri Mantra*[30] with its meanings thus :

> *"O Lord! O Personification of True Existence, Intelligence and Bliss! Everlasting, Holy, Allwise, Immortal. Thou art Unborn, without any symbolical distinction and organisation, Omniscient, Sustainer and Ruler of the Universe, Creator of all, Eternal, Protector and Preserver of the Universe. O All-pervading Spirit! O Ocean of mercy! Thou art the Life of the Creation. Thou art an All-blissful Being the very contemplation of whom wipes off all our pains and sorrow."*

After learning the *Mantra* with its meanings, the children should be taught the method of Divine worship (*Sandhyopasana*) with all its preliminaries and accessories such as bathing, *Achman*[31] and *Pranayama.*[32] Both girls and boys should be taught *Pranayama.* The *Sandhyopasana* should be performed in a solitary place with great concentration. It should be the responsibility of the teachers to teach children all that is necessary about diet, dress and proper behaviour towards elders and juniors.

The children should daily perform *Devayajna, i.e.*, the feeding of fire with boiled pure butter, and aromatic substances for sanitary. purposes. Swami Dayananda describes in detail the processes of the *Devayajna* and wants that the children should carefully pick up the same for practising them daily.

According to the *Manusmriti* (Chapter-III, I) Swami Dayananda wants that a student should observe *Brahmacharya*[33] and study the *Vedas* with their subsidiary subjects for 9, 18, 36 years or until they are completely mastered. Swami Dayananda quotes from the *Taittireya Upanisad* (VII, 1-4) and explains how a teacher should instruct his pupils to lead a virtuous life. The teacher should say :

> *"My children, speak the truth. Lead a virtuous life. Never be negligent in learning and teaching. Devote yourself to the*

procuring of the knowledge of physical and spiritual sciences. After making your knowledge perfect give to your preceptor anything that he needs. After this go and get married. Follow the path of truth and religion. Never neglect your health. Never be indifferent to the acquisition of wealth and power, etc. Never neglect your studies. Serve your mother, father, teacher and guest. Love virtue and shun vice. Imbibe our virtues, not our faults and imperfections. Always keep the company of learned and pious Brahmans and trust them fully. Be charitable. Give in faith or without faith. Give for fame or through shame. Give whether through fear or public opinion or simply for keeping your word. Always give. If you are even in doubt follow the virtues of those Brahmans who are free from prejudices, charitable in disposition, and well-versed in philosophy and physical and spiritual sciences, and keen to further the cause of righteousness. This is the advice, commandment and the mandate of the *Vedas*. Moreover, this is the law. Act according *to this advice. Obey this law.*"[34]

Swami Dayananda says that teachers should inculcate in the minds of the pupils the belief that it is only, after abstaining from the acquisition of wealth and from having eternal pleasures that one can attain the knowledge of true religion. In this connection he draws his authority from the *Manusmriti* and further suggests that the teachers should not neglect the education of princes, and other *Ksatriyas, Vaisyas* and *Sudras*. If all the classes of society are well educated and cultured, no one will try to set any false practice. Therefore, all persons of all classes should be given sound education and instructed in the principles of true religion.

The Principle of Physical and Mental Austerity

Swami Dayananda advocated a life of physical and mental austerity for a student. He wanted the student to lead a life of hardhood and endurance so that he may be prepared for the worst kind of future. The following words well express Swami Dayananda's point of view:

"Children should be able to understand the prospective, hardship of life, and where will they receive training for it if not in the school? ... If our young man cannot cope with the varying situations of life our educational system is to be blamed. We should so train him so as to equip him for the worse in life... A Brahmachari... is a soldier in the making. He sleeps on a hard bed, takes a coarse meal, braves the oddities of weather, lives on the bare necessities of life, eschews all temptations ... and all these help him in presenting himself as the most serviceable and self-sufficient unit in the social organism ..."[35]

As in the ancient times, Swami Dayananda wanted to extend the above principles of austerity to the mental life as well. This he wants to accomplish through the practice of *Yoga* which means:

"... a harnessing of the senses and mind from the falsely manifold objects and thoughts, and at the same time a union with the unitary blissful self..."[36]

Yoga aims at suppressing all lower activities:

"When cease the five senses—knowledge, together with the mind, and the intellect stirs not... This they consider as Yoga."[37]

Seclusion of the School Premises

Swami Dayananda wanted that an educational institution should be at least four *Kosas* or eight miles or about 12 km away from towns and cities because he wanted the students to be kept away from the distractions of city life. He apprehended that even the parents would interfere with the studies of the student if they were to see him during the period of study. Therefore he says:

"The parents should not meet their children, nor children their parents, nor should there be a communication between them, so that they might be entirely free from the cares of the world and devote themselves exclusively to their studies."[38]

The Criteria of Testing Knowledge

Swami Dayananda recommends that all that is learnt should be carefully examined by the following five tests :

1. The *Veda* and Nature of God—All that is found according to the teachings of the *Vedas,* nature and attributes and characteristics of God is right, the reverse is wrong.
2. Laws of Nature—All that tallies with the laws of nature is true, the reverse is untrue.
3. The practices and teachings of *Aptas, i.e.*, the pious and learned men.
4. The purity and conviction of one's own soul. What is good for you is good for the world. What is painful to you is painful to others. This ought to be the guiding principle of one's conduct towards others.
5. Eight kinds of Evidence, *viz.* (i) Direct cognisance, (ii) Inference, (iii) Analogy, (iv) Testimony, (v) History, (vi) Deduction, (vii) Possibility, (viii) Non-existence or Negation.

On the basis of *Nyaya Sastra*, Swami Dayananda explains the above five criteria to a great length, and believes that it is only by means of these five that one can ascertain what is true or untrue and right or wrong. He advises that teachers should examine everything that they teach to the students according to these criteria. The students should also follow this method before accepting any thing; otherwise, they will be only crammers, and not profound scholars. Teachers should examine a book by these five tests before teaching it to students.

The Scheme of Studies

1. Swami Dayananda recommended that first of all the children should be taught Panini's phonetics. It is the responsibility of the parents and teachers to teach their children and pupils to pronounce letters correctly with the right amount of 'effort' and the right 'accent'.

2. After phonetics, the children should be taught grammar which includes *Astadhyayi*, *Dhatupath* (Book of roots). *Ganapath* (book of groups); *Unadikosh* (Book of prefixes and suffixes, etc.); *Mahabhasya* (Exposition of the above four books of Panini and Patanjali)[39]. The study of grammar may be learnt in three years.
3. After grammar, the students should read *Nighantu* and *Nirukta* (Book of *Vedic Vocabulary and Philology*) written by Yask. This study should not take more than six to eight months.
4. Thereafter the students should study *Chandograntha* (prosody) by Pingal in order to learn the rules that govern poetry. This study may be finished within four months.
5. Then the students should study *Manusmriti, Valmiki Ramayana, Vidurniti,* and similar selections from *Mahabharat* in order to get rid of evil habits and become cultured. This study should not take more than a year.
6. Then the students should study six *Sastras* (erroneously known as the six Schools of Philosophy) with the expositions of *Risis*—the great ancient seers. But before studying the *Vedanta Sastras* students should learn the ten *Upanisads*. The study of all these books should be finished within two years.
7. After that, the students should study the four Vedas together with their four Brahmanas[40]. Proper attention must be paid to accents and meanings, both theoretically and practically. The study should be finished within six years.
8. After the study of the *Vedas*, the students should study the *Upavedas* (or sub-*Vedas*) which are four in number, *viz.* *Ayurveda* (medical science), *Dhanurveda* (the science of Government), *Gandharva Veda* (the science of Music), *Artha Veda* (the science and practice of mechanical arts).

Thus Swami Dayananda wanted the student to learn the nature and properties of all substances both theoretically and practically.

After the study of the *Upavedas*, Swami Dayananda wanted the student to learn *Jyotisha Shastra*, which should consist of arithmetic, algebra, geometry, geography, geology and astronomy. The students should also have all types of practical training in these sciences. It should be noted that Swami Dayananda was against the study of astrology, because he considered this science a fraud.

Swami Dayananda urged both the teachers and students to master all the sciences and arts in twenty or twenty-one years in order to become cultured for leading a happy life.

Swami Dayananda advises that both the teachers and the students should try to avoid any hindrance that comes up in the way of acquiring knowledge, *viz.*, company of wicked persons, forming bad habits, child marriage, want of perfect *Brahmacharya*, indifference of rulers, parents and learned persons for the dissemination of knowledge, over-eating, keeping late hours and sloth in learning, etc. He remarks that those Indians who are involved in such false and wicked practices are devoid of the advantages of *Brahmacharya* and education. He also attacked the sectarian selfish Brahmanas of his days because of their false teachings and attempt to keep the Ksatriyas and other classes illiterate in order to retain their selfish grip over them intact. He emphasises that it is the duty of both the rulers and the ruled to see that these hindrances are removed in order to enable the male and female students of all classes to acquire the necessary and right knowledge of truth and religion.

Dayananda on Women Education

From the foregoing account it is clear that Swami Dayananda was in favour of women education. He asserts that nowhere in the *Vedas* it is mentioned that the women are not qualified to study the *Vedas*. He believes that both men and women have equal right to education. He quotes from the *Atharva Veda*[41] to prove that girls should also practice *Brahmacharya* and receive education. He said that for conducting the affairs of the State, the administration of justice, the duties of married life both the men and women should be educated. He recommended the Brahmana and Ksatriya women to acquire all kinds of knowledge; Vaisya women to learn trade and some practical arts; and the Sudra women, the art of cooking, etc. As the men should acquire the knowledge of grammar, *Dharma* and their profession, similarly women should learn grammar, *Dharma*, medical science, mathematics and the practical arts at least which are very necessary for them for ascertaining truth, proper behaviour towards their husbands and other persons, reproducing, upbringing and instruction to their children, and proper managing of domestic affairs. Therefore, Swami Dayananda has all praise for those parents who do their best in making both their sons and daughters practice *Brahmacharya,* acquire knowledge and perfect their character in all respects.

Dayananda on Co-Education

Swami Dayananda was against co-education. He, therefore, laid down that the boy's schools should be at least two *Kosas* (four miles or 6 km) away from those of girls. He suggested that only men teachers and men servants should be allowed in a boys' school and women teachers and maid servants in girls schools. No boy above the age of five years should be allowed in a girls school and *vice versa.* Thus Swami Dayananda was not in favour of any contact between the opposite sexes during the period of school life.

> *"They should, keep themselves aloof from eight kinds of sensualities—looking at a person of opposite sex, contactual relation, private meetings, conversation, love-story telling, intercourse, contemplation of tempting object and company. The teacher should also keep them away from the above mentioned things, so that they may increase their happiness by attaining sound education, training, refined manners, good habits, and strength of body and soul."*[42]

One can charge Swami Dayananda of unnaturalness when he thus excludes the opposite sex from the life of a student—whether male or female. Its seriousness becomes all the more greater when it is noted that a student is not permitted to go home or go into the outside world for the entire period of his education.

Some Essential Features of Dayananda's System of Education

Thus, Swami Dayananda laid great emphasis on character-building by giving to the young, religious and moral training. He had no sympathy for a system of education which was divorced from this essential feature. He believed that formation of character was not possible if the students were not taught their duty to God and man.

Another essential feature of Dayananda's educational philosophy was his insistence of a long course of eighteen years arduous study by enforcing a life of celibacy. The emphasis that he lays on it is not found in the history of any other country. For a students' life he advocated *Tapasya* (penance), not indulgence; sacrifice, not selfishness; simplicity, not luxury; *Dharma,* not godlessness; service, not enjoyment; duty, not pleasure. These indeed are high virtues of character which would ultimately build the national character. At a time of history when we are passing through the turbulent times marked with greed for wealth and lust for power and a yearning for enjoyment of worldly pleasures, these virtues of service and sacrifice for suffering humanity and an emphasis on the higher spiritual values will undoubtedly go a long way in mitigating some of the glaring shortcomings of our times and thus making a healthy impact on our educational system as well.

When we look to the daily routine which Swami Dayananda prescribed for a student in a school, we find that he considered practical personal hygiene as an essential part of education. In this respect he required the student to follow the routines of a disciple in the ancient *Gurukula*, such as, rising early in the morning, daily bath, prayer and practice in *Pranayama* (deep correct breathing) and doing most things outdoor. The health of our students is sure to be better if they are urged to acquire some of these excellent habits. Thus, the practical personal hygiene may be considered as the third essential feature of Swami Dayananda's scheme of education.

In his system of education Swami Dayananda regarded the rich and the poor, the prince and the peasant, the high and the low, the Brahmana and the so called lower castes, as equal. The State should provide free and universal education not only upto the primary stage, but for all the eighteen years, *i.e.*, upto the highest stage. According to Swami Dayananda, in exceptional cases the State should give education upto the age of thirty-six or forty-eight years. Thus he gives us a unique concept of the duty of the State for educating its citizens. The elimination of all the distinctions of caste and class and sex in matter of education and the advocacy of financing education at all the stages by the State are based on fundamental principles of democratic socialism. The foundations of what we have now adopted as the socialistic pattern of society were laid more than three-fourth of a century ago by the principles preached by reformers like Dayananda. Hence, we can rightly regard that democratisation of education was a notable contribution of Swami Dayananda to the educational philosophy in India.

The emphasis that Swami Dayananda laid on the intimate relationship between the teacher and the taught on the ancient *Gurukula* pattern may be regarded as the fifth unique feature of the educational system advocated by him. He wanted that the student should find in the teacher the love of the parents, and the teacher should accept the student as a member of his family to all intents and purposes. Thus the teacher is to bestow on the student all the loving care of a mother. This, indeed, is a noble example of teachers' duty towards his pupils.

Swami Dayananda condemned the use of a foreign language as the medium of instruction. This may be accepted as another essential feature of his educational philosophy. Like a true educationist he rightly realised that a foreign language cannot be a suitable medium of instruction. While he opposed the use of a foreign language as a medium of instruction, he did not oppose Indians going abroad in quest of knowledge. He encouraged people to gather knowledge from all corners and sources. But at the same time he believed that a sound system of education must make a student feel proud of his language, his country, his cultural heritage, his nation's achievements. He was of the conviction that this could never be achieved, if the Indian languages and Sanskrit were not given their proper place in the scheme of education in the country.

Efforts to put Swami Dayananda's Ideas into Practice

Swami Dayananda had emphasised a system of national education. Wherever he went he urged people to establish Sanskrit schools and to learn *Vedas.* In the eight Principles of the Arya Samaj, as we have already studied, dispelling of ignorance and diffusing of knowledge have been advocated. Therefore, the Samaj became engaged both in educational reconstruction and religious propaganda. In order to put his educational programme and educational ideas into practice two premier institutions, at first, were established in Northern India. The one at Lahore, named Dayananda Anglo Vedic College in the year 1886, and the other near Hardwar, named Gurukula Kangri in the year 1902.

The institution at Lahore had been a great success and a splendid example of indigenous enterprise in the field of education. Lala Hansraj was the principal architect of this institution. A few years after the establishment of this institution some of its founders felt that they had drifted much towards the Westernization of education and they were forgetting the Dayananda's ideals. In fact, they wanted to run an ideal institution on the lines indicated by Swami Dayananda. This group of Dayananda's disciples founded another institution named Gurukula at Kangri near Hardwar under the leadership of Mahatma Munshi Ram, later known as Swami Shraddhananda. Needless to mention that Mahatma Munshi Ram, the actual founder of the *Gurukula*, derived the inspiration of his fundamental principles from Dayananda. Thus the Gurukula, though an ancient system, was again brought into the minds of the people by Swami Dayananda, who through his *Satyartha Prakash* explained the underlying principles in the light of the modern thought that he could command.

The D.A.V. College of Lahore ceased to be a part of India after the partition of the country in the year 1947, and by that time it had deviated from the Dayananda's ideals by conceding to run practically on the Western pattern of education. The Gurukula Kangri still retains its Dayananda character in many respects. Let us look into this institution along with some other modern institutes which are trying to follow the Dayananda's ideals of education upto some extent.

The Hardwar and Brindaban Gurukulas

The Gurukula Kangri (near Hardwar) and the Brindaban Gurukula (near Mathura) are the two notable institutions in India which are trying to put into practice some of the ideals of education advocated by Swami Dayananda. Accordingly, these institutions are endeavouring to revive the ancient Indian Vedic philosophy and literature. They aim at producing such citizens who may be fit to preach Vedic religion. During one of his visits to these *Gurukulas* Sir James Meston says:

> *"The Gurukula is one of the most original and interesting experiments carried on. One of the most wonderful, interesting and stimulating institutions; we have a hand of ascetics devoted to their duty, and working in the wilderness following the traditions of the ancient Risis, combined with the most modern scientific methods, and working practically for nothing, and a set of students of strong physique, obedient, loyal, thoughtful, devoted, extraordinarily happy, and extraordinarily well fed ..."* [43]

As practised in the ancient *Gurukula*, these institutions are residential in character. They are away from the influences of the city life. They are amidst natural surroundings. They try to bring the atmosphere of a *tapovan* (hermitage) to the students. However, it has not been a part of this study to investigate their suitability and say how far they are able to live up to their professed ideals.

Trying to adhere to the principles laid down by Swami Dayananda these two institutions admit children between the ages of six and eight years. They offer many separate courses— each of fourteen years' duration. Hindi is the medium of instruction. Special attention is paid to the study of Hindu culture and Sanskrit literature. These *Gurukulas* are against co-education. Every student is required to undergo certain bodily and mental discipline as advocated by Swami Dayananda (or as practised in the ancient *Gurukulas*). Each student is required to take a vow of *Brahmacharya* and remain a bachelor till the age of twenty-four years, if not longer. The student is expected to be a vegetarian and shun all stimulants.

Now these institutions claim that they are trying to modernize themselves. Accordingly, they are now trying to introduce the studies of some modern arts and sciences, but they are still quite different from the other universities in the country which are run on the modified Western pattern. These institutions now call themselves full-fledged universities. However, the spirit of Swami Dayananda or that of the ancient *Gurukulas* can be sensed up to some extent in them especially because of their location in the natural surroundings.

The Dehradun, Baroda and Sasani Kanya Gurukulas

Mention may be made here of the three of the other *Gurukulas* meant exclusively for girls—(1) The Kanya Gurukula of Dehradun, (2) The Arya Kanya Mahavidyalaya of Baroda, and (3) The Kanya Mahavidyalaya, Sasani (Aligarh). The spirit of Swami Dayananda may also be seen in these three *Gurukulas* for girls. The students of these *Gurukulas* are urged to observe strict *Brahmacharya* vows, and they are not allowed to marry before the age of sixteen. These *Gurukulas* profess to emphasise the type of education which is especially suited to the needs and requirements of woman. The Arya Kanya Mahavidyalaya of Baroda claims to lay special emphasis on physical training.

The Dayananda Anglo-Vedic Colleges and Schools

Besides the above five institutions, in the country, there are a host of other Dayananda Anglo-Vedic Colleges and Dayananda Anglo Higher Secondary Schools in Northern India. It is true that these institutions are not at all working on the educational patte.n as designed by Swami Dayananda, and for convenience, they have succumbed to the many influence of the educational system engineered by the British much against the spirit of Swami Dayananda. However, these institutions, too, claim to keep the spirit of some of the ideals of Swami Dayananda alive and in some of their workings. For example, prayers are offered every morning and on some special occasions; religious or moral instructions are given on some days, and the routine of students in some of the hostels etc. reflects the spirit of Swami Dayananda upto some extent.

NOTES

1. A monk.
2. Mythological.
3. Sri Aurobindo: *Bankim-Tilak-Dayananda*, p. 57.
4. Sri Aurobindo: *Bankim-Tilak-Dayananda*, p. 57.
5. Dayananda Commemoration Volume, P.V.—Quoted in K.C. Vyas's. *The Social Renaissance in India*, p. 85.
6. *The Caves and Jungles of Hindustan*.
7. *Satyartha Prakash*, p. 79.
8. *Ibid*.
9. *Ibid*., pp. 110-111.
10. Opposed to righteous conduct.
11. Indulging in sinful deeds.
12. Engrossed in filthy acts.
    NB : All these three terms stand for those who are inhuman in their behaviours. As regards the degree of intensity these three terms are mentioned here in the ascending order.
13. The non-infliction of pain (*Ahimsa*).
14. The practice of truth (*Satya*).
15. Non-stealing (not even mental) of other's property (*Asteya*).
16. Non-attachment (*Asang*).
17. Modesty (*Hri*).
18. Want of storing for the future (*Asanchaya*).
19. Faith in religion (*Astikya*).
20. Abstinence (*Brahmacharya*).
21. Silence (*Maun*).
22. Steadiness (*Sthairya*).
23. Forgiveness (*Kshama*).
24. Fearlessness (*Abhaya*).
25. *Satyartha Prakash*, p. 42 (footnote).
26. *Ibid*., p. 43.
27. *Satyartha Prakash*, Chap. 11., p. 34.
28. The first and the sixth are regarded as mental intercourse with members of the opposite sex.
29. The Sacred Thread ceremony.
30. A hymn of the *Yajur Veda*, XXXVI, 3, an invocation to the Almighty God, Quoted in *Satyartha Prakash*, Chapter 111, pp. 37–38.
31. This consists in taking up a little water in the palm of *one's* hand and applying it to the lips in order to relieve the irritation of the throat or possible dryness thereof.
32. A very well organised and systematised process of deep breathing which burns of all impurities and exalts the soul.
33. *Brahmacharya* means observance of perfect celibacy and abstinence from the eight types of intercourse with the opposite sex.
34. *Manusmriti*, Chap. II, p. 13.
35. *Satyavrata* : *Fundamental Principles of the Gurukula System*, p. 6.

36. R.E. Hume: *The Thirteen Principal Upanisads,* p. 68.
37. *Kathopanisads*, 6, pp. 10-11.
38. *Satyartha Prakash*, p. 57.
39. Two great authorities of grammar and literature in ancient India.
40. *Aitreya, Satapatha, Sama and Gopatha.*
41. It consists of righteousness, justice, honesty, proper discharges of one's duties in all fields.
42. *Satyartha Prakash*, p. 56.
43. Quoted in *Lajpat Rai: Arya Samaj*, p. 209.

4

SWAMI VIVEKANANDA (1863—1902)

His Life

Swami Vivekananda was born in 1863 in Calcutta. Before he became a monk, his name was Narendra Nath Datta. He belonged to the Ksatriya caste. While he was a college student, seventeen years of age, when he came under the influence of Sri Ramkrishna. During his college days he was a gay youth taking part in many activities, like boxing, wrestling, swimming, riding, etc.; but at the same time he was very eager to gain all kinds of knowledge. He was an earnest student of philosophy and poetry. He studied all the systems of Western philosophy and became very well acquainted with the contemporary philosophy of Herbert Spencer and John Stuart Mill. Wordsworth and Shelley were his favourite poets. His teachers could very well recognise the genuis hidden in him. Once the principal of his college Mr. Hastie remarked :

> *"Narendra Nath is really a genius. I have travelled far and wide, but I have never yet come across a lad of his talents and possibilities, even in German Universities amongst philosophical students. He is bound to make his mark in life."*[1]

It was from this Englishman, Mr. Hastie, that Narendra Nath learnt about Ramkrishna Paramhamsa. On the advice of Mr. Hastie, Narendra Nath went to see Ramkrishna and was conquered, and from here began a new chapter in the history of Hinduism.

Swami Vivekananda did for the gospel of Sri Ramkrishna what St. Paul did for the gospel of Christ. He spread the truths of Vedanta in India; Europe and America, as realised in the experiences of

Sri Ramkrishna. He demonstrated to the world that the great Indian spiritual tradition was still alive and vigorous. He showed both the precept and by example that, if the ancient Vedanta were reinterpreted in the light of Sri Ramkrishna's spiritual experiences and applied to modern life, India would be able to solve many of her problems and would rise once again to deliver a message to humanity. Therefore, while he was explaining the philosophy of Vedanta to the public in America and Europe he asked his countrymen to put those truths into practice. He declared that the most practical form that the Vedanta could take in India was the uplift of the masses. His life from the time of the death of his Master to his own death had been one prolonged cry for the upliftment of the toiling and starving millions of his beloved Motherland. He had full sympathy for the poor and the downtrodden in India. In this respect he was a true forerunner of Mahatma Gandhi. He was not a politician, but he wanted to make the Indian masses strong and self-reliant. He vehemently pleaded for social reform in India as he did for religious freedom in the West. To him an ideal society should combine the spiritual culture of India and the secular culture of America and England.

Swami Vivekananda advocated that Vedanta could open its gates to all without any distinction of caste, colour, creed or sex. He thought that it should be practicable everywhere—liberalizing religion in the West and elevating society in the East. He repeatedly told his countrymen till his death in 1902 at the age of thirty-nine, that they had become weak and poor because they did not apply their Vedanta to life. He deplored that Indians had lost faith in themselves. According to him, strength alone was the crying need of the hour in India.

Through his foreign tours he rightly realised that it was foolish to expect any substantial help from outside for helping the starving people of India. He became convinced that India must stand on its own two feet and solve its various problems by itself, i.e., the Indian people must become self-reliant. This self-reliance could come only through self-confidence. He wanted the Indian youth to banish their feeling of inferiority. He thus urged the young men in India :

"Make your nerves strong. What we want is muscles of iron

and nerves of steel. We have wept long enough. No more weeping but stand on your feet and be men. It is a man-making religion that we want. It is man-making all-round education that we want."[2]

Swami Vivekananda also realised that the foreign rule had a degenerating influence on the Indian people, and that the spirit of self-confidence and self-reliance could not grow unless the people were made proud of their heritage and culture. The Swami himself was proud of his race, religion and motherland. He did not believe that the Indian people would be elevated by imitating the West.

Swami Vivekananda saw the West rolling in opulence and prosperity, but he saw no hope for the Western civilization if it was deficient in spiritual values. He thought that the spirituality lacking in the West could be supplied only by the East and particularly by India. He believed that the excessively spiritual life of the East was in need of a dose of the Western materialism in order to raise standard of life; and the Western material, civilization needed the spirituality of the East. Therefore, he suggested an exchange of spiritual values and material wants between the East and the West on an equal footing. Once lecturing in Colombo, he[3] declared:

"Once more the world must be conquered by India. This is the dream of my life and I wish that each one of you who hear me today should have the same dream. They will tell you everyday that we had better look to our homes first, then go to work outside. But I will tell you in plain language that you work best when you work for others ... This is the great ideal before us, and everyone must be ready for it... the conquest of the world by India ... Let them come and flood the land with their armies, never mind. Up, India and conquer the world with your sprituality. Aye, as had been declared on this soil, first love must conquer hatred, hatred cannot conquer itself. Materialism and all its miseries can never be conquered by materialism. Armies when they attempt to conquer armies only multiply and make brutes of humanity. Spirituality must conquer the West. Slowly they are finding it out that what they want is spirituality to preserve them as nations. They are

> *waiting for it, they are eager for it. Where is the supply to come from? Where are the men ready to sacrifice everything so that this message shall reach every corner of the world? ... Such heroic workers are wanted to go abroad and help to disseminate the great truths of Vedanta."*

The above words were uttered by Swami Vivekananda in a combative tone. But this tone did not imply any desire to conquer. In fact, it meant only to shake off the lethargy of his countrymen and infuse in them a missionary spirit for the good of themselves and for the rest of the world. We may summarise the message of Swami Vivekananda in the following manner :

1. No religion is inferior to any other. All religions lead to the same goal. So one must adhere to one's own religion.
2. God is Omnipresent and Impersonal. He is manifested in all the creatures on the earth.
3. The reformers must not try to weed out any part of Hinduism. Every aspect of Hinduism is of value and must be retained.
4. Hindu civilization is good, beautiful and spiritual. The interpretations of missionaries about Hinduism are misleading.
5. The Hindu nation will again lead the whole world, as it had led in the past, in the realm of spiritualism.
6. The Hindus must not try to imitate the European nations and Western civilisation blindly.
7. The Indians must be self-reliant for improving their lot.[4]

After his return from his travels abroad Swami Vivekananda organised the Ramkrishna Mission on May 1, 1897 on purely spiritual and humanitarian basis. The Ramakrishna Mission has carried on three types of activities :

1. Charitable work among the poor;
2. Missionary work for diffusing the principles of the Vedanta and the teachings of Sri Ramkrishna; and

3. Organisation of education in order to bring enlightenment to the people.

The organisation of education as carried by the Ramkrishna Mission has been greatly influenced by the educational philosophy of Swami Vivekananda, and even today his followers try to interpret, and propagate his views on various educational problems.

Educational philosophy of Swami Vivekananda has been derived from his philosophy of life. So it is in fitness of things that we first consider his philosophy which has been derived from the Vedanta.

His Philosophy of Life

Swami Vivekananda regards the Vedanta as perfectly impersonal. To him the Vedanta philosophy, as it is known today, includes the various sects that are found in India. Consequently, various interpretations of the Vedanta philosophy have been forwarded, from the dualistic (or *Dvaita*) to the non-dualistic, (or *Advaita*). Swami Vivekananda considers all these interpretations progressive. The Vedanta is eternal. It is not originated by any person or prophet. So it is not built around any particular individual at the centre. However, it does not criticise those philosophies which have been propounded by certain individuals. Swami Vivekananda regards the *Dvaita*, the *Visistadvaita* and the *Advaita* as the different expressions of the Vedanta. So, to him, they are not opposed to each other. He does not consider them as absolute to proceed progressively towards the realisation of higher and higher ideals till everything is merged in that wonderful unity which is reached in the *Advaita system.*

As a staunch Vedantist, Swami Vivekananda gives only three attributes to God—He is Infinite Existence, Infinite Knowledge and Infinite Bliss. He believes that these three are one.

> *"Existence without knowledge and love cannot be; knowledge without love, and love without knowledge cannot be; What we want is the harmony of Existence, Knowledge and Bliss Infinite, for that is our goal. We want harmony, not one-sided*

> *development. And it is possible to have the intellect of a Sankara with the heart of a Buddha, I hope we shall all struggle, to attain that blessed combination ...*"[5]

What a great ideal Swami Vivekananda places before man! Swami Vivekananda's interpretation of the Vedanta is based upon a scientific analysis. He says:

> "*When the scientific teacher asserts that all things are the manifestation of one force does it not remind you of the God of whom you hear in the Upnishads? As the one fire entering into the universe expresses itself in various forms, even so that one Soul is expressing itself in every soul and yet is infinitely more besides ...*"[6]

Thus the Swami believes that both the Vedanta and science maintain common principles.

Swami Vivekananda believes that the same methods of investigation that are applied to sciences and knowledge today should be applied to the science of religion, because thereby it will become as scientific, at least, as any of the conclusions of physics or chemistry, and will have greater strength, because physics or, chemistry do not have that internal mandate to vouch for their truth, which religion has.[7] Therefore, one must not deny the efficacy of any rational investigation into religion.

Swami Vivekananda thinks that the same omnipresent and omniscient soul resides in everyman and in every animal, however weak, small or great.

> "*The difference is not in the soul, but in the manifestation. Between me and the smallest animal, the difference is only manifestation, but as a principle he is the same as I am, he is my brother, he has the same soul as I have.*"[8]

Thus Swami Vivekananda believes in universalism and spiritual brotherhood. He asserts that the Vedanta as a religion must be intensely practical. He urges people to apply it to every aspect of their lives. He regards the difference between various religions as fictitious and says that they must cease. Such is his conviction about the universalism he preaches.

Swami Vivekananda has intense faith in man and he realises the dignity and diversity of human beings. In fact, he finds the manifestation of God in man.

> *"The only God to worship is the human soul, in the human body. Of course, all animals are temples too, but man is the highest, the Taj Mahal of temples. If I cannot worship in that, no other temple will be of any advantage. The moment I have realised God sitting in the temple of every human body, the moment I stand in reverence before every human being and see God in him—that moment I am free from bondage, everything that binds vanishes, and I am free ..."*[9]

To him the ideal of the Vedanta is to know man as he really is, this is the message of the Vedanta. He asks :

> *"If you cannot worship your brother man, the manifestation of God, how can you worship a God who is un-manifested? ... If you cannot see God in the human face, how can you see Him in the clouds, or in images made of dull, dead matter, or in mere fictitious stones of your brain? I shall call you religious from the day you begin to see God in men and women ..."*[10]

Thus the Swami teaches the eternal communion of man with the Infinite through a religion of universal oneness and cosmopolitanism. He is completely consistent when he urges people to believe in a universal religion. He does not regard the various religions as contradictory. To him the various—

> *"religions are different forces in the economy of God, working for the good of mankind ..."*[11]

He thinks that every religion is progressive. He believes that universal religion exists in the same way as the universal oneness between man and man is already existing. He regards the realisation of Divinity, or the knowledge of Brahman as the ultimate goal for man. But he says that man cannot remain absorbed in Brahman all the time. The absorption in the Brahman can be only for some exceptional moments which do not last long. That is why the saint after having realised that the Self sees the Self in all creatures. Therefore, he devotes himself entirely to the service of all beings. It is because of this that Swami Vivekananda has emphasised universalism and spiritual brotherhood.

Swami Vivekananda believes that perfection is one's heritage. He declares :

> *"Perfection is not to be attained, it is already within us, immortality and bliss are not to be acquired, we possess them already, they have been ours all the times ..."*[12]

All through his life the Swami strove wholeheartedly to make his fellow-being realise this truth.

His Philosophy of Education

Knowledge Resides Within the Individuals

Swami Vivekananda believes that knowledge resides within the individual himself. He simply discovers or realises it. Similarly, as noted above, he holds that perfection is already inherent in man, and education is the manifestation of the same. Everyone is entitled to perfection. In fact, everyone is in the process of perfection, and education is a means towards this end. Swami Vivekananda believed that it is under this framework of philosophy that education should be conducted.

The Child Does His Own Growing

Swami Vivekananda says :

> *"Each of us is naturally growing and developing according to our own nature; each will in time come to know the highest truth, for after all men must to teach themselves. What can you and I do? Do you think you can teach even a child? You*

cannot. The child teaches himself. Your duty is to afford opportunities and to remove obstacles. A plant grows. Do you make the plant grow? Your duty is to put a hedge round it and see that no animal eats up the plant and there your duty ends. The plant grows of itself."[13]

Thus Swami Vivekananda believes that the child learns through self-education. Each one must teach oneself. Things will be made clearer to the child by his own power of perception and thought. Like Froebel, Swami Vivekananda thinks that the child develops his own nature. Just as the plant grows by itself, and all that the gardener need do is to protect it; similarly, all that the teacher can do for the child is to arrange the necessary atmosphere for him so that he may do his growing. Tne teacher is not to be a taskmaster. He has just to be a guide and helper. He will probably harm the child if he adopts the role of a tutor. Man has all the knowledge. He requires only an awakening. So the teacher has only to see that the child applies his intellect and the various senses properly.

Nothing should be forced on children. They should be left free to carve out their own path. Children have infinite tendencies which must be given full scope for satisfaction. Any undue domination exercised on them will mar their development. The children must not be scolded every now and then. Kindness and encouragement will help them bloom. Positive ideas should be given to them. It is better to guide them as to how they should work in order to avoid mistakes. Only pointing out their mistakes will be harmful. We should also let them know that they are progressing and that they have to strive further in order to achieve greater progress.

Education According to Tendencies of the Child

The teaching should be adjusted according to the needs of children. These needs should be determined in terms of the tendencies inherent in children, and not according to what the parents or teachers think. Swami Vivekananda says that it is foolish for the parents or teachers to think that they can determine the path which the child should follow. He advises us to regard every soul as the soul of God, and every child as God. One can only serve God. So the teacher has only to serve children.

Concentration is the Essence of Education

> *"There is only one method by which to attain ... knowledge, that which is called concentration ... The strength and force of blow come through concentration. There is no limit to the power of the human mind. The more concentrated it is, the more power is brought to bear on one point; that is the secret."*[14]

Thus Swami Vivekananda regards concentration as the only method to attain knowledge. He considers concentration of mind as the essence of education. Everyone wants this power of concentration for success in his life. Men and animals differ in their power of concentration. Animals forget things very soon. Those who train animals experience this difficulty. There is also a difference in the power of concentration between man and man. A man is called superior to another if he has greater power of concentration. The treasure house of knowledge can be opened only through the key of concentration. Swami Vivekananda considers the concentration of mind as the essence of education. The collection of facts is not education. Facts should be collected only after developing the power of concentration.

Brahmacharya for Concentration

Swami Vivekananda says:

> *"... simply by the observance of strict Brahmacharya (continence) all learning can be mastered in a very short time— one has an unfailing memory of what one hears or knows but once. It is owing to this want of continence that everything is on the brink of ruin in our country."*[15]

Thus, according to Vivekananda, *Brahmacharya* or complete, continence is necessary for developing the power of concentration. The sexual energy should be sublimated into spiritual energy. This sublimation is the process of *Brahmacharya*. Swami Vivekananda believes that by observing strict *Brahmacharya* all learning can be mastered within a very short time. Chastity in thought, word and deed is *Brahmacharya*. In his opinion every boy should be trained to practise this chastity or *Brahmacharya* in order to develop his power of concentration which is the basis of all education.

Qualities for the Teacher

Swami Vivekananda attaches great importance to the personal life and character of the teacher. He thinks that only a *Tyagi* (the one who has renounced his personal desires and the one who has dedicated his life to the service of others) can be a good teacher. In India the imparting of knowledge has always been through *Tyagis* or men of renunciation. Our modern teachers must imbibe this virtue if they want to be teachers in the true sense of the term.

The teacher should be of a very high character. He must be pure in mind and heart, only then his words[16] will be valuable. The teacher has not only to stimulate the spirit of intellectual curiosity in the child, in fact, he has to transfer something to the child and that is his blemishless character.

> *"The function of the teacher is indeed an affair of the transference of something, and not of mere stimulation of the existing intellectual or other faculties in the taught. Something real and appreciable as an infuence comes from the teacher and goes to the taught. Therefore the teacher must be pure."*[17]

The teacher must love his pupils. Without love he cannot contribute anything to them. He should have no ulterior selfish motive of any kind. Love should be the only guiding principle for him. Love is the best medium to transmit the spiritual force. Any selfish motive on the part of the teacher will destroy this medium. Therefore the teacher must work for his pupils only out of love.[18]

The teacher must have full sympathy for his pupils. He can never teach if he is devoid of sympathy. Swami Vivekananda says:

> *"The true teacher, is one who can throw his whole force into the tendency of the taught. Without real sympathy we can never teach well."*[19]

It is only through sympathy that he can bring himself down to the level of his pupils and act according to their inherent tendencies. Placing a lofty ideal before teachers, Swami Vivekananda further says :

> *"The only true teacher is he who can immediately come down to the level of the student, and transfer his soul to the student's soul and see through the student's eyes and hear through his ears and understand through his mind. Such a teacher can really teach and none else."*[20]

The Qualities for the Pupil

Just as the teacher must have certain virtues, similarly, the pupil, too, must have some qualities. The pupil must be pure in thought and speech. He must have a perseverance and real thirst for knowledge.[21] He must be a *Brahmachari*. He must continuously struggle to grapple his basic nature; only then he can achieve victory and acquire true knowledge.

Aims of Education

From what we have studied we can understand the aims of education as believed by Swami Vivekananda. Needless to mention that these aims are only corollaries to his philosophy of life and that of education.

Faith Created in One's Own Self

Swami Vivekananda believes that faith in one's own self must be created through education. He regards faith in one's own self as the first step towards advancement. To him it is the function of education to make one conscious of one's latent powers which are always quite potent and can make one's life sublime and divine. Education must teach that a man can do everything if he has courage. Education must give one the *Mantram* (the faith): "Arise, awake and stop not till the goal is reached" (*Kathopanisad*, I, III, IV). This has been the core to all that Swami Vivekananda has taught throughout his whole life, and he wants to make this as the corner stone of education.

Sraddha or Faith

Swami Vivekananda regrets that the existing system of education in India produces a broken-down youngman who lacks in *Sraddha*[22] or faith. The *Sraddha*, which is the key-note of the Veda and the Vedanta, must be created in man. It is this *Sraddha* which moves the world. Hence its annihilation is to debase man, and its infusion is to make human life sublime. The man who is devoid of this *Sraddha* runs to ruin. In order to create *Sraddha*, the first requisite is self-knowledge. This self-knowledge, according to Swami Vivekananda, does not mean matted hair, staff, *Kamandala*[23] and mountain caves. On the contrary by this term he means knowledge of one's latent powers and potentialities, creation of self-confidence and self-reliance which alone can bring material prosperity as well as freedom from the bondage of wordly existence. Education must aim at this kind of knowledge of the "self" and at creation of self-confidence and self-reliance.

Education not to Ignore Practical Side of Life

Swami Vivekananda deplores the wretched poverty of his countrymen, and says that the Vedanta, today in India, should mean to feed our starving millions. Education which does not prepare man to attend to this primary want of the people is worthless. Hence education must not overlook the practical side of life. By the practical side of life or by material prosperity Swami Vivekananda does not mean that one should strive only to a mass wealth. All that he means is that everyone must be able to get his primary needs satisfied. Education must give this ability to everyone, and it must also give one the sense of universal brotherhood so that one does not interfere with other's fulfilment of these primary needs, i.e. one must not think of exploiting others.

Swami Vivekananda wanted to open a centre in the capital of each State in India from where the much-needed education would spread throughout the whole country. In these centres he recommended training be given in agriculture and industry so that one might know how to make a living. He wanted to establish know-how to make a living. He wanted to establish workshops for the furtherance of arts. Thus he gave practical suggestions for the solution of the immediate problem of hunger in the country.

To Promote Self-Reliance and Universal Brotherhood

Swami Vivekananda believes education must promote the spirit of self-reliance and universal brotherhood. The acquisition of this spirit is the first step towards the ultimate ideals of freedom, dispassion and renunciation, which must also be imbibed by man as a result of the education given to him. Education must ultimately teach man that the *Atman* (soul) is the same in all—from the ant to the perfect man, the difference being only in its manifestation. This means that the Dualist, Qualified-Monist, Monist, Saiva, Vaishnava, Sakta, the Buddhist, the Jain, the Christian, the Muslim and all others are one—that infinite power is lying hidden in this *Jivatman* (individualised soul). Swami Vivekananda believes only that education is worth the name which imparts this spirit to man. The imbibing of this spirit in the heart of man would mean the annihilation of all misery from this earth, and education has to strive for this annihilation. Swami Vivekananda asserts that "from the highest God to the meanest grass the same power is present in all—'whether manifested or not". Education has to call forth this power in every man.

Book-learning is not Education

To Swami Vivekananda book-learning is no education. To him, "the training by which the current and expression of will are brought under control and become fruitful is education." That is not education which makes man a machine. That is not education which chokes the will by force. In fact, that is education which develops the will and enables one to realise the divinity latent in him. Education must aim at the development of infinite energy, infinite zeal, infinite, courage, and infinite patience in man.

The Teacher to make the Pupil Conscious of Perfection

Swami Vivekananda says that, the Vedanta does not recognize any sin. It recognizes only error. According to the Vedanta the greatest error is to say that you are weak, that you are a sinner, a miserable creature, and that you do not possess power and you cannot do this or that. Evidently, according to Swami Vivekananda, the teacher must not dishearten the pupil, he must not scold him for his errors; on the contrary, he must make him conscious of his inner powers. The Swami has immense faith in man. To him 'man is higher than all animals, than all angels, none is greater than man. Even the gods will have to come down again and attain salvation through a human body', and the teacher has to make the pupil conscious that he has to reach his perfection. Education must be directed towards the fulfilment of this aim.

The Spirit of Renunciation

Education must generate the spirit of renunciation in man. Without the spirit of renunciation none can work for others. The man of renunciation views all alike. Today India needs men of this spirit of renunciation. This has been the clarion note of Swami Vivekananda's life. Education must inculcate in man the feeling that we are all debtors to the world and the world does not owe us anything. It is a great privilege for one to be able to do something to the world.

Swami Vivekananda says :

> *"I look upon religion as the innermost core of education — Mind, I do not mean my own, or any one else's opinion about religion. I think the teacher should take the pupils starting point in this as in other respects, and enable them to develop along their own life of least resistance."*[24]

As regards religious education, he further recommends that the children should be taught about lives of great saints of all lands. He observes that temples and churches, books and forms are simply the Kindergarten of religion. They are mere preliminaries. In fact, one must enter into the heart of religion, that is, one must realise it in one's own life.

"We can talk and reason all our lives, but we shall not understand a word of truth, until we experience it ourselves. You cannot hope to make a man a surgeon by simply giving him a few books. You cannot satisfy my curiosity, to see a country by showing me a map; I must have actual experience. Maps can only create curiosity in us to get more perfect knowledge. Beyond that, they have no value whatever. Clinging to books only degenerates the human mind. Was there ever a more horrible blasphemy than the statement that all knowledge of God is confined to this or that book? How dare men call God infinite and yet try to compress Him within the covers of a little book."[25]

Thus according to Swami Vivekananda religion must be a living experience with oneself. Only intellectual education cannot give the necessary training to the child for developing towards perfect manhood. Training of the heart is also necessary, and this training is possible by giving examples from the lives of great saints and by providing opportunities to the pupils to act accordingly. This will be the true religious education which must be imparted to our children. Teaching of doctrines and creeds of particular religions should not form a part of religious education in schools. All religions must be accepted, and only their essential spirits should constitute the religious education to be given to children.

Women Education

Swami Vivekananda was greatly pained at the miserable condition of women in India. He was conscious that a nation could rise only paying proper respect to women. He quotes from the *Manusmiriti*[26] (III, 56) :

"Where women are respected, there the Gods' delight; and where they are not, there all works, efforts come to naught."

He further, says :

"There is no hope of rise for that family or country where

> *there is no estimation of women, where they live in sadness. For this reason, they have to be raised first..."*[27]

So he recommends that daughters should be brought up and educated just as sons. He wants that the ideal of chastity should be emphasised for women, because this ideal would bring them strength for reaching perfect womanhood. He places the ideal of Sita before the Indian women. He remarks that any attempt to modernize women which takes the women away from the ideal of Sita is vicious and need be stopped. To Swami Vivekananda, Sita is a symbol of purity; she is purer than purity itself, she suffered without a murmur, she is our ideal, and she must remain so. Indian women must be taught to follow the ideal of Sita.[28]

Swami Vivekananda was against child marriage, as this practice stood in the way of the fullest development of personality of children married prematurely. In this connection he was particularly against the early marriage of girls. He deplores that girls in India are married at the age of eleven years. They should, he believed, also observe *Brahmacharya* like boys and should be educated by their parents. He believes that there can be no hope of well-being of the country unless the condition of the women is bettered.[29] He says :

> *"Women must be put in a position to solve their own problems in their own way. No one can or ought to do this for them. And our Indian women are as capable of doing it as any in the world."*[30]

Thus Swami Vivekananda had immense faith in Indian women. He did not like them to imitate the West. Speaking on virtues that the Indian women must cultivate, he says :

> *"With regard to domestic virtues I have no hesitation in saying that our Indian methods have in many ways the advantage over all others."*[31]

He further says :

> *"... To the women of this country I would say exactly what I*

say to the men. Believe in India and in our Indian faith. Be strong and hopeful and unashamed."[32]

Swami Vivekananda wants to give such an education to the Indian women as to :

"Bring to the need of India great fearless women—women worthy to continue the traditions of Sanghamitra, Lila, Ahalya Bai, and Mira Bai—women fit to be mothers of heroes, because they are pure and selfless..."

Thus he wanted to give a type of education that may make women fearless and brave. He wanted to give women an education which may form character and may increase the strength of mind and may enable them to stand on their own feet. He remarks :

"With such an education women will solve their own problems. They have all the time been trained in helplessness, servile dependence on others and so they are good only to weep their eyes out at the slightest approach of a mishap or danger. Along with other things they should acquire the spirit of valour and heroism. In the present day it has become necessary for them also to learn self-defence. See how grand was the Rani of Jhansi."[33]

If we organize the education for women with the aim of making them fearless and self-dependent, we shall in due course have mothers who will produce ideal citizens.

Swami Vivekananda had all admiration for those who worked for the spread of female education in India. He says :

"... Female education is to spread with religion as its centre. All other training should be secondary to religion. Religious training, the formation of character and observance of the vow of celibacy—which has obtained up till now in India, it is religion that has been made a secondary concern."[34]

Swami Vivekananda wanted to teach some women the ideals

of renunciation, so that they may take up the vow of lifelong dedication to God. He believes that :

> *"If even one amongst the women becomes a knower of Brahma, then by the radiance of her personality thousands of women. would be inspired, awakened to truth, and great well-being of the country and society would ensue."*[35]

The Swami wanted to train some *Brahmacharinis* who would take up the education of women ...

> *"Centres have to be started for teaching women. Brahmacharinis of education and character should take up the task of teaching at these different centres."*[36]

According to him women should be taught history and the *Puranas* (mythologies), housekeeping and the arts, the duties of homelife and principles that make for the development of an ideal character. These subjects should be taught with the help of modern science. He wanted that girls be trained in ethical and spiritual life. He further says :

> *"We must see to their (women's) growing up as ideal matrons of home in time. The children of such mothers will make further progress in the virtues that distinguish the mothers. It is only in home of educated and pious mothers that great men are born ... The uplift of the women, must come first and then only can any real good come about for the country, for India."*[37]

Thus we see that the Swami has a very high ideal of education for women.

Education of the Masses

Swami Vivekananda felt very distressed at the pitiable condition of the common man in India. He says,

> *"The poor, the low, the sinner in India have no friends, no*

help—they cannot rise ...they sink lower and lower everyday, they feel the blows showered upon them by a cruel society..."[38]

He further says :

"So long as the millions live in hunger and ignorance, I hold everyman a traitor who, having been educated at their expense, pays not the least heed to them."[39]

Thus Swami Vivekananda regarded the neglect of the masses as a great national sin. He observes :

"No amount of politics would be of any avail until the masses in India are once more well educated, well fed, and well cared for."[40]

Swami Vivekananda believes that the root cause of all evils in India is the poverty of the people. He considers education as the sole remedy for improving the condition of the poor in the country. By education he wants to develop their lost individuality. He regrets that nothing substantial has been done for educating the poor. He is an ardent advocate of mass. emancipation. He says :

"Priest-power and foreign conquests have trodden them down for centuries, and by now the poor of India have forgotten that they are human beings. They are to be given ideas; their eyes are to be opened to what is going on in the world around them, and they will work out their own salvation ...Our job is to put the chemicals together, the crystallisation comes in the law of nature. Our duty is to put the ideas into their heads, they will do the rest."

Thus Swami Vivekananda points to the very urgent need with regard to mass education in the country. He believes that a nation advances as education and intelligence spread among the masses. He deplores that education in India is monopolised by a handful of men, and the education of the masses is ignored. He suggests that first of all everything possible should be done so that the common man in India may recover his lost individuality. The gems of spirituality stored in our sacred books should be brought to the common man. This can be done by spreading education among the masses through the medium of mother-tongue. Ideas can easily be understood and assimilated even by the commonest man, if they are taught through their own mother-tounge.[41]

Swami Vivekananda says :

> *"If the mountain does not come to Mahomet, Mahomet must go to the mountain. If the poor boy cannot come to education, education must go to him. There are thousands of single-minded, self-sacrificing sanyasins in our country, who must go from village to village, teaching religion. If some of them can be organised as teachers of secularism also, they will go from place to place, from door to door, not only preaching but teaching also."*[42]

Such is the abiding faith of the Swami in mass education.

An Ardent Advocate of a National System of Education

Swami Vivekananda considered education as a very important means to regenerate the country. He wanted to reorganise education on a national basis. The national system of education according to Swami Vivekananda should begin by acquainting the child with the home where he resides, the community in which he moves, the country to which he belongs and ultimately his understanding and sympathy for the humanity at large must grow. With such an education Swami Vivekananda wanted to train the children in the various aspects of Indian customs, manners, culture and philosophy and then acquire the knowledge of various civilisations of the world. He desired that education in the country should be wholly national in spirit. When Sister Nivedita expressed a desire to come to India and work to educate Indian women and girls, he asked her to adopt the Hindu ways when working for them. He told her :

> *"You have to set yourself to Hinduise your thoughts, your needs, your conceptions and your habits. Your life, internal and external has to become all that an orthodox Brahmacharini ought to be. The method will come to you, if only you desire it*

sufficiently. But you have to forget your own past and to cause it to be forgotten. You have to loose even its memory."[43]

This shows that in matters of education he was not only a staunch nationalist, but also a practical advocate who thought it necessary, perhaps even before Mahatma Gandhi did so, that the millions of this country could better be taught by person who live and behave like the people themselves.

NOTES

1. Quoted by Sharma in *The Renaissance of Hinduism*, p. 258.
2. *The Complete Works of Swami Vivekananda*, Vol. Ill, p. 224.
3. Quoted by Vyas, K.C., in *The Social Renaissance in India*, p. 107.
4. Volumes may be written on the glory and immortal works of Swami Vivekananda who did so much to reinterpret India both to the West and to the Indians themselves. But our scope here is very limited. Evidently, it is not possible for us to give here an adequate account of what this intellectual giant, accomplished in his short life-span of thirty-nine years.
5. *The Complete Works of Swami Vivekananda,* Vol. II, p. 143.
6. *Ibid.*
7. *Ibid.*
8. *Ibid.*
9. *Ibid.*, Vol. II, p. 319.
10. *Ibid.*, p. 324.
11. *Ibid.*, Vol. Il, p. 364.
12. *Ibid.*, Vol. II, p. 348.
13. *Ibid.*, Vol. Il, p. 383.
14. *Ibid.*, Vol. I, pp. 130-131.
15. *Ibid.*, Vol. VII, p. 222.
16. *Ibid.*, Vol. III, p. 50.
17. *Ibid.*, Vol. III, p. 51.
18. *Ibid.*
19. *Ibid.*, Vol. VII, p. 97.
20. *Ibid.*, Vol. IV, p. 179.
21. *Ibid.*, Vol. IV, p. 22.
22. Self-regarding sentiment, *Ibid.*, Vol. III, p. 444.
23. A special kind of utensil generally carried by monks in India.
24. *Ibid.*, Vol. V, p. 161.
25. *Ibid.*, Vol. I, p. 185.
26. *Ibid.*, Vol. VII, p. 213.
27. *Ibid.*
28. *Ibid.*, Vol. III, p. 256.
29. *Ibid.*, Vol. V, p.23.
30. *Ibid.*, Vol. V, p. 159.

31. *Ibid.*, Vol. V, pp. 160-161
32. *Ibid.*, p. 162.
33. *Ibid.*, pp. 257-258.
34. *Ibid.*, Vol. VII, p. 218.
35. *Ibid.*, Vol. VII, p. 217.
36. *Ibid.*, Vol. VI, p. 444.
37. *Ibid.*, Vol. VI, pp. 444-445.
38. *Ibid.*, Vol. V, p. 11.
39. *Ibid.*, Vol. V, p. 45.
40. *Ibid.*, Vol. V, p. 152.
41. *Ibid.*, Vol. III, p. 291.
42. *Ibid.*, Vol. IV, p. 309.
43. Quoted by Vyas : *The Social Renaissance in India*, p. 14.

5

ANNIE BESANT (1847—1933)

Her Life

Mrs. Annie Besant was the pupil of Madame Helena Petrovna Blasvatsky, one of the founders of the Theosophical movement in modern times. During her lifetime she had been a great dynamic force behind the Theosophical movement. She had been the President of the Theosophical Society from 1907 till her death on September 20, 1933. She was Irish and a free thinker. Before she joined the Theosophical Society, she had been a great admirer of Hindustan and often claimed that she must have been a Hindu in her former birth. She loved India and her people from the core of her heart. She had been one of the most outstanding figures in the history of the Hindu Renaissance of the nineteenth century. She regarded India as her own motherland and she looked upon the Indian people, as her own people.

At the age of forty-six, she came to India on the 16th November, 1893. After coming here, she made India her home. She wore the Hindu dress. She adopted the Hindu way of life and worked for the next forty years for the revival of Hinduism and uplift of the Indian nation till her death.

Like a true Hindu she went on a pilgrimage in 1901. Like a pious Hindu, she loved to reside in the holy city of Banaras (now known as Varanasi) where she founded the Central Hindu College which became the nucleus of the Benaras Hindu University. At Benaras she delivered her illuminating and inspiring lectures on Hindu ideals, translated the *Gita*, and wrote admirable summaries of the *Ramayana* and the *Mahabharata* and very lucid textbooks on Hindu Religion and ethics.

Mrs. Besant was a wonderful and captivating orator. She was also a great organiser. She used all her energy and powers in the service of her "beloved motherland"—India. For about three decades she travelled throughout the country, and made many voyages to Europe, America and Australia for delivering various lectures. She tried to make Indians feel the greatness of their religion and great cultural heritage. She tried to organize every form of activity which would make India great. She regarded religion, education, politics, journalism and social reforms as means for enabling India to rise to its great height. In each of these fields she showed tremendous energy and driving power.

Mrs. Besant's generosity knew no bounds. She dedicated all her wealth to her dear Central Hindu College and ultimately she made a gift of this college to Pandit Madan Mohan Malviya so that it might form the nucleus of the Banaras Hindu University.

Overwhelmed by her services to the cause of the Indian nation, and her courage and devotion in advocating Home Rule for India, the Indian National Congress elected her its President in 1918. This was the highest honour at that time which political India could give to any person. Unfortunately, it could not be possible for her to sympathize with the Non-cooperation movement started by Gandhiji in 1919, and consequently she lost her influence and leadership in the political field. But we must agree with Mrs. Sarojini Naidu when she says: "If Annie Besant had not been, Gandhiji could not be." Gandhiji,[1] too, had remarked :

> *"As long as India lives, the memory of the magnificent services rendered by her (Mrs. Annie Besant) will also live. She endeared herself to India by making it her country of adoption and dedicating her all to it."*

Thus we see that Mrs. Annie Besant endeared herself to India by her many-sided activities for the uplift of the Indian people whom she considered her own. Hinduism had a tremendous influence over her and all her public lectures and writings were imbued with Hindu ideals and Hindu way of life. By basing education of the Indian youth on the great ancient Indian traditions, she wanted to make the youth of the country conscious of the great

Indian heritage and the part that they could play in transmitting the spiritual light for the benefit of the whole humanity. However, she was not blind to the needs of the modern society, and so she wanted to conduct education in such a way as to enable the student to stand on his own two feet in various situations of life. With these aims in view she laid down certain ideals and principles of education together with a national scheme of education for India. In all these conceptions she had been very much influenced by the great Indian ideals of education which were practised in the ancient *Ashramas* and *Gurukulas* of India (the ancient forest-schools). By founding the Central Hindu College at Banaras in 1898 and by nourishing it with utmost sincerity for nearly two decades she tried to put her educational ideals into practice. The great Theosophical institution at Adyar, Madras, had also been very much influenced by her noble ideals.

We shall now discuss her philosophy of life and her ideals and conception of education for India. Since it is from one's philosophy of life that one's educational ideas are drawn, we shall first consider Annie Besant's philosophy of life.

Annie Besant's Philosophy of Life

Annie Besant believed in the creeds of the Theosophical Society, of which she had been a president in India. Her philosophy of life, though derived from these creeds, is basically Hindu in conception. We can classify[2] the basic teachings of this Society under four heads—Religious, Philosophical, Scientific and Ethical.

1. *Religious :* The Theosophists believe that God is one and He is Absolute. They further believe in the trinity corresponding to Ishwara, Hiranyagarbha and Virat in the Hindu Philosophy. According to them there is a hierarchy of spiritual intelligences ranging from the highest gods to the lowest gnomes and fairies.
2. *Philosophical :* The soul is immortal. Man is subject to rebirth. Matter is subordinate to mind.
3. *Scientific :* Corresponding to the Hindu conception of seven Lokas the universe consists of seven planes. Man's

constitution consists of seven sheaths. One will have to reap the consequences of his action (Law of *Karma*)—a similar doctrine has been taught by Hinduism and Buddhism. The world is always on the march of evolution. The various races of man and individuals of each race undergo well-marked stages of evolution.

4. *Ethical :* One should strive towards the realization of universal brotherhood. One must pay complete obedience to the law of evolution. The man may develop his spiritual powers through meditation, thought-control, love and service.

It should be noted that Theosophy recognised the equality of all religions, still it tended more towards the teachings of Hinduism and Buddhism. For creating the feeling of universal brotherhood the Society considers the comparative study of religions very necessary. This organisation is not a sect or religion. Its members are free to follow any religion. There is no specific religious or prayer book. Scriptures and prayers of all religions are chanted at its gathering.

Annie Besant passionately claimed that she was a Hindu in her former birth. Speaking about her a biographer says :

> *"There is a sublime pathos as well as passion in all her references to her love of India, which she looked upon as her own motherland, to her love of the Indian people, whom she looked upon her own people, and to her love of Hinduism and Hindu scriptures, which she looked upon as a sacred heritage and, above all, in her devotion to that most baffling Beloved of the Hindus—the Avatar of the Bhagavad Gita."*[3]

Consequently, Annie became a Hindu in spirit and in the ways of her life; and her philosophy of life has been essentially Hindu. Accordingly, she has written :

> *"In the ideal figure of Sri Ram Chandra we have the perfect man, the man who in every relation of life—son, husband,*

> *brother, king—set an example of nobility and purity—great as human imagination can depict... in Sri Krishna there is something more, some subtle gleam of divinity, of half-heard melody, of elusive fleeting grace, scarce seen but sensed.*"[4]

As a Hindu she went on a pilgrimage in 1901 to Amarnath, 16,000 feet above the sea, in the Himalayas. During this pilgrimage she walked barefoot through the snow and bathed in the ice-cold stream beside the temple.

As a staunch Hindu, Annie Besant believed in the fundamental principles of *Karma*, Reincarnation, *Yoga* and Spiritual Evolution. So her philosophy of life hinges round these fundamental concepts of Hinduism. It is from her Hindu philosophy of life that her educational philosophy has been evolved. That is why she has been an upholder of ancient Hindu traditions and spirit in the field of education in India.

Annie Besant's Philosophy of Education

The Old Gurukula Freedom to be Restored

Annie Besant wanted to apply the Indian ideals to the salvation of modern education and culture in India. She urged that once again learning must be inspired by the ancient ideals which should be embodied in new forms of the present day. These new forms should be expressions of modem Indian life, and this is possible only if the old academic freedom which existed in the ancient *Gurukulas* and *Ashramas is* restored to the educational institutions in the country.

Mrs. Annie Besant felt that :

> *"Here is an Indian ideal that it would be well to revive... It (India) must have a few representatives (of the ancient Ashrama) if she is to rise to her former level in supreme intellectual and spiritual achievement.*"[5]

The kings in ancient India gave all help to the *Gurukulas* and

Ashramas, but they claimed no authority on them. Similarly, the government today should give all help to the educational and cultural institutions, so that they may produce learned and skilled men and women for all walks of life in order to carry on the various tasks efficiently.

Education to be All-sided

Annie Besant deplores modern Indian education which attends to the training or intellect alone, and ignores the physical, emotional, moral and spiritual aspects of the student's life. Such an education can never build the personality of the child. This education produces only such individuals who think especially of their own aims, and are careless of the welfare of the nation as a whole. Such men have well-developed intelligence but are wanting in self-respect, in character, in public spirit and in straightforward and upright behaviour. This is the result of neglect of religion and morality in education. Annie Besant asks :[6]

> *"What do we find in modern India? An education directed to one part of the boy's nature only, developing the intelligence, training the intellect, but leaving entirely on one side the spiritual nature, and the moral or emotional nature, disregarded... Such an education ... can never build up a true man of the world, able to discharge his duties in the world ... What sort of a nation can you have where the education given to its young is but one quarter of what it should be... ?"*

Thus she emphasises an all-round education for the fullest and multi-demensional personality of the pupil.

The Ideal of Brahmacharya

Annie Besant regrets that the ancient ideal of *Brahmacharya* is now absent in the modern schools of India. Now the students in schools and colleges are not *Brahmachari*. This is against the old ideals, and this means ruin of India. Annie Besant urges the Indian people to become conscious of this grave shortcoming and rise again by education and by restoring the old ideals of *Brahmacharya.* She says:

> *"A student ought not to be mixed up with the cares of household life... The life of a student should be that of Brahmacharya—celibacy—until the student days are over. He should not be called upon to take up the burden of household life before finishing his education."*[7]

The Duties of the Teacher

On the duties and responsibilities of the teacher Annie Besant says that the teacher should realise that the pupil is an immortal soul. The pupil is not conscious of his great past heritage and the glorious future which he has before him if he realises his latent powers. The teacher has to make him aware of all these. The teacher has to be a friend of the soul of the child and not only of his body. He should believe that the body is only a vehicle for the soul, an instrument of the soul's great ends. He must not force the child into line with his own standard. He must respect the individuality of the child and make him conscious of his soul which is other than the material body.

The teacher should not disregard the education of emotions. Through education of emotions the teacher should create the spirit of universal brotherhood, the spirit of unity, the spirit of generosity, compassion, happiness and peace. If emotions are not educated, mind will become hard and narrow. Therefore, the teacher must prevent this undesirable outcome.

Annie Besant urges teachers in India not to look towards the West for inspiration, because she believes that India has still enough to inspire and lead one to lofty ideals in life. Hence she remarks that education of the West can never be the ideal for the East. The teacher in India must have this faith and act accordingly.

The Ideal for the Student

Annie Besant emphasises the importance of the life of the *Brahmachari* for an Indian student. On the basis, of the ancient ideals of Indian education[8] she says that service, study, simplicity and self-control should be the motto of the student. She remarks that this motto refers to the four aspects of human nature. The idea of service becomes clear to us when we look to the needs and importance of our physical body. We need to serve our body if we want any service from it. Our body cannot serve us to our satisfaction if we fail to attend to it properly.

Apart from the body, there are feelings, emotions and appetites which always influence our behaviour. These make up the second major aspect of human nature, and may be called the emotional nature of man. The mind which helps us to observe, reason and remember is the intellectual nature of man. This is the third division of the human constitution. Besides these three states, there is the spiritual nature of man, the fourth state. The spirit within the individual owns the body, the emotions, and the mind.

These four aspects of human nature must be taken into consideration in any scheme of education if that is to be complete and worthwhile. The *Brahmachari* or the ideal student in India needs this kind of all-round and worthwhile education. We shall consider below the qualities that a student, according to Annie Besant, should imbibe.

Annie Besant deplores that in modern times service to the *Guru* (teacher) has lost its old significance. She wants that the student should owe to his teacher obedience and affectionate respect and trust. The student should also serve his parents. Annie Besant says:

> *"He (the student) should avoid harsh criticism of them (the teachers) and all disorderly behaviour; it should be his pride to be orderly in class, courteous in his learning; he should not entertain suspicions of the teachers' goodwill, nor resent the discipline he may impose. Service to the parents should also form part of the Brahamachari's life."*[9]

To Annie Besant, the object of study should not be only to pass examinations. She criticises the present system of education which is only identified with the passing of examinations. She says:

> *"The gold does not gain its value from the hallmark; the*

hallmark is placed on it because it is already valuable. And so the knowledge does not gain its value from the examination; but the examination marks it as having a certain value. The passing of examination should be a proof that the student possesses a certain amount of knowledge; but only too often today the hallmark is stamped on base metal, for the knowledge has been gained by cramming ..."[10]

The object of study is not only to gain knowledge. In fact, the real object of study is to draw out, train and discipline the faculties of the mind. The study must evolve and train the power of observing, reasoning and judging. Thus the study should aim at the development of all faculties—physical, moral, intellectual and spiritual.

Simplicity is the symbol of the virtues of the *Brahmachari* or the ideal student. Without this trait he cannot imbibe the various virtues required of him. Annie Besant adds that the virtue of obedience, of physical and moral courage, of endurance, of the team-spirit and of self-control must be acquired by the student. These are the virtues[11] which the ancient Aryan scheme of education tried to inculcate, in the student. Annie Besant wants that the Indian youths should be inspired by the same sentiments which pervaded an ancient *Gurukula* in India. But she urges that the Indian youths must not indulge into vanity over the past. She observes that the past should be a matter of inspiration and not of boast.

Annie Besant's Principles of Education[12]

Annie Besant recognizes the importance of time and place in the application of any principle of education. She says :

"The principles of Education, its natural bases in the human constitution, are paramount while their applications must be local, adapted to the conditions of time and place. Hence while the Natural Law of Education must be recognized, there should be freedom in experiment and flexibility in application, so that we may discover the best methods available to us for the moment, and use them until we find better ones."[13]

Therefore, she is prepared to allow freedom for experiments in the field of education. She regards education as a science, and not a haphazard process of instructing children. Knowledge is not to be forced from outside. In fact, children should be helped to unfold and utilize their inborn capacities. Annie Besant thinks that this is possible only if an atmosphere of happiness and love is created in the home and the school.

Annie Besant regards man as a spiritual being, manifesting Activity, Emotion and Intelligence. She believes that education must train the organs of Activity, Emotion and Intelligence. In other words, education must be physical, mental, religious and moral. If education omits any of these four aspects of human nature, it will develop only a deficient human being.

Annie Besant reminds[14] us that education should not be the training of an isolated individual. An individual must be considered in the context of the society in which he has to live. The society is a group of inter-dependent individuals, everyone of whom has to perform certain functions. Therefore, education must regard the individual as the embryonic citizen who has social obligations and responsibilities. Education must see the individual in relation to his environment, the home and the school. From the very beginning the child should be given the consciousness that he is a part of his country with certain responsibilities and duties. A sense of duty should be evoked in the child, duty to parents, sisters, brothers, and servants who have protected him during his helplessness. Similarly, a sense of responsibility towards others should be evoked in him.

Annie Besant has hinted at the objectives of the various types of education—physical, mental, religious and moral.

Objectives of Education

Physical Education

The objective of physical education is to secure a perfect development of the body in order to provide a good physical basis for mental, religious and moral activities. All these activities are conditioned by the body. Therefore, it is very necessary, above all, to attend to physical education of the child.

Mental Education

The objective of mental education is to train the powers of intelligence, such as observation, memory, reasoning, judgement and the clarity of thought.

Religious Education

The objective of religious education is to remove those hindrances which come between man and his love for God.

Moral Education

The objective of moral education is to develop and train the powers of emotions. Moral education should ultimately result in harmony between thought, word and deed. This will bring in social virtues, the sense of duty and responsibility. It will create an attitude of love for all.

The Three Natural Periods of Education

According to Annie Besant, the early evolution of the individual falls into three natural periods of seven years each, ending at the ages of seven, fourteen and twenty-one. Education of the individual should cover these twenty-one years. At the age of twenty-one the person should become fit to shoulder the social duties and responsibilities. We shall see now Annie Besant's suggestions as regards the nature of education during these three periods.

The First Period—From Birth to Seven

Education during this period should be chiefly physical. The various senses should be trained by accurate observation of natural objects. The child should be given the greatest possible freedom so that his natural capacities may develop to the utmost extent. The body should be given a balanced nutrition in order to secure a healthy development.

The Second Period—From Seven to Fourteen

This period is chiefly emotional, because emotions colour most of the activities of the individual. Hence education during this period should be directed towards training and control of emotions. The reasoning capacity begins to germinate during this period, so it must not be overstrained. Mental education during this period should consist of accumulation of facts based on one's observation and experiments. Memory may also be, trained by attempting a coordination between the facts thus learnt.

The Third Period—Fourteen to Twenty-one

During this period the mind is most active. This is the time for developing and training of the faculty of reasoning and judgment. During this period the serious study of logic, philosophy, science and art may be undertaken.

Besides the above principles, Annie Besant has also outlined a scheme of national education for India. No account of hers as an educational philosopher will be complete without a mention of this scheme.

Annie Besant's Scheme of National[15] Education for India

The General Scheme

Annie Besant recommends that the mother-tongue of the district should be the medium of instruction. English should be compulsory as a second language upto the secondary and high school stage. The school should work from 7 a.m. to 6 p.m. The school hours should vary in different parts of India according to local convenience. The main study-work should be done between 7 and 10 and 2 and 4; and food, rest and games between 10 and 2 and 4 and 6. The work of the school should begin and end with a short religious service and singing.

The school education should be divided into Primary Class—1, A and B, ages 5–7; Lower Secondary—Classes II, III and IV, ages 7–10; Higher Secondary—Classes V, VI, VII and VIII, ages 10–14; High Classes—Classes IX and X, ages 14–16. There should be an examination at the end of the Higher Secondary Education. The High School should be closed by a school-leaving examination. Students entering into professions like engineering, agriculture, business, commerce, science and medicine, etc., will devote an additional year to a university preparatory class. Only then they will enter into the degree course which will be of three years duration, i.e., upto twenty years of age. They will enter the post-graduate studies after the degree course.

At the primary and secondary stages there will not be much difference between the girls' and boys' education, except that needle work, music, cookery, household economy, hygiene, home science and first aid will find special place in the scheme of studies for girls.

The Outline of Studies

The First Period

Annie Besant suggests that during the first period (from birth to seven) which is chiefly physical, the care of the body should be the major consideration. The infant should be looked after with care, but he must not be carried around for a long time. He should be allowed full freedom to move as he chooses. Brightly coloured objects should be scattered around him in order to awaken curiosity in him and to stimulate him to exert. He should be encouraged to learn about his body parts. At about the age of three, increased opportunities of choice should be placed in his way. At four his play may be organised a little. The small child should not be scolded for that will frighten him.

The child's play should give him an idea of interdependence. The child should be encouraged to help all around him, to be kind to animals and plants and to be clean in body.

In the primary school, play should be the chief method of teaching. Annie Besant is in favour of the Pestalozzi's, Montessori's and Froebel's principles of teaching, and advises that the parents, teachers and guardians should be familiar with these principles.

Stories should be the chief means of teaching religious and moral lessons in the primary classes. The children should be taught drawing and modelling. Through objects the four rules of arithmetic should be taught.

The school should maintain small gardens where the children should observe birds, insects and flowers. It should, however, be seen that the child does not get overtired. The child is very imitative and receptive during this period, so teachers of good character, manners and habit's should be selected.

The Second Period (Lower Secondary School)

This period is chiefly emotional and extends from seven to ten years of age. For religious education moral stories, hymns and incidents from lives of great religious teachers should be narrated. The intellectual education of students should consist of a good knowledge of mother-tongue, very elementary knowledge of Sanskrit, Pali or Arabic, English through conversation and story telling, nature-study through observations and experiments, history and geography through pictures and stories and through making of models and maps, beginning with the immediate neighbourhood arithmetic through solving easy problems.

The moral education should consist of stories illustrating truth, devotion, courage and honour, self-sacrifice, duties towards elders, and kindness to animals and plants.

The Physical education should emphasise the value of healthy body, self-control, gymnastic exercise, concerted exercises with music.

The Second Period (Higher Secondary School)

Religious education during this period should aim at teaching to the children the fundamental unity of all religions. Intellectual education should consist of more advanced teaching of mother-tongue, Sanskrit, Pali or Arabic, English, nature-study, history, geography, higher arithmetic and elementary algebra and geometry. At this stage emphasis should be placed on the political, economic and industrial conditions. Students at this stage should be guided to help and teach children in the lower classes. The moral education should mean fuller teaching of the virtues we associate with a good man and good citizen.

In the physical education scheme instructions in the physiology of animal and human should be given. The importance of *Brahmacharya* should be emphasised. The body should be trained in muscular strength. Carpentary, basket work, use of tools and first aid should be taught.

The Third Period (High School)

During this period the mind is most active. The religious education of this stage should mean fuller teaching of the chief doctrines of the student's religion. The students should be taught that all religions are great in themselves. Education to develop the mind during the Classes IX and X will depend upon the careers for which the students want to prepare themselves. This means that a certain specialization may be introduced at this stage. But at the same time, certain subjects will be common to all High Schools. The common subjects will include more advanced studies of the mother-tongue, English, general science, history, geography, first-aid and an elementary course in psychology.

As regards the special subjects, a high school should teach Sanskrit, Arabic or Pali, a more specialized course in (1) Mother-tongue, (2) English, (3) History and Geography. The science section of the high school will specialise in mother-tongue, English, physics, chemistry, algebra and geometry including trigonometry and mensuration and elements of surveying. Teachers at the high school must give special emphasis on pedagogy, school management, principles of physical training, etc.

A commercial high school at this period will teach useful foreign languages, business-forms, book-keeping, commercial arithmetic, office methods, commercial law, typewriting and shorthand, etc. Food supplies and cooking will be taught specially to girls.

A technical high school should teach the same subjects as science section of a high school omitting Sanskrit, Arabic and Pali, and adding elementary engineering, mechanics, electricity and industrial history.

An agricultural high school should teach all subjects with special reference to their relation to rural life. Mathematics, experimental physics, domestic science and elements of mechanics, nature-study and gardening should be taught showing their relation to agricultural output.

Annie Besant has suggested that the above outlines may be further improved according to the needs of the students, and that other types of schools, e.g. art high school, for fine arts and music, etc., might also be opened.

The moral education during the third period should consist of training in aesthetic development. The chivalrous spirit in boys should be encouraged by all means possible.

The physical education during the third period should consist of manual training, shop practice and laboratory work. Essential dignity of all true labour should be emphasized.

An Attitude of Service to be Developed

The high school and college students should be guided to take interest in the life of the poor in the neighbourhood. They should be trained to give help to the people in fairs, festivals, in accidents and in teaching at primary and night schools. They should be encouraged to develop an attitude of rendering service to the poor and the needy, and to the Motherland. Towards this end the boys in the schools should be inspired to join the Indian Boy Scout Movement and those in college to join the Cadet Corps.

Annie Besant was also alive to the needs of the village community as regards education of rural children. She also suggested the lines on which a school in a village should be organized as below :

The Organization of A Village School[16]

The village school should be organized according to the surroundings of the village. The various subjects should be taught with special reference to the locality from which the children hail, e.g., geography should be started by a map of the village. At the age of eight or nine years, the children should be required to work in the small plots attached to the school. They should be taught the science of agriculture according to their level of comprehension. Besides small agricultural plots, the school may maintain carpenter's or weaver's workshop also according to the needs of the students concerned. At the age of ten the village boys and girls should be taught the principles of first-aid and sanitation. The girls should be taught domestic hygiene, cookery and washing, while the boys should be engaged in the workshops. The special talents of any student must be marked in order to make the necessary provision for their further development. The attitude of service to the Motherland must be developed both in boys and girls.

Annie Besant: A Great Educator and Emancipator

The ideals and principles of education and a national scheme of education for India envisaged by Mrs. Besant indicated that she was quite alive to the fundamental principles of education. She had a deep psychological insight to understand the problems of education in India, and also to understand the needs of modern India. With this insight combined with unbounded sympathy for the Indian masses she at once captured the hearts of the people and evoked great admiration, love, respect and reverence. Her great devotion and efforts for the emancipation of the Indian people have left a permanent mark in the history of modern India.

Throughout her life in India, Annie Besant strove for the establishment of institutions for national education in India, just as the Arya Samaj did in Northern India. She realised the need for moral and religious education. She rightly felt that the prevailing educational system was not suitable for promoting the growth of the Indian nation. So she wanted a national system of education based on the fundamental principles of Indian culture and that too, through the medium of mother-tongue of the people. Furthermore, she urged that the students should be made conscious and proud of the glory and the greatness of their country. Her national scheme of education gave primary importance to the teaching of Indian culture, religion, history and literature. She gave only a secondary place to a foreign subject. She wanted to infuse in the students a spirit of patriotism through her national scheme of education and for this purpose she opened a number of schools and colleges.

No history of modern India will be complete without a full account of the part played by Annie Besant for the emancipation of India. Annie Besant stands as a unique figure both as an educator, and a social reformer, and above all, as one of the makers of modern India. It is difficult to pay by mere words the debts that India owes to Annie Besant. So Indians should pay their homage to her by living up to the ideals she stood for so that India may become great as she wanted it to be.

NOTES

1. Quoted by Sharma in *The Renaissance of Hinduism*, pp. 221-222.
2. Vyas, K.C.: *The Social Renaissance in India*, p. 122.
3. Sharma, D.S.: *The Renaissance of Hinduism*, p. 201.
4. Annie Besant, *Hindu Ideals*, pp. 152-153.
5. *The Besant Spirit*, Vol. 11, pp. 48-50.
6. *Ibid.*, pp. 61-62.
7. Anniversary Address, 1911 at the Central Hindu College by Annie Besant.
8. *The Besant Spirit*, Vol. 11, p. 82.
9. *Ibid.*, Vol. II, p. 88.
10. *The Besant Spirit*, Vol. II, pp. 89-90.
11. *Ibid.*, Vol. 1I, pp. 93-105. .
12. Annie Besant, *National Education Pamphlet* No. 1, pp. 1-14.
13. *Ibid.*, p. 1 .
14. *Ibid.*, p. 107.
15. *Ibid.*, pp. 15-49.
16. *Ibid.*, pp. 50-54

6

SRI AUROBINDO (1872—1950)

His Life

Sri Aurobindo was born in 1872 in Calcutta. His father sent him to England for education while he was only seven years of age. He remained there for fourteen years to complete his education both at London and Cambridge. He was instructed by his father to keep away from the Indian and Eastern culture while in England. His father wanted to anglicise him completely. Accordingly, he mastered Greek and Latin and obtained record marks in these languages at the Indian Civil Service Examination. In order to be able to reading great authors in original he also learnt French, German and Italian. Thus he received a purely occidental education. Yet it is surprising to note that no other Indian of the present age has shown such a profound knowledge of the soul of India as he displayed in his later life.

Sri Aurobindo passed the Indian Civil Service Examination in 1890, but he was disqualified for the Service, because he did not present himself at the riding examination. He left for India in 1893. After coming to India, he remained in the service of the Gaekwar of Baroda for thirteen years, from 1893 to 1906. During this period he prepared himself for his future work. He learnt Sanskrit and several modern Indian languages and assimilated the spirit of Indian civilization and Hindu religion. At the time of the partition of Bengal in 1905 he resigned his Baroda job and went to Calcutta to direct the newly awakened spirit of nationalism. He worked in the political field only for four years, but even during this short period he revolutionized the political thought in the country through his writings, speeches and famous journals—

The Bande Mataram, *The Karma Yogin* and *The Dharma*—which were short lived.

Sri Aurobindo's Nationalist Party did not agree with the Moderates' policy of begging and petitioning the British Government. So Sri Aurobindo declared *Swaraj* (Self-Government) as the goal for India. For his revolutionary political activities he was prosecuted several times and in 1908 was put in the Alipur Jail for about a year as an under-trial prisoner, but he was acquitted because of the brilliant advocacy of Chittaranjan Das. From his own words we judge that the period of detention in the Alipur Jail was the most momentous period in his life. In jail he had a profound religious experience which completely changed the course of his life. He has written that one day he had a vision of the spirit of God which urged him to work in the spiritual realm after his release and to carry the message of spiritual India to all mankind. He obeyed this command and retired from public life in 1910 and settled down in Pondicherry (then a French possession in Southern India), where he spent the whole of his remaining life. He died here in 1950. We shall study in brief his philosophy through which he aimed to give the message of India to the whole world.

It will be beyond the scope of this study to paint a complete picture of Sri Aurobindo's philosophy. But since his educational philosophy is only a corollary to his philosophy, we will take into account the fundamentals of his philosophy in general. Needless to mention that this account is only a very brief outline of his views.

Sri Aurobindo's Philosophy

Consciousness about Indian Renaissance and India's Greatness

While Sri Aurobindo was working in the political field he was conscious that India was passing through a period of Renaissance. He published a series of Articles in the *Arya* from August to November, 1918, and in the first article he says :

> *"Now the ... reawakening has come, India will certainly keep her essential spirit, will keep her characteristic soul, but there is likely to be a great change of the body. The shaping for*

> *itself of a new body, of new philosophical, artistic, literary, cultural, political, social forms by the same soul rejuvenescent will ... be the type of the Indian renaissance."*[1]

He himself answers the question, "What is this ancient spirit and characteristic soul of India?"

"Spirituality is indeed the master-key of the Indian mind; the sense of the infinite is native to it."[2]

He further asserts that :

> *"The note of spirituality is dominant, initial, constant, always recurrent; it is the support of all the rest. The first age of India's greatness was a spiritual age when she sought passionately for the truth of existence through the intuitive mind and through an inner experience and interpretation both of the psychic and the physical existence. The stamp put on her by that beginning she has never lost, but rather always enriched it with fresh spiritual experience...."*[3]

And Sri Aurobindo gave his entire self towards the enrichment of this stamp of spirituality that India bears. He has been quite conscious of the almost unimaginably prolific creativeness of India, because he rightly believed that India's spirituality did not flourish in the void. He says :

> *"For three thousand years at least ... she has been creating abundantly and incessantly, lavishly, with an inexhaustible many-sidedness, republics and kingdoms and empires; philosophies and cosmogonies and sciences; creeds, arts and poems ... systems of yoga, arts spiritual, arts worldly ... the list is endless and in each item there is almost a plethora of activity."*[4]

Sri Aurobindo's own life has been only a symbol of this plethora of activity for prolific creativeness.

Besides prolific creativeness of India, Sri Aurobindo speaks of the third characteristic of Indian genius which is 'a strong intellectuality'. To him it is an intellectuality "at once austere and rich, robust and minute, powerful and delicate, massive in principle and curious in detail." He sums up the greatness of Indian culture thus :

> *"An ingrained and dominant spirituality, an inexhaustible vital creativeness and gusto of life, and, meditating between them, a powerful, penetrating and scrupulous intelligence, combined of the rational, ethical and aesthetic mind at a high intensity of action created the harmony of the ancient Indian culture."*[5]

Sri Aurobindo says that at the time of decline, all these great powers of India deteriorated. Consequently, during the period of decadence, in every sphere of activity in India, in place of creation there was lifeless imitation, instead of intelligent appreciation there came in the despotic authority of rules and the balanced spiritual synthesis was replaced by over-emphasis on certain spiritual truths.

He regarded diseased spirituality as the root cause of all decadence in India. He urged that this state of affairs must end and put forth a programme for Indian Renaissance in the following words :

> *"The recovery of the old spiritual knowledge and experience in all its splendour, depth and fullness is its first, most essential work; the flowing of this spirituality into new forms of philosophy, literature, art, science and critical knowledge is the second; an original dealing with modern problems in the light of Indian spirit and the endeavour to formulate a greater synthesis of a spiritualised society is the third and most difficult. Its success on these lines will be the measure of its help to the future of humanity."*[6]

No wonder then that Sri Aurobindo set himself completely to the renovation of the decayed spirituality of India. He does not want only to enlarge and enrich the Indian culture but to give it a spiritual direction as well. He says :

> *"The greatness of the ancient Indian civilization consists in the power with which it did this work and the high and profound wisdom and skill with which, while basing society, ordering*

> *the individual life, encouraging and guiding human nature and propensity, it turned them all towards the realization of its master idea, and never allowed the mind, it was training, to lose sight of the use of life as a passage to the infinite and a discipline for spiritual perfection."*[7]

But in order to reach this goal Sri Aurobindo suggests that we must know our culture fully well and understand all its implications.

The Veda

Like Swami Dayananda, Sri Aurobindo regards the *Veda* as 'India's Rock of Ages'. He agrees with Dayananda's contention (1) that the Veda contains truth of science and truth of religion, (2) that it glorifies the one God of many names and powers, (3) that it celebrates the Divine law and man's aspiration to fulfil it, and (4) that it means to give us the Law of the Cosmos. Sri Aurobindo says that the hymns of the *Rig Veda* represent the gospel of the ancient Indian mystics. Therefore, they are essentially spiritual and psychological, and they should not be regarded as merely full of rituals and mythological details. He believes that the whole Vedic symbolism is woven around the two main parables—the *Angiras* legend and the *Vrtra*. So, in order to understand the *Veda,* we must be clear about the meaning of these parables. He observes :

> *"If Vrtra and the waters symbolize the cloud and the rain and the gushing forth of the seven rivers of the Punjab, and if the Angiras are the bringers of the physical dawn, then the Veda is a symbolism of natural phenomenon personified in the figure of Gods and Rsis and maleficent demons ... If on the other hand, this is a symbolism of struggle between spiritual powers of Light and Darkness. Truth and Falsehood, Knowledge and Ignorance, Death and Immortality, then that is the real sense of the whole Veda."*[8].

Sri Aurobindo regards the *Rig Veda* as the high aspiring song of Humanity. He thinks that *Chandogya*, the *Brhadaranyaka*, the *Taittiriya* and the *Aitareya Upanishadas* which may be considered the earlier Vedanta represent more faithfully the psychology of the Vedic Rsis. He finds the later Vedanta more ascetic in character and standing for a different set of values. He thinks that earlier Vedanta represents a balanced view of life by standing for a healthy integration of God and the world, renunciation and enjoyment, freedom of the soul and action of nature. Being and Becoming, the One and Many, *Vidya* and *Avidya,* knowledge and work, and birth and release. Instead of this integration, the later Vedanta imposes the impression that the world is a snare and meaningless burden on the soul itself, and the soul must get rid of this as soon as possible.

The Gita

Sri Aurobindo is of the conviction that it is this integral view of the earlier Vedanta which is admirably exposed in the *Gita*. He explains this in his two series of '*Essays on the Gita*'. He primarily regards the *Gita* as a gospel of *Yoga*, or fellowship with God. He is not content to regard it merely as a gospel of humanitarian work teaching man the sanctity of social duty and service. He says that the fellowship with the God which the *Gita* implies must generate in man an idea of new birth and a new idea of work. Thirdly, from the *Gita* a man must get the impression that the fellowship with God can be achieved only by disinterested action in society, by never-ending meditation, by self-forgetting devotion and by feeling a kind of unity of all things with God.

In the *Gita* Sri Aurobindo finds a synthetic *Yoga* wherein *Karma*, *Bhakti*, *Dhyana* and *Jnana* have been given due place. The *Karma Yoga* that the *Gita* teaches wants the surrender not only of the fruit of action (the *Phal*) but all the actions (the *Karma*) and its agency (the doer). Sri Aurobindo says that in order to attain self-liberation one must get rid of the agency. One must feel that it is Nature that acts and not the soul. After having realised this, one must surrender this agency of Nature to the Divine Power (*Sakti*). When the soul reaches this stage, it attains its full liberation. When one knows One's own nature and acts accordingly, his action is full of ease and spontaneity. This is exactly what the *Gita* means by *Svadharma* which is dependent upon *Svabhava* (one's own nature). By *Svadharma*, the *Gita* does not mean caste dictated duty, but the work which is organically dependent on one's own nature. By the terms one's own nature or *Svadharma,* the *Gita* implies the natural endowments of man and not the profession of one's parents—the son of a carpenter being a carpenter and the son of a warrior being a warrior for all the time. Thus the *Gita* stands for the evolution of man's action according to the inner law of nature.

Sri Aurobindo further states that the ideal man of the *Gita* is he who transcends his nature as well, and not merely confines himself within the bonds of his own nature. Transcending one's nature means rising above the qualities of Nature—*Sattva, Rajas* and *Tamas* and surrendering himself completely to God. The one who has reached this status is *Trigunatita*, i.e., one who has raised himself above the three attributes of nature. A *Trigunatita* attains union with God in body, mind and soul. This union results in the descent of the Divine power upon the person and by this descent the person becomes the instrument of God for fulfilling his cosmic purpose, and he is no longer himself. 'Now the Divine energy flows into the world through him.'

Sri Aurobindo gives his own interpretation about the three *Purusas* of the *Gita*, viz., *Ksara, Aksara* and *Uttama*. He regards *Ksara* as the individual soul subject to Nature. *Aksara* is the Lord having a vigilant eye over the work of nature and the *Uttama* is that supreme spirit (the *Purusottama)* which pervades Nature and goes beyond it.

A Reassertion of the Integral View of Life

In his interpretation of the *Tantras* Sri Aurobindo finds similar views. To him the *Tantras*, too, stand for the integral view of life culminating in synthetic *Yoga*. He points out that with all their shortcomings, the *Tantras* assert throughout that the liberation is to be achieved in this world and not outside and that this liberation consists in making oneself a perfect instrument of the Divine Power working in the world. The main purpose of Sri Aurobindo's life has been to reassert the integral view of life as implied in the *Veda,* the *Isa Upanisad*, the *Gita* and the *Tantras* and also to find out once again the ancient *Sadhana* and to make it available to all his fellow beings irrespective of caste, creed, colour and sex so that mankind may reach a higher level in the spiritual evolution.

The Supermind

Sri Aurobindo sets forth his philosophy in *The Life Divine*. We can only attempt to give a rough outline of what he propounded in this monumental work. His source of philosophy is the original Vedanta of the *Upanisads*, and not the schools of metaphysical philosophy. He believes that logical reasoning cannot help one to reach great spiritual truths. It is through intuition that one can reach them. So intuition should be connected by more perfect intuition and not by logical reasoning. Man's mind is an imperfect instrument—therefore, it cannot catch the full integral truth. Sri Aurobindo believes that the errors of the conceptual mind must be corrected by the Supermind which is the intermediary link between *Sachchidananda* and Universe, Knowledge and Ignorance. He says:

> *"We call it Supermind or Truth-Consciousness because it is in principle superior to mentality and exists, acts and proceeds in the fundamental truth and unity of things, and not like the mind, in its appearance and phenomenal divisions."*[9]

Sri Aurobindo regards it a knowledge—will or conscious-force. It is the dynamic aspect of God Himself. It is a self-force of God. Supermind is the divine gnosis which creates, governs and upholds the world. It is all-inclusive. It is the Lord within. In it there is no distinction of Knowledge, Knower or Known.

According to Sri Aurobindo, Supermind is a state of consciousness. One can acquire it gradually. After acquiring it one must use it for transforming one's entire being—body, mind and soul. When the man attains the supermind he becomes a superman, a *Jnani* or a gnostic individual. In the concluding chapter of *The Life Divine* he describes the nature of the gnostic individual and his way of life. He says:

> *"The gnostic individual would be the consummation of the spiritual man; his whole way of being, thinking, living, acting*

would be governed by the power of a vast universal spirituality ...He would feel the presence of the Divine at every centre of his consciousness ... All beings would be to him his ownselves... The gnostic individual would be in the world and of the world, but would also exceed it in his consciousness and live in his life of transcendence above it."[10]

Sri Aurobmdo translates the three Vedantic terms *Sat*, *Chit*, and *Ananda* as Pure Existent, Consciousness-Force and the Delight of Existence. Thus he does not interpret *Chit* as consciousness alone. He adds *force* to it, because to him force is inherent in the Eternal Being and this force may be immobile or mobile, for "the immobile and the mobile Brahman are both the same Reality."[11] To Sri Aurobindo the consciousness aspect of the Absolute is in its nature:

"*A self-expressive force capable of infinite variation in phenomenon and form and endlessly enjoying the delight of that variation.*"[12]

He says :

"*The Divine descends from pure Existence through the play of Consciousness-Force and Bliss and the creative medium of Supermind into cosmic being; we ascend ,from matter through a developing life, soul and mind and the illuminating medium of Supermind towards the divine being. The knot of the two, the higher and the lower hemisphere, is where mind and Supermind meet with a veil between them. The rending of the veil is the condition of the divine life in humanity; for by that rending, by the illuminating descent of the higher into the nature of the lower beings and the forceful ascent of the lower being into the nature of the higher, mind can never recover its divine light in the all-comprehending supermind, the soul realises its divine self in the all-blissful Ananda, life repossess its divine power in the play of omniscient Consciousness-Force and matter open to its divine liberty as a form of the Divine Existence.*"[13]

In this passage we find a beautiful summary of the whole of Sri Aurobindo's philosophy. He believes that it is through the intervening stages of mind and life that the spirit descended into matter. He further says that various worlds other than our own, originated as a result of this descent of spirit into matter. These worlds consisted of world of pure mind unhampered by life, and worlds of pure life unhampered by matter. He believes that these higher worlds are acting upon and are in communication with our own plane of being.[14]

Sri Aurobindo points out in the following manner the contrast between the working of the mind and that of the supermind :

> *"The mind acts by intellectual rule or device or by reasoned choice of will or by mental impulse or in obdience to life impulse: But supramental nature does not act by mental idea or rules or in subjection to any inferior impulse; each of its steps is dictated by an innate spiritual vision, a comprehensive and exact penetration into the truth of all and the truth of each thing; it acts always according to inherent reality, not by the mental idea, not according to an imposed law of conduct or a constructive thought or perceptive contrivance. Its movement is calm, self-possessed, spontaneous, plastic; it arises naturally and inevitably out of harmonic identity of the truth which is felt in the very substance of the conscious being, a spiritual substance which is universal and therefore, intimately one with all that is included in its cognition of existence."*[15]

Thus Sri Aurobindo, finds a wide gulf between the ordinary mind and the supermind. He suggests that this gulf should be bridged by *Yoga*.

Yoga

Sri Aurobindo defines *Yoga* as :

> *"a methodised effort towards self-perfection by the expression of the potentialities latent in the being, and a union of*

individual with the universal and transcendent existence we see partially expressed in man and in the cosmos."[16]

To him *All Life is Yoga.*[17] He says that the human and the cosmic evolution follow the same line. Therefore, *Yoga* is a compressed form of the method of evolution in Nature.[18] It is with an idea of integral Divine that he speaks about his integral Yoga. Thus the integral *Yoga* is based on integral philosophy, but is not subordinated to philosophy. However, in a way, he finds *Yoga* and philosophy correlative to each other.

To Sri Aurobindo the aim of *Yoga* is not to escape nature, but to become free from birth and death. The *Yoga* aims at divinizing the whole man, bringing down the supermind in order to transform the human mind, life and body. When this aim is fulfilled in a man's life, the man becomes a superman—the consummation of the spiritual man, and individual universal in nature but "free in the universe, individual but not limited by separate individuality". This is within the reach of any individual who practices *Yoga*. The aim of the spiritual man is to establish the Kingdom of God on earth. Therefore, first of all he will try to create a community of perfected individuals for raising the life of humanity. Therefore, Sri Aurobindo advises us to reform our minds before we try to reform the world. We should think in terms of unity, not of diversity; of harmony, not of discord; of All, not of Each. He repeats to us the teaching of the *Upanisad*— "Happiness lies in the infinite, not in the finite."

The greatness of Sri Aurobindo does not lie so much in his restatement of the integral spiritual ideal of the *Rig Veda,* the early *Upanisads* and the *Gita*, as in his actual practice of *Purna Yoga* by which the supramental consciousness comes down to influence the mental, vital and physical being of man. The methods of Yoga that he prescribes are free from the difficult feats of physical postures (*Asana Pranayama*) and mechanical exercises in concentration. His method is profoundly religious and spiritual. He recommends an absolute and unconditional surrender to God (*Atmasamarpana*) as the first step of *Yoga*; and this condition has to be maintained throughout. Man can achieve nothing on his own, unless he is helped by God. So man must surrender himself to God so that His grace may enter, purify and uplift him.

Life

Sri Aurobindo considers life as a form of the one cosmic Energy, a dynamic movement of current of it, positive and negative, a constant act or play of the force which builds up forms, energises them by an unceasing process of disintegration and renewal of their substance. Thus disintegration and renewal, status and change, birth and death, all are the processes of the same life. To Sri Aurobindo life is everywhere whether it is secret or manifest, organised or elemental, involved or evolved. He regards life as universal. It is all-pervading and imperishable. It differes only in form and organization. The same common force is engaged in each form. Sri Aurobindo finds no essential difference between the life in plant or in animal or man. Everywhere he finds the same birth, growth, nutrition, productivity and sterility, sleep and waking. The force that is fundamentally acting behind all this as the *Cit-Tapas* or *Cit-Sakti* of the Vedanta.

To Sri Aurobindo life is a universal organisation of conscious-force acting sub-consciously in matter. He finds three stages in this operation—material life, vital life and mental life—the subconscious, the conscious and the self-conscious.[19] Life is a connecting link between matter and mind. It is not like the mind, but it possesses all conscious-force behind it and it is this conscious-force that acts in created things.

The Law of Karman

Sri Aurobindo does not believe in the popular notion of the law of *Karman* in the sense of material rewards and punishments. He believes that even the heredity and environment are determined by the present and past actions of man. To him man is the maker of his own destiny. Man reaps the consequences not of his action alone, but sometimes he shares the results of the actions of others and *vice versa*, because all existence is continuous.

Sri Aurobindo finds a continuity between different births. He points out that sometimes it may be difficult to sense justice in nature's laws but on the whole the doctrine of *Karman* is valid. According to him even thoughts and feelings have corresponding results, though action has the greatest amount of result, because life consists more of action. Moreover, it is on actions that man exercises more control than on thoughts and feelings.

Sri Aurobindo is not a fatalist. He says that the law of *Karman* does not determine the destiny of the soul. It is the soul which uses the law as one of its instruments. Thus *Karman* cannot work as an impediment to spiritual freedom. As one proceeds towards higher and higher evolution, the grip of the mechanical law gradually breaks down and the individual attains more and more spiritual freedom. Sri Aurobindo says :

> *"Prakriti is the field of law and process but the soul the 'purusa' is the giver of the sanction, 'anumanta', and if ordinarily it chooses to remain a witness and concedes an automatic sanction, it can be, if it wills the master of its Nature, 'Iswara'."*[20]

The soul wants to grow out of ignorance. Therefore, it seeks self-expression and experience in the body. Furthermore, it wants the development of the nature through cosmic experience. Sri Aurobindo further says:

> *"All the secrets of the circumstances of rebirth centre around one capital need of the soul, the need of growth, the need of experience that governs the line of its evolution and all the rest is accessory."*[21]

Thus we come to the philosophy of rebirth as propounded by Sri Aurobindo.

The Philosophy of Rebirth

Sri Aurobindo does not believe that it is the law of *Karman* which determines rebirth. He regards rebirth as an indispensable machinery for working out a spiritual evolution. Hence birth and death are predetermined processes in the scheme of evolution. They are not sheer accidents. Human life must not be regarded as a chance product. It is through the human life that the secret spirit in the universe fulfils its purpose gradually by the enlarging and ascending individual soul-consciousness in the body. It should be noted that soul is not a byproduct of body, life or mind. It may take different forms according to its various manifestations. Sri Aurobindo remarks :

> *"The soul is not bound by the formula of mental humanity; it did not begin with that and will hot end with it; it had a prehuman past, it has a superhuman future."*[22]

Thus the individual soul grows through form to form till it reaches the human form which is only a stage to yet higher levels. Hence, the normal law is the reoccurrence of birth in new human forms. This reoccurrence does not stop, because the soul has to realise yet higher possibilities. Therefore, rebirth is an absolute necessity. Our world is not the only world, so the soul need not enter body immediately after death. There might be an interval between birth and death depending upon the unique experience of the soul which needs assimilation. This interval may be a passage to other worlds. After death the soul may choose to stay temporarily in some imaginary desire constructions. Thus births and deaths are intermediaries between the same process of evolution of the soul.

Sri Aurobindo's Philosophy : A Synthesis

Thus, it may be said that Sri Aurobindo gave us a philosophy through which we can find solutions of many problems of human life. His philosophy may be regarded as a happy synthesis of old and new. East and West, realism and idealism, pragmatism and spiritualism. Sri Aurobindo has asserted that it is the synthetic or integral approach to the problems of human life that can serve humanity. He has shown the path which will lead to the regeneration of mankind.

Sri Aurobindo's Educational Philosophy

Sri Aurobindo has explained his educational philosophy in the weekly *Karmayogin* published from February 12 to April 2,1910. It is true that Sri Aurobindo is one of the greatest educators of humanity of all times, in the sense that he dedicated his life in showing man the path to the supreme spiritual advancement which alone can give solace to mankind. But here it is proposed only to understand what Sri Aurobindo has to say about the training of young children as expressed in his articles.

The Four Layers of the Mind

Sri Aurobindo regards the mind (or *Antahkarana*) as the chief instrument of the teacher. He thinks that the mind consists of four layers. The past mental impression (*Chitta*), or the store house of memory is the foundation on which the other three layers rest. It is from the *Chitta* that the active memory selects its requirements at times. Sometimes this selection is properly made, and sometimes irrelevant things are selected. Sri Aurobindo thinks that the passive memory or the *Chitta* needs no training, because it is automatic and naturally sufficient for its purposes. Hence it is the active memory which needs training and improvement.

The mind proper or *Manas* is the second layer. It is in this layer that all the other layers are collected. The function of the mind is to receive the images coming from the five senses—touch, smell, taste, sight and sound and translate them into thought-sensations. Sri Aurobindo believes that the mind is also capable of receiving images of its own direct grasping. The mind transforms these images into mental impressions. These sensations and impressions are the materials of thought. For making the thought efficient it is very important that these materials are sufficient and perfect. Therefore, it is the duty of the teacher to see that the six senses, i.e. sight, sound, taste, smell, touch and mind (which receives images of its own grasping), are so trained as to make them as keen, subtle and sensitive as possible. Sri Aurobindo says :

> *"It is, therefore, the first business of the educationist to develop in the child the right use of the six senses; to see that they are not stunted or injured by disuse, but trained by the child himself under the teacher's direction to that perfect accuracy and keen subtleness of which they are capable."*[23]

In this training the help of the organs of action should be utilised. For example, the hand should be encouraged to reproduce what the eye sees and the mind senses. Similarly, speech should be trained to express the knowledge contained by the whole *antakharana* or the whole mind.

The intellect or *buddhi* is the third layer. It is the real instrument of thought. It is the intellect which arranges and rearranges the elements of knowledge coming to the mind. Sri Aurobindo thinks that this third layer or the intellect is the most important for the educationist. It is the intellect which has the comprehensive, creative, synthetic, critical and analytical faculties. The comprehensive, creative and synthetic faculties of the intellect may be regarded as its right hand. This right hand judges, imagines, memorises, observes, commands and manipulates. Sri Aurobindo believes that the critical and analytical faculties of the intellect may be regarded as its left hand. The left hand or the critical faculties "distinguish, compare, classify, generalise, deduce, infer and conclude".[24] Thus these faculties are the essentials of logical reasoning. The right hand mind is the master of knowledge, because it penetrates deeply into its very soul. The left hand mind is only the servant of the mind, because it only touches the body of knowledge. The left hand tries to ascertain the truth, whereas the right hand grasps even those elements which are not yet ascertained and verified. Both the right and left hands of the mind are essential for human reason. So both these hands of the mind must be perfectly trained to the highest possible degree, otherwise the education of the child will remain incomplete and one-sided.

Sri Aurobindo is of the opinion that the fourth layer of the mind is the power of 'intuitive perception of truth'; 'a direct vision of knowledge's amounting to revelation and making a man a 'prophet of truth'. He says that this power of the mind is not yet fully developed in man, and it is still in the process of a gradual and wider development. He considers this power as rare, and many possess it imperfectly or by flashes. The critical reason of man is not prepared to accept this power, because "the admixture of error, caprice, or a biased imagination" may distort its perfect working. Yet Sri Aurobindo is convinced of the existence and manifestation of this power. He argues that if it were not so the humanity would not have advanced to its present stage.[25] He thinks that the educationists have not yet grappled with the problem of developing this intuitive power which may be manifested in the genius of a pupil. An ideal and liberal teacher is he who encourages and welcomes this intuitive power in the pupil.

This faculty of intuitive power is so important to humanity that it must not be left out of consideration. This faculty must be encouraged and developed by carefully eliminating, "the admixture of error, caprice and biased fancifulness".[26] But here the teacher cannot do anything directly for the pupil. In fact, the pupil is to be encouraged to develop according to his own nature; and the teacher is only a guide. Similarly, in relation to the development of the intuitive faculty in the pupil, the teacher is to allow him to grow his own way to perfection. Sri Aurobindo says :

> *"The teacher is not an instructor or task-master, he is a helper and a guide. His business is to suggest and not to impose. He does not actually train the pupil's mind, he only shows him how to perfect his instruments of knowledge and helps him and encourages him in the process. He does not impart knowledge to him, he shows him how to acquire knowledge for himself. He does not call forth the knowledge that is written; he only shows him where it lies and how it can be habituated to rise to the surface."*[27]

Sri Aurobindo strikes here one of the fundamental principles of education as have been repeatedly asserted generally by many naturalists and pragmatists.

The Nature of True Education

To Sri Aurobindo only such education is true and living which helps one to develop his latent powers and enables him to enter into the right relation with life, mind, and soul of his nation as well as with the total life, mind and soul of humanity. He[28] says that man has developed certain vital propensities—an ego, a mind and a reason. Therefore, his whole life and education should be so guided as to satisfy these propensities under the control of a trained mind and reason. The education which tries to do this is true.

Education must not be 'a machine made fabric'. It should aim at building the powers of the mind and spirit of the human being. Sri Aurobindo recognises a universal mind and a soul of humanity. Between these there is an intermediate power, the mind of a nation. The education which takes into consideration all these three minds is true.[29]

The acquiring of various kinds of information is not all that is wanted. In fact, the central[30] aim of education should be to assist man to build the power of his mind and spirit. For the fulfilment of this central aim, the human mind at all the stages of development—infancy, childhood, adolescence and adulthood—must be understood. The human mind receives images of things through the five principal source or gateways of knowledge, viz., sight, sound, smell, taste and touch. The mind translates these images into thought sensations. These thought—sensations are the material of thought, not thought itself. The mind is also capable of receiving images of its own direct grasping. These images are later on transformed into mental impressions. Above all the teacher should see that the child is able to use his five senses accurately and is able to form correct mental impressions.

We have noted that besides the ordinary mind, Sri Aurobindo recognizes a Supermind which exists beyond the mind, life and matter. Just as mind, life and matter manifest themselves on the earth, similarly the Supermind, too, manifests itself in this world of Matter. The development of consciousness of this Supermind, and the utilization of this Supermind for the development of an integrated human personality is the true aim of education.

To Sri Aurobindo, the real meaning of life is to rise above ego and become our true self, i.e., to be conscious of our real being. To possess the self is the ultimate meaning of life on this earth. Only that education is true which helps one to realise his real being—the self. Sri Aurobindo advises us to accept the ancient idea that man has within him not only the physical soul or *Purusa*, but also a vital, mental, psychic, supermental, supreme spiritual being.[31] Only that education is true which helps one to become actively conscious of these powers. Sri Aurobindo says :

> *"The first necessity for the building up of a great intellectual superstructure is to provide a foundation strong enough to bear it."*[32]

He deplores that the modern system of education does not provide this foundation and that it mainly emphasises on giving information about various subjects. He believes that in this state of affairs, a fundamental error, has been committed. He says:

> *"Informaton cannot be the foundation of intelligence, it can only be a part of the material out of which knower builds knowledge, the starting point, the nucleus of fresh discovery and enlarged creation. An education that confines itself to imparting knowledge, is no education."*[33]

Therefore, Sri Aurobindo believes only that education is true which not only equips the various faculties of the mind with the relevant tools and materials but trains them also :

> *"To bring fresh materials and use more skilfully those which are in possession. And the foundation of the structure they have to build, can only be the provision of a fund of force and energy sufficient to bear the demands of a continuity growing, activity of the memory, judgement and creative power."*[34]

Only that education is true which helps the child to develop his intellectual and moral capacities to their highest limit. Hence education must be based on the psychology of child-nature. The child should not be regarded as an object to be handled and transformed by the teacher as per his own whims. It must be noted that each human being is self-developing soul. The parents and the teacher must enable the child to educate himself, to develop his own practical, intellectual, moral and aesthetic capacities, and to grow independently as an organic being. The education which helps the child in this supreme task is true.

One must know that man is a soul within, and a conscious power of the divine. The evocation of this conscious power of the divine within is the real aim of education, and the education which does this is true. The fulfilment of the individual does not consist in the utmost growth of his egoistic intellect, vital force, physical welfare and the maximum satisfaction of his physical, emotional and mental cravings, but the development of the divine in him to the maximum limit of power, love, wisdom and universality. It is through this development that he will attain the maximum realisation of all the possible beauty and delight of existence. The education which helps a child to thus develop is true.

Training of the Senses

Sri Aurobindo recognises the six senses which help one to receive knowledge—sight, hearing, smell, touch, taste and mind. Except for the mind all the other five senses are dependent for their activity on the organs of the eye, ear, nose, skin and palate. Sri Aurobindo attaches great importance to the training of these senses and advises that their training should be the first care of the teacher.[35] Our senses must be accurate and sensitive and if there is any hindrance in making them so, that hindrance must be removed. In order to make the senses perfect, the cause of their imperfection must be understood.

The unobstructed activity of the nerves is necessary for making the senses accurate and sensitive. In themselves the organs have a tendency to do their work perfectly. It is only when obstructed that they fail to serve us. The obstacle may be in the nerve current.

The nerves are channels which carry information to the brain. In that case the help of some physician must be sought.[36]

Sri Aurobindo believes that if the defects in the senses are not due to physical injury or some physiological inadequacy or deformity, they can be removed by the purification of the nerve system, i.e., by the regulation of breathing. The regulation of the breathing is called nerve-purification or *Nadi-Suddhi* according to the Yogic discipline.

If there is no defect in the organ, and the nerve channels are clear, the defective functioning of the senses may be due to the inadequate functioning of the mind, the sixth sense. The mind (the *Manas*) is in itself like a channel similar to the nerves. It is a channel for communicating with the Buddhi or brain-force. The mind is both a sense organ and a channel. As a sense organ it is as perfect as the other five senses; but as a channel it is liable to obstruction or distortion.[37]

The mind, as a sense organ receives thought impressions from outside and from within. These impressions are perfectly correct in themselves, but in their reporting they may not reach the intellect at all or may reach it in a distorted way thus, giving false impressions. The full development of the sensitiveness of the mind is called *Sukshmadrishti*, or subtle reception of images in *Yogic discipline*. Sri Aurobindo deplores that the development of the sixth sense has never been included in the system of education of man. He advises that mind should be so trained as to give a correct report to the intellect in order to enable us to start our thinking correctly.

He further observes that man often looks at things with a bias which he holds because of his environment. Therefore, man is prone to interpret acts according to his habitual ways of looking at them. It is only a more developed mind which can interpret first impressions without an unconscious bias. In order to make oneself free of bias while interpreting impressions, one must purify one's mental and moral habits, i.e., one must attain '*Chitta-Suddhi*'. This is a preliminary process of *Yoga*, and Sri Aurobindo[38] regrets that this should be considered out of place in a modern system of education. He emphatically states that this source of disturbance in the functioning of the mind will continue unless some of the principles of the old Indian system are incorporated in the system of modern education. He further remarks that our national education should not be controlled wholly by European ideas, and in the matter of developing the sensitiveness of the mind (the sixth sense) we must accept our old Indian system.[39]

Sri Aurobindo says that insufficient use might be another cause of the inefficiency of the senses. Sometimes, it so happens that we do not observe sufficiently and a sight, sound smell, even touch or taste do not fall within our perception. In fact, one ought to be accustomed to catch the various sense-impressions promptly and be able to distinguish their nature and mark their properties and sources and finally so arrange them in the mind as to recall them in future at will. But experiments have shown that the faculty of observation is very imperfectly developed in men, because of the want of due care in the use of senses and the memory.[40] This faulty observation can be removed by training the senses to work efficiently; and for this the child should be encouraged to use his various senses in appropriate situations.

Training of the Mental Faculties

Sri Aurobindo emphasises the training of the mental faculties.[41] The pupil should be encouraged to develop the power of attention. By attention he does not mean only centring the mind on one thing at a time. He believes that it is possible to develop the power of double concentration, triple concentration, multiple concentration. He admits that the tendency of the mind is to attend to one thing at a time, but he insists that through steady natural practice attention may be equally distributed over a number of circumstances in such a way as to learn everything perfectly. Towards this goal, the teacher must try to see that the student learns to observe accurately and concentrate his attention on things in a gradually increasing degree.

Like the faculties of observation and attention, memory and judgement should also be trained.[42] The student should not be required to repeat the same lesson for a number of times in order to commit it to memory. This is a mechanical and unintelligent way of training the memory. Instead, the pupil should be encouraged to observe something carefully and concentrate his attention thereon in order to reach a judgement about the same. Thus he will acquire a habit of observing the similarities of things and their differences. Sri Aurobindo advises that the teacher must take every care to encourage this habit in the pupil. He[43] believes that with the help of the powers of observation, attention, judgement and memory, the pupil will learn botany through flowers and plants, astronomy through stars, geology through earth and stones, etc., entomology and zoology through insects and animals. Sri Aurobindo thinks that every scientific subject may be taught by training of faculties to observe, compare, remember and judge various classes of objects. It is not always necessary to take recourse to formal teaching of a particular subject in a classroom.

Sri Aurobindo considers the faculty of imagination as the most important and indispensable instrument of education. He divides imagination into three functions :

"1. the forming of mental images,
2. the power of creating thoughts,
3. the appreciation of the soul in things, beauty, charm, greatness, hidden suggestiveness, the emotion and spiritual life that pervades the world."[44]

The teacher must see that the pupil is able to exercise these three functions of imagination. Sri Aurobindo recommends that:

> *"The mental faculties should first be exercised on things, afterwards on words and ideas."*[45]

The Training of the Logical Faculty

Sri Aurobindo realises the necessity of training the logical faculty.[46] For this he recognizes three steps. The first step is to make the child interested in drawing inferences from facts, tracing cause and effect. The second step is to mark its success and failure and the third step is to find out the cause of the success and failure. In this way the mind can be trained to reason correctly. Sri Aurobindo is not in favour of teaching formal logic in order to train a child in reasoning at an early age. Therefore, he advises to postpone it for a later stage, when it can be mastered in a very brief period.

Principle of Teaching

Sri Aurobindo[47] believes that the mind must be consulted in the process of its growth. Therefore, the child must not be moulded according to the desire of the parents or teacher. To do so is barbarous. The child himself must be left free to grow according of his own nature. It is a folly of the highest magnitude on the part of parents to expect that their child should develop particular qualities, capacities, ideas and virtues. The child must never be prepared for a prefixed career. To force the child to abandon his own nature (*Svadharma*) is to do a permanent harm to him, to mutilate his growth and deface his perfection. Everyone has something divine within him, something his own. The task of education is to discover, develop and use this something. The principal aim of education is to help the growing soul to its best form and to be devoted to a noble cause.

According to Sri Aurobindo another principle of teaching is "to work from the near to the far, i.e., from that which is to that which shall be".[48] Heredity and environment are the basis of man's nature. Therefore the educator must constantly keep in view these two basic factors which condition the growth of an individual. We must accept the heredity as it is, but the environment may be arranged according to the needs and interests of the child. If this is done then true foundation is laid for a genuine development. Sri Aurobindo says: "The past is our foundation, the present our material, the future our aim". In any system of education all the three, i.e., the past, present and future, should have their due place. In other words, it may be said that the past, i.e., the heredity and the cultural heritage of an individual must not be ignored. The present, i.e., the nature of the individual and the needs of the modern society must be the guiding principles while striving to reach our chosen goals which must be designed in the best interest of both the individual and the society in which he happens to live.

The Early Training of the Child[49]

Sri Aurobindo wants that above all the child should be made interested in life, work and knowledge. In order to do this his instruments of knowledge, i.e., the senses, should be developed properly, and then he should be helped to acquire the mastery of the medium that he must use. The medium that he must use should be his mother-tongue. The child should be successively introduced to the most interesting and vitalizing parts of his country's literature and history and the life around him. The child should be encouraged to know the living and human parts of his nation's history. Every child wants to inquire, investigate, analyse and anatomise. He should be helped to acquire the scientific attitude unconsciously. The intellectual curiosity of the child should be used to help him to enter into metaphysical inquiry, so that he may begin to understand the world and himself. Every child has a natural power of imitation and imagination. This power should be used to develop in him the faculty of the artist.

Moral and Religious Education

Sri Aurobindo says :

"In the economy of man the mental nature rests upon the moral,

> *and the education of the intellect divorced from the perfection of the moral and emotional nature is injurious to human progress*"[50]

Thus, he believes that an intellectual education divorced from the perfection of the moral and emotional nature defers human progress. He admits the difficulty of providing moral and religious training in the modern schools and colleges, and he says that the study of moral and religious textbooks is a vanity and delusion, because the heart is not necessarily educated by the instructing mind, though the mind can influence the heart up to some extent. But the danger of moral textbooks is that through them the understanding of high thoughts becomes mechanical and artificial, and hence the same cannot but put into actual practice.

Emotions, 'formed habits and associations'[51] and nature[52] are the three chief aspects to be dealt with in connection with a child's moral nature. In order to make the child moral, he must be guided to get habituated to the right emotions, the noblest associations and to follow the fundamental impulses of his basic nature to right action. As in the education of the mind, so in the education of the heart, the best way to help the child is to put him on the right road to his own perfection and to encourage him to follow it and in no way should the child be interfered with in this process. Sri Aurobindo remarks :

> *"The old Indian system of the Guru commanding, by his knowledge and sanctity, the implicit obedience, perfect admiration, reverent emulation of the student was a far superior method of moral discipline. It is impossible to restore that ancient system; but it is not impossible to substitute the wise friend, guide and helper for the hired instructor or the benevolent policeman which is all that the European system usually makes of the pedagogue."*[53]

Thus according to Sri Aurobindo moral education can be given only if the teacher assumes the role of a friend, guide and helper and not that of one who imposes. Therefore, he thinks that in moral training it is the suggestions which are more helpful, and not commands and impositions. The personal example in all the walks of life within the reach of the child is the best suggestion. The child should be given an opportunity to put into action the moral impulses that arise within him. Sri Aurobindo says:

> *"The thirst for knowledge, the self-devotion, the purity, the renunciation of the Brahmin—the courage, ardour, honour, nobility, chivalry, patriotism of the Kshatriya—the beneficence, skill, industry, general enterprise and large openhandedness of the Vaisya—the self-effacement and loving service of the Shudra"*[54]

are the chief qualities of the Aryan. These are the qualities that should form the moral attitude of our youngman. For developing this attitude it is necessary to train our youngman in the Aryan traditions.

With regard to religious education, Sri Aurobindo says that the teaching of dogmas to children is no religious training worth the name, because dogmas cannot help them to become pious and moral. In fact, religion must be lived and experienced, and not learnt as a creed. He says:

> *"No religious teaching is of any value unless it is lived, and the use of various kinds of Sadhana, spiritual self-training and exercise is the only effective preparation for religious living."*[55]

He further believes that the ritual of prayer, homage and ceremony may be helpful to spiritual progress if they are not made an end in themselves. It is unimportant whether any distinct training in any form of religion is given or not. In fact,

> *"The essence of religion, i.e., to live for God, for humanity, for country, for others and for oneself in these."*[56]

is the real religious ideal which must be propounded in every school and college.

Sri Aurobindo Ashram

With the educational philosophy of Sri Aurobindo as the guiding spirit. The Mother[57] has tried to conduct the affairs of the Sri Aurobindo Ashrama—with which Sri Aurobindo hardly interfered because of lack of time, as he devoted himself entirely to the understanding of the spiritual realm. She organized a school and an International University in the *Ashrama* at Pondicherry. It is true that we cannot think of the Ashrama without thinking of Sri Aurobindo, but in this treatise it is not proposed to examine the workings of the Ashrama and of the school and the International University centre in terms of Sri Aurobindo's educational philosophy.

NOTES

1. *Sri Aurobindo: The Renaissance in India,* 4th Ed., p. 6.
2. *Ibid.*, p. 8.
3. *Ibid.*, pp. 21-22.
4. *Ibid.*, pp. 10-11.
5. *Ibid.*, p.15.
6. *Ibid.*, p. 27
7. Quoted in D.S. Sharma's *The Renaissance of Hinduism*, p. 317.
8. *Ibid.*, p. 320.
9. *The Life Divine*, Vol. 1, Second Edition, p. 174.
10. *The Life,* Vol. II, pp. 1035-36.
11. *Ibid.*, Vol. II, p. 1250.
12. *Ibid.*, Vol. II, p. 129.
13. *Ibid.*, Vol. 1, p. 404.
14. *Ibid.*, Vol. II, p. 755.
15. *Ibid.*, Vol. II, p. 1026.
16. *The Synthesis of Yoga*, First University Edition, p. 4.
17. *Ibid.*, p. 7.
18. *Ibid.*, p. 5.
19. *Ibid.*, Vol. I, Second Edition, p. 225.
20. *The Life Divine,* Vol. II, Second Edition, p. 629.
21. *Ibid.*, p. 637.
22. *Ibid.*, p. 581.
23. *Sri Aurobindo: A System of Nation*, 4th Ed., p. 9.
24. *Ibid.*, p. 10.
25. *Ibid.*, p. 12.
26. *Ibid.*
27. *Ibid.*, p. 3.
28. *Integral Education,* compiled by Dr. Indra Sen, p. 1.

29. *Ibid.*, p. 3.
30. *Ibid.*, p. 5.
31. *Taittiriya Upanisad.*
32. *Sri Aurobindo : The Brain of India*, p. 12.
33. *Ibid.*, p. 13.
34. *Ibid.*, pp. 13-14.
35. *Ibid.*, p. 31.
36. *Ibid.*, p. 33.
37. *Ibid.*, p. 35.
38. *Ibid.*, p. 38.
39. *Ibid.*, p. 42.
40. *Ibid.*
41. *Ibid.*, pp. 45-52.
42. *Ibid.*, pp. 47-48.
43. *Ibid.*, p. 49.
44. *Ibid.*, p. 51.
45. *Ibid.*, p. 52.
46. *Ibid.*, pp. 53-57.
47. *Integral Education,* compiled by Dr. Indra Sen, p. 6.
48. *Ibid.*
49. *Ibid.*, pp. 27-28.
50. *Ibid.*, p. 13.
51. *Samskaras, Ibid.*, p. 14.
52. *Ibid.*
53. *Ibid.*, p. 17.
54. *Ibid.*, p. 18.
55. *Ibid.*, p. 21.
56. *Ibid.*
57. A French lady who dedicated herself to the realiazation of Sri Aurobindo's ideals in her own life.

7

MAHATMA GANDHI (1869—1948)

His Life

Mohandas Karamchand Gandhi was born on 2nd October, 1869 at Porbandar in Kathiawar. His father and grandfather were the Prime Ministers of the State of Porbandar. His father became the Prime Minister of the other two Kathiawar States—Rajkot and Vankaner also. Gandhiji's mother was a saintly woman and she had a strong influence on his life. Gandhiji passed his Matriculation examination in 1887 and sailed for England on September 4,1887 to study law. Gandhiji stayed in England as a student for three years and nine months. He passed his Law Examination and on June 10,1891 was called to the bar.

Gandhiji returned home in 1891 only to discover that his mother had passed away. He tried to set up practice in Bombay, but he could not earn sufficient to live on. So he went to Rajkot to try his luck in the local court there.

In April, 1893 Gandhiji went to South Africa in connection with a big law case. He hoped to come back to India within a year. Little did he know that he would spend twenty years of his life there and find a spiritual weapon to fight for the regeneration of India and for gaining political freedom for his countrymen. It is not the purpose of this chapter to describe the political activities of Gandhiji for the emancipation of his countrymen in South Africa and for the liberation of India from the British rule, nor to describe his greatness as a social reformer or his greatness as a man. By his unparallel sacrifice Gandhiji has become a legend not only of India but in human history of the whole world. He commanded universal respect and when on January 30, 1948, Nathuram Godse, a Hindu, shot him dead, the whole world was plunged into deep and indescribable grief. At his death the *New York Times* wrote :

> *"He left as his heritage a spiritual force that must in God's good time prevail over arms and armaments and dark doctrines of violence"* (January 31,1948).

On his death Mr. H.S. Suhrawardy[1] wrote :

> *"I feel as if the bottom of the world has fallen out. Who is there who will now assuage the anguish of the oppressed, who is there who will now wipe their tears? To him we had learnt to turn for guidance and for advice in all our difficulties and he never failed us."*

To understand Gandhiji's educational philosophy we must understand his philosophy of life which is at the root of all his ideas—social, political and educational.

Gandhiji: Philosophy of Life

Gandhiji says :

> *"I do not claim to have originated any new principle. I have simply tried in my own way to apply the eternal truths to our daily life and problems. Well, all my philosophy, if it may be called by that pretentious name, is contained in what I have said. You will not call it "Gandhism," there is no "ism," about it. And no elaborate literature or propaganda is needed about it."*[2]

Thus Gandhiji himself has not claimed that he is an original thinker of new ideas, and so his ideas do not constitute a system of new philosophy in the strict academic sense. He learned what he called *eternal truths* from the great religions of the world. He applied these truths to life and thus developed a kind of new philosophical outlook.

In the words of Lionel Curtis :

> *"Few men, if any, in my generation have commanded so great a following, have so changed the course of events, and so influenced thought in more than one continent than Mr. Gandhi."*[3]
>
> *"In M.K. Gandhi is to be found an integration of life. He is never standing apart, the spiritual superior aloof. If he is a Mahatma or Great soul, he is also a man of the people, amongst the people. Clear sighted, keeping much silence before God, humble-minded in the essential sense, the spiritual man of prayer and vision; he is also the man of much physical work, very approachable, lovable and humorous—moral and religious, social and political."*[4]

In a nut-shell B.G. Ray observes Gandhiji, the philosopher, as under:

> *Gandhiji starts from his Hindu religion; and the metaphysical solution of eternal problems from a Hindu angle of vision forms the basis of his philosophy. He has not sought to answer or solve the problems from an independent perspective, of experience or of reason."*[5]

However, Gandhiji approached the problems of life in his own way which is undoubtedly based on Hinduism. But he did not regard Hinduism as the only true religion. He considered all religions as different paths leading to the same destination. He says :

> *"I do not believe in the exclusive divinity of the Vedas. I believe that Bible, the Koran and the Zend-Avesta to be as divinely inspired as Vedas."*[6]

He further observes :

> *"All religions are founded on the same moral laws. My ethical religion is made up of laws which bind men all over the world."*[7]

It was this cosmopolitan and catholic attitude of Gandhiji which has endeared him not only to the Indian people but to the whole world.

The Nature of Reality

To Gandhiji the nature of reality is Truth. He believes that God can be realised only through Truth. Wherever there is Truth there is God. God exists because Truth exists. Thus he regards Truth and God as one. To him truth includes beauty and goodness as well. He says :

> *"A true art must help the soul to realise its innerself ... All truths, not merely true ideas but truthful faces, truthful pictures or songs are highly beautiful. People generally fail to see beauty in truth ... Whenever men begin to see beauty in truth, then true art will arise."*[8]

He further remarks :

> *"Truth is not only truthfulness in word, but truthfulness in thought also, and not only the relative truth of our conception, but the absolute truth, the Eternal principle that is God."*[9]

Thus Gandhiji considers *Truth* as Absolute, fixed and unalterable which can never be destroyed.[10] To him Truth means reality. He regards Truth as the 'real existent', God. To realise God, he believes that one must plunge into active social service. He wants to see God in His works and Truth in action. To him God is Truth, Goodness and Beauty (*Satyam, Sivam, Sundaram*). So in order to realise God one must be true, good and beautiful in thoughts and deeds. Thus Gandhiji's concept of reality affirms :

> *"The existence of absolute values which are neither the projection of individual minds, nor the product of the social process."*[11]

His Conception of God

To Gandhiji, God is the all-pervasive Reality, immanent in man and also in the world which he considers as His manifestation and creation. But he thinks that God is also transcendent. He is in the world and beyond it. Thus he has a comprehensive conception of God. He says:

> *"I believe Him to be creative as well as non-creative ... From the platform of the Jainas I prove the non-creative aspect of God, and from that of Ramanuja the creative aspect. As a matter of fact, we are to know the Unknown, and this is why our speech falters, is inadequate and even often contradictory. That is why the Vedas describe Brahman as "not this, not this". But if He or It is not this, He or It is ... He is one and yet many; He is smaller than an atom, and yet bigger than the Himalayas."*[12]

Evidently, Gandhiji tries to include within his conception the diverse elements of various religious teachings and regards them as the various aspects of the same Reality whose limitless richness is beyond our comprehension, Therefore, he describes God on different occasions from different angles, but his basic idea of God as the All Pervasive Reality is visible in all his expressions. He gives an eloquent description of his conception of God when he says :

> *"God is that indefinable something which we all feel but which we do not know. To me God is Truth and Love, God is Ethics and Morality. God is Fearlessness. God is the source of light and life and yet He is above and beyond all these. God is conscience. He is even the atheism of the atheist. He transcends speech and reason. He is a personal God to those who need His touch. He is the purest essence. He simply is to those who have faith. He is long suffering. He is patient but He is also terrible. He is the greatest democrat the world knows, for He leaves us unfettered to make our own choice between evil and good. He is the greatest tyrant ever known for he often dashes the cup from our lips and under cover of free will leaves us a*

margin so wholly inadequate as to provide only mirth for himself at our expense. Therefore, it is Hinduism that calls all this sport—Lila, *or calls it an illusion—Maya.*"[13]

In the above synthetic outlook Gandhiji imposes a great strain on the customary channels of thought. But today when scientific inventions are overcoming space and time and there is a great desire for common understanding between people in isolated areas, the necessity of this synthetic outlook is all the more important.

God and Evil

Thus we may infer that Gandhiji includes within his conception of God not only the benign aspects of the world but also its tyranny, terror and atheism. Thus he would like to face the problem of evil rather than sacrifice the infinity and total reality of God. Therefore, he is realistic enough to take into account His aspects of suffering, tyranny and terror. However, he feels that he cannot give an explanation of evil, because man is not capable of understanding fully the motives of all actions of God. This is clear from the words of Gandhiji :

"I cannot account for the existence of evils by any rational method. To want to do so is to be co-equal with God. I am therefore humble enough to recognize evil as such. And I call God long-suffering and patient precisely because He permits evil in the world. I know that He has no evil."[14]

God is Truth

To Gandhiji God is Truth and Truth is God. He says:

"I would say with those who say God is Love, Love is God. But deep down in me I used to say that though God may be God, God is truth above all ..."[15]

Upanisads, which influenced Gandhiji so much, also depict God, Brahaman, as Truth, Knowledge and Infinite. Jesus also says,

"I am the way, and the truth, and the life".[16] It is in this sense that Gandhiji declares God is Truth, Love and Conscience. "Truth is God" implies that "Truth should be the object of Worship". Undoubtedly, Gandhiji worshipped Truth as such throughout his life.

Gandhiji wanted to realize God through service to man. He says:

> *"Man's ultimate aim is realization of God, all his activities, social, political, religious have to be guided by the ultimate aim of the Vision of God. The immediate service of all human beings becomes a necessary part of the endeavour, simply because the only way to, find God is to see Him in His creation and be one with it... This can only be done by service to all".*[17]

Thus, Gandhiji endeavoured to seek God through serving man, and realizing the truth through action. Gandhiji says:

> *"I believe in absolute oneness of God and therefore also of humanity. What though we have many bodies? We have but one soul. The rays of the sun are many through refraction. But they have the same source."*[18]

Thus to Gandhiji God is the one binding force for all individuals. Man can live without food but not without God.[19] Gandhiji, however, does not believe in a personal God. He says:

> *"My Ram, the Ram of our prayers is not the historical Ram, the son of Dasharath, the King of Ayodhya. He is the eternal, the upborn, the one without the second. Him alone I worship."*[20]

Gandhiji regards God as benevolent. He says:

> *"I see, God is purely benevolent, ,for, I can see that in the midst of untruth, truth persists, in the midst of darkness, light persists. Hence I gather that God is Life, Truth, Light. He is love—Supreme Good".*[21]

Thus Gandhiji's belief in God is very rational and it will be difficult for anyone to deny belief in such a God. He has said:

> *"You believe in some principle, clothe it with life, and say that it is your God ... I should think it enough."*[22]

Inner Voice

Some explanation is needed about Gandhiji's 'inner voice' or 'God's Voice' which has mystified many. There were many occasions when he heard the inner voice.

> *"Everyone who wills can hear the voice. It is within every one. But like everything else, it requires previous and definite preparation."*[23]

Gandhiji's mind was ever awake and used to observe the ever changing surroundings. While his mind was working in a çertain direction, then, quite unexpectedly at a certain moment,

> *"A decision came to him as if in a flash, as an intuition, or to use his own phrase, as voice of God or the inner voice."*[24]

Radhakrishnan has pointed out that :

> *"Intuition is not opposed to intellectual or discursive process of thought but is often the crowning result of that process."*[25]

Romain Rolland also says :

> *"What we call inspiration is the development of reason ... No genuine, inspiration ever contradicts reason. Where it does it is no inspiration."*[26]

In the case of Gandhiji the 'inner voice' was intuition or inspiration which used to come only through inner reasoning of which he was not quite conscious.

His Conception of the World

Gandhiji regards the world as real. He does not believe in renouncing it, because he believes that the practice of *Ahimsa* (non-violence) is meaningful in society alone. He says :

> *"... The world is changing every moment and is therefore unreal, it has no permanent existence. But though it is constantly changing, it has something about it which persists and it is therefore to that extent real...."*[27]

It is because of this belief that he participates in so called wordly affairs. He says :

> *"Realization of truth is impossible without a complete merging of oneself in, and identification with, this limitless ocean of life. Hence, for me, there is no escape from social service, there is no happiness on earth beyond or part from it."*[28]

Thus Gandhiji believes that this world is real and one must perform one's duties here on this earth in order to realize happiness.

Morality

Gandhiji regards morality as the very basis of life. The progress of individuals and society depends upon morality. Morality checks discord, strife and ruin and it promotes harmony, peace and happiness. Thus morality may be regarded as the very essence of religion.

Love

No morality is possible without love. Love is the surest approach to God. Through love an individual is able to widen his narrow self and takes within his fold others.

Love makes all duties pleasant. Gandhiji says:

> *"My life is one indivisible whole and all activities run into*

one another, and they all have their rise in my insatiable love of mankind."[29]

Thus to Gandhiji love (*Ahimsa*) is the essence of morality.

Knowledge

Gandhiji attaches great importance to knowledge. To him knowledge is necessary for liberating love from its narrow limits. Quite naturally, then, he regards knowledge necessary for morality. He says:

> *"No action, which is not voluntary can be called moral. So long as we act like machines, there can be no question of morality. If we want to call an action moral it should have been done consciously and as a matter of duty. Any action that is dictated by fear or by coercion of any kind ceases to be moral."*[30]

Thus a mechanical action performed under blind impulse cannot be regarded as moral by Gandhiji. Evidently, morality implies conscious volition which is not possible without a thorough knowledge of relevant conditions. One must study the motive behind an action. Gandhiji says:

> *"Our desires and motives may be divided into two classes—selfish and unselfish. All selfish desires are immoral, while the desire to improve ourselves for the sake of doing good to others is truly moral."*[31]

Thus he regards self-analysis as a regulating factor in one's morality. So whenever he was in doubt he used to retire in seclusion for self-analysis and if he found himself wrong he was always prepared to confess his error. But along with self-analysis he also gave much weight to the opinion of others. So he used to say: "We must also try to see as other see us."

The End and The Means—The Truth and Non-Violence

Gandhiji believes that the end and the means are convertible terms.[32]

To many persons "the end justifies the means", that is, in order to achieve a desirable end one may take recourse to any means, even bad ones. But to Gandhiji the end and the means are inseparable. The two must be equally just and pure. A good end loses its goodness if bad and immoral means are employed for its achievement. Bad means have their inevitable bad results. Therefore, means must be moral. In fact, means are everything to Gandhiji.[33] He emphasises the goodness of means, because he believes that man can only strive, but he cannot be sure of results. "We have always control over the means and never on the ends."[34] He thinks that the end springs out of the means. He remarks :

> *"The means may be likened to a seed, the end to a tree; and there is just the same inviolable connection between the means and the end as there is between the seed and the* tree."[35]

Gandhiji says: "As the means so the end".[36] Therefore, Gandhiji believes that "if one takes care of means, the end will take care of itself."[37] In the form of *Satyagraha* (resistance for the sake of truth) for freedom of India he gave a concrete expression to his above belief and this has been the most unique contribution to the philosophy and technique of revolution in the modern age.

To Gandhiji non-violence (*Ahimsa*) is the means, and truth (*Satya*) is the end. So he is not so much the votary of non-violence as of truth. He is prepared to sacrifice non-violence for the sake of truth, but not truth for anything on earth or heaven.[38] He says:

> *"The jewel of non-violence was discovered during the search for and contemplation of truth."*[39]

He believes that if he ignores the truth he will never be able to solve this mystery of non-violence (*Ahimsa*).[40] He considers truth as the highest law, and non-violence the highest duty.[41] He thinks that truth is not conditioned by time and space, whereas non-violence exists only on the part of finite beings.[42] Non-violence divorced from truth will be demoralizing. Gandhiji says:

> *"Without truth there is no love; without truth it may be affection as for one's country to the injury of others; or infatuation, as*

of a young man for a girl; or love may be unreasoning and blind, as of ignorant parents for their children."[43]

He further says:

"Ahimsa *(non-violence) being the means, we are naturally more concerned with it in our daily life. It is* Ahimsa, *therefore, that our masses have to be educated in. Education in truth follows from it as a natural end."*[44]

Gandhiji regards non-violence also as omnipotent, infinite and synonymous with God. He considers it as a soul-force or the power of God within us. Soul can exist independent of the physical body. Similarly, non-violence (*Ahimsa*) also transcends time and space. It may act independently of any physical aids like truth, non-violence is a matter of faith and experience. It is not a matter, for argument. "It is not so much a mental or intellectual attitude as a quality of the heart and soul".[45] Gandhiji believes that the universe is governed by non-voilence or love.

He writes :

"We all are bound by the tie of love. There is in everything a centripetal force without which nothing could have existed... even as there is cohesive force in blind matter, so much there be in all things animate and the name of that cohesive force among animate beings is love ... Where there is love there is life; hatred leads to destruction."[46]

Non-violence thus pervades everything. It is applicable to every situation in life without exception. Therefore, Gandhiji insists that non-violence must pervade the entire fabric of life and must not be applied to isolated acts.[47] To Gandhiji "*Ahimsa* (non-violence) consists in allowing others the maximum of convenience at the maximum of inconvenience to us".[48] To him—

"Every act of injury to a living creature and endorsement of such act by refraining from non-violent effort, whenever possible to prevent it, is a breach of Ahimsa.*"*[49]

Thus perfect *Ahimsa* implies complete freedom from *Himsa* (violence); that is, freedom from hate, anger and ill-will and an unbound love for all. Gandhiji says :

> *"Non-violence cannot be taught to a person who fears to die and has no power of resistance ..."Before he can understand non-violence he has to be taught to stand his ground and even suffer death, in the attempt to defend himself against the aggressor who bids fair to overwhelm him. To do otherwise would be to confirm his cowardice and take him further away from non-violence. Whilst I may not actually help anyone to retaliate, I must not let a coward seek shelter behind so called non-violence"*[50]

Evidently, Gandhiji's non-violence is a weapon of the brave, and not of the coward. It is infinitely superior to violence, requiring a higher form of courage than does violence, the courage of dying without killing. Gandhiji advises that the person who does not have this courage must kill and be killed rather than run away from protection in the name of non-violence.

Truth and non-violence are not new ideals. These are eternal laws of life preached since the very beginning of civilization. But these ideals lacked that vitality in the past which they possess today. In the past they were regarded as a mere mask for the weak and coward. No doubt, they were accepted as correct ideals but were dismissed as impracticable in the course of human life. It was believed that truth could not work in trade, commerce and in professions like law and politics. Similarly, non-violence, even after Buddha and Christ, was seldom thought of as a correct method of resolving conflicts. Only isolated individuals and groups were sometime noted to use it. It is remarkable that Gandhiji has demonstrated the use of these fundamental laws in terms of modern life. He has shown by actual practice that these ideals are for all humanity to follow in every situation of human existence. Furthermore, he has demonstrated that truth and non-violence are the mightiest weapons in the hands of man.

Belief in Rebirth

Gandhiji's belief in soul leads us to his belief in the doctrine of rebirth. Gandhiji has written:

> *"I believe in rebirth as much as I believe in the existence of my present body. I, therefore, know that even a little effort is not wasted."*[51]

It is because of this belief that Gandhiji thinks that if his dream does hot materialise in one year, "He is equally prepared for it within the course of several centuries."[52]

Aim of Human Life

To Gandhiji, Human life is an inspiration. Its mission is to strive after perfection, which is self-realization."[53] He regards perfection or self-realization as a heritage of everyone. Therefore, he says:

> *"The ideals that regulate my life are presented for acceptance by mankind in general. I have not the shadow of a doubt that any man or woman can achieve what I have, if he or she would make the same effort and cultivate the same hope and faith."*[54]

Gandhiji wants to attain self-realization working within society. He does not feel that necessity of seeking the shelter of a cave.[55] He believes that this self-realization cannot be achieved unless '*Sarvodaya*—greatest good of all' is materialised. Therefore he fully participates in the so called mundane affairs.

Gandhiji believes in the 'inborn non-violent nature of man, because to him love is the law of human existence.'[56] Because of this belief some people called him a visionary. Gandhiji replies,

> *"I am not a visionary...... I claim to be a practical idealist. The religion of non-violence is not meant for the Risis and saints. It is meant for the common people as well. Non-violence is the law of our species, as violence is the law of the brute. The spirit lies dormant in the brute, and he knows no law but*

that of physical might. The dignity of man requires obedience to a higher law, to the strength of the spirit."[57]

Gandhiji's aim of human life is beautifully summed up in the following words of Radhakrishnan:

"Gandhiji is the prophet of a liberated life wielding power over millions of human beings by virtue of his exceptional holiness and heroism. There will always be some who will find in such rare examples of sanctity the note of strength and stark reality which is missing in a life of general goodwill, conventional morality or vague aesthetic affection which is all that many modern teachers have to offer. To be true, to be simple, to be pure and gentle of heart, to remain cheerful and contented in sorrow and danger, to love life and not to fear death, to serve the spirit and not to be haunted by the spirits of the dead, nothing better has ever been taught or lived since the world first began."[58]

Such has been Gandhiji's aim of life and his unique achievement.

Satyagrahi

For the realization of Truth, Gandhiji has evolved a technique—the technique of *Satyagarh*. He wants that everyone must be a *Satyagrahi*. A *Satyagrahi* is one who has faith in truth, non-violence, *Brahmacharya* (continence), control of palate, fearlessness, non-possession.[59]

"The Central quality which is ever the principle of conduct of every true Satyagrahi is courage. Not only is that courage to be used in facing one's own lower nature, but also against the temptations which come from a world where lust is mistaken for love, and greed flourishes as a necessary force in the competition of life; where the fittest to survive are the successful competitors who use the force of wrath, however, subtly disguised, against their opponents. At every turn we need the

Courage of Soul that proceeds from our identification with the Spirit of Universe."[60]

Thus the life of a *Satyagrahi* implies strict discipline.

A *Satyagrahi* is the ideal man for Gandhiji. But can masses lead the life of this ideal man? It is extremely difficult, if not impossible. But an ideal must remain an ideal. The moment it is reached, it ceases to be an ideal. Gandhiji says :

"Between the ideal and practice there must be an unbridgeable gulf. The ideal will cease to be one if it becomes possible to realize it."[61]

But should we cease to strive for it, simply because it is hard to realize it? Gandhiji says :

"Let us be sure of our ideal. We shall ever fail to realize it. But should never cease to strive for it."[62]

Conception of Society

Gandhiji believes that the individual has a divine origin. Therefore, to him the aim of the individual must be spiritual and not material. This aim can be realised only if the individual is not used as a means. He must be considered as an end unto himself. The individual must not be forced to follow a particular direction. He must enjoy the freedom to chalk out and follow his own path. He has to work out his perfection in a society which is based on the principles of love, non-violence, truth and justice. A society which is based on these principles can give no place to any kind of exploitation—economic, social, political or religious. Gandhiji gives expression to his conception of society thus :

"I shall work for an India in which, the poorest shall feel that it is their country in whose making they have an effective voice; an India in which, there shall be no high class and low class of people; an India in which all communities shall live in perfect harmony. There can be no room in such an India for the curse of untouchability or the curse of intoxicating drinks

> *and drugs. Woman will enjoy the same rights as men. Since we shall be at peace with all the rest of the world, neither exploiting nor being exploited, we shall have the smallest army imaginable. All interests, not in conflict with the interests of dumb millions, will be scrupulously respected, Personally, I hate the distinction between foreign and indigenous. This is the India of my dreams.*"[63]

Thus the society that Gandhiji wants is that which is free from all kinds of exploitation. But this society can be established only if economic, political and social life are based on non-violence, truth and justice. If any of these principles are absent there is bound to be exploitation. When there is exploitation the individual is used as a means and his divine dignity is offended. Therefore, Gandhiji does not like any kind of concentration of powers, Social position or worldly goods in the hands of the few. He wants a classless society of workers. But when he says that he believes in the caste-system he means only the division of labour and specialisation of functions according to an individual's nature and natural and acquired skill. He says :

> "*I believe that everyman is born in the world with certain natural tendencies. Every person is born with certain definite limitations which he cannot overcome. From a careful observation of those limitations the law of 'Varna' was deduced. It establishes certain spheres of action for certain people with certain tendencies. This avoided all unworthy competition. While recognizing limitations the law of 'Varna' admitted no distinctions of 'high and low' on the one hand it guaranteed to each the fruits of his labours and on the other it prevented hurt from pressing upon his neighbour. This great law has been degraded and fallen into disrepute. But my conviction is that an ideal social order will only be evolved when the implications of this law are fully understood and* given effect to."[64]

Dignity of Labour

For promoting the feeling of equality of man Gandhiji wanted to create a sense of dignity of labour in every individual. Therefore, he says, "Everyone must be his own scavenger". He does not want that unwholesome work should be the exclusive domain of any particular class. He believes that if everyone does some type of physical work he will keep himself fit and will appreciate and promote the dignity of labour. He wants that everyone must do his 'bread-labour,' that is, everyone must do some sort of physical labour to earn his bread. This need not necessarily mean tilling of soil, because for everyone it may not be possible. Therefore one may take spinning, weaving, carpentry or smithery and so on. Gandhiji finds support to his theory in the *Bible* which reads, "In the sweat of thy brow shall thou eat thy bread." The *Gita* also says that he who eats, food without labouring for the same, eats stolen food.

Economic Equality

Gandhiji is of the conviction that all work necessary for society must be regarded as sacred and should be performed by those who have the special aptitude and interest for the same. But he believes that everyone should get equal wages. He says:

> *"The lawyer, the doctor or the teacher was entitled to no more than the Bhangi (i.e. Scavenger). Then only would division of work uplift the nation or the earth. There was no other royal road to true civilization or happiness."*[65]

He was conscious that he was putting too high an ideal to be achieved in a short span of time. But he wanted that every country must strive towards this goal for ushering in economic equilibrium, peace and happiness. If the ideal of equality of wages is put into effect there would be a natural tendency in every individual to do the type of work for which he is most suited by aptitude, ability and interest.

Labour and Capital

Gandhiji regards labour superior to capital. But he does not like to incite labour against capital for it is against his principle of non-violence (*Ahimsa*). No society can exist on the basis of hatred and violence. Just as it is immoral for the capitalist not to give legitimate wages to the labourers, it is equally immoral for the labourers to destroy the industries and trouble the capitalists by exaggerated demands. So Gandhiji "wants marriage between capital and labour"—a harmonious co-operation between the two. He advises the capitalist to act as trustee of the people's wealth and spend it for the welfare of the people.

The Evil of Industrialization

Gandhiji admits that machines are necessary for saving labour in those countries where there is dearth of labourers, but it is not so in India. In India the question is how to employ its millions of people. So machines in India mean throwing workers out of employment in cottage industries, manual labour and agriculture in villages. The unemployed persons can be engaged only by starting other industries to produce various kinds of goods. This will ultimately result in multiplication of the evils of industrialization. Gandhiji thinks that the life in a highly industrialized society becomes a mechanical drudgery. Thus Gandhiji thinks that industrialization mechanizes, dehumanizes and demoralizes man, because in this process human energy is engaged in search of pleasures which goes against the pursuit of spiritual values.

Machines

From the above it must not be inferred that Gandhiji is opposed to machines. He is conscious that even the spinning wheel which he wants to introduce into every Indian home is a machine. He says:

> *"Machinery has its place, it has come to stay. But it must not be allowed to displace necessary human labour."*[66]

Her further says :

> *"What I object to is the craze for machinery, not machinery as such ... Men go on "saving labour," till thousands are without*

work and thrown on the open streets to die of starvation. I want to save time and labour, not for a fraction of mankind, but for all; I want the concentration of wealth, not in the hands of few, but in the hands of all. Today machinery merely helps a few to ride on the back of millions. The impetus behind it all is not the philanthropy to sane labour, but greed. It is against this constitution of things that I am fighting with all my might... I am aiming not at eradication of all machinery, but limitation... The supreme consideration is man".[67]

Decentralization

Gandhiji is against the anarchic individualism of the capitalist system, nor does he like the crushing concentration of power of some political systems. He wants to build a social and economic structure on the basis of decentralized agriculture and industry. Therefore, he favours cottage and village industries based on limited private property. He believes that this system will develop decentralized and autonomous village communities in natural and healthy surroundings leading individuals to live simpler lives and to acquire more of social sense. He says :

"I suggest that, if India is to evolve along non-violent lines, it will have to decentralize many things. Centralization cannot be sustained and defended without adequate force. Simple homes from which there is nothing to take away require no policing....."[68]

The Place of Man and Woman in Society

Gandhiji believes that man and woman are complementary to each other and each one is to fulfil his or her distinct obligation in terms of his or her inherent nature. Man is to support and protect the family and a woman is equipped by nature to be a mother and take care of children and the home. Thus one cannot live without the other and the work of each is essential for human existence. Gandhiji is against woman's doing the work of man in so many sphere. He wants that the woman should perform her duties with a sense of dignity. "There is as much bravery in keeping one's house in good order and condition as there is in defending it against attack from outside". Gandhiji believes that there is a fundamental spiritual unity between man and woman, though one may easily exaggerate the distinction between the two. He says:

> *"The division of the spheres of work being recognized, the general qualities and culture required are practicably the same for both the sexes ".*[69]

Therefore he advocated the equality of men and women in educational, civic and spiritual matters. He struggled to remove many of those evil customs which distracted the full development of womanhood. Consequently, he found many women as excellent co-workers in the political emancipation of India. But in spite of this he firmly believed that married life with a spiritual direction was the ideal life for most women. He says:

> *"It is no doubt an excellent thing for girls to remain unmarried for the sake of service, but the fact is that only one in a million is able to do so".*[70]

Therefore, he regarded marriage as quite natural. Speaking on marriage he says that it is wrong—

> *"To consider it derogatory in any sense. When one imagines any act a fall, it is difficult, however hard one tries, to raise oneself. The ideal is to look upon marriage as a sacrament. Marriage in Hinduism is one of the four ashrams.*[71] *In fact the other three are based on it."*[72]

He further says:

> *"The ideal that marriage aims at is that of spiritual union through the physical. The human love that it incarnates is intended to serve as a stepping stone to divine or universal love."*[73]

He is of the firm conviction that the woman, as mother,

possesses the infinite capacity for real love and sacrifice, and therefore it is the woman who can be leader. He says :

> *"Let her transfer that love to the whole of humanity, let her forget that she ever was or can be the object of man's lust. And she will occupy her proud position by the side of man as his mother and maker and silent leader."*[74]

Such was his faith in the capacity and role of woman in general.

Gandhiji's Philosophy of Education

Some Fundamental Aspects

To Gandhiji education is an activity which is necessary not only for social progress but also for moral, political and economic development. It must be remembered at the very outset that the Wardha Scheme as such does not include the total philosophy of education as envisaged by Gandhiji, because this scheme is concerned only with the education of children between the age of 7 and 14. While discussing his philosophy of life we have seen that he wants to establish a spiritual society on the basis of truth, non-violence and justice. So he has evolved a philosophy of education as a dynamic side of this philosophy of life. Gandhiji gives his meaning of education thus:

> *"By education I mean an all-round drawing out of the best in child and man, body, mind and spirit. Literacy is not the end of education nor even the beginning. It is one of the means whereby man and woman can be educated. Literacy in itself is no education."*[75]

In the words of Mahadev Desai, Gandhiji wants education to :

> *"Draw the whole man out of the boy and the girl, and no education could be sound that does not make useful citizens, whole man, of boys and girls."*[76]

Thus in his philosophy of education he stands for a harmonious development of all the four aspects of human personality—body, heart, mind and spirit. To Pestalozzi, too, "education is to provide the condition under which ... development can take place ... harmoniously".[77]

Gandhiji says:

> *"True education is that which drows out and stimulates the spiritual, intellectual and physical faculties of the children."*[78]

Thus to him education must not ignore any aspect of human development.

After thus fixing the objectives of education Gandhiji speaks about the method that should be followed for realising these objectives. He remarks that the existing system of education is:

> *"Not only wasteful but positively harmful. Most of the boys are lost to the parents and to the occupation to which they are born. They pick up evil habits, affect urban ways and get a smattering of something which may be anything but education. What then should be the form of primary education? I think the remedy lies in educating them by means of vocational or manual training."*[79]

Education through vocational training is the most important aspect of Gandhiji's *philosophy of education*. He further says :

> *"I would therefore begin the child's education by teaching it a useful handicraft and enabling it to produce from the moment it begins its training. I hold that the highest development of the mind and the soul is possible under such a system of education. Only every handicraft has to be taught not merely mechanically as is done today. But scientifically, i.e., the child should know the why and the wherefore of every process."*[80]

Thus Gandhiji makes handicraft as the centre of the method. He wants to give all education through the medium of productive industry. Hence according to him all the subjects should be taught through a vocation, but this vocation has to be used only as a means and the school is not to be transformed into a productive factory where boy-workers are engaged in producing things. It is the whole personality of the child which is to be developed through a vocation. Hence, the schools cannot come down to the level of factories. The children will have to learn other subjects as well. These subjects are not to be supplemented by manual training. In fact, manual training is made the means of literary and intellectual training.[81]

Gandhiji has a self-supporting aspect in his educational philosophy. He thinks that the handicraft chosen as a means of education will make education self-supporting. The term self-supporting aspect of education is generally taken in two senses; viz., education that will make a student self-supporting after he finishes his education, and education which is self-supporting in itself, meeting the teachers' salaries. There cannot be much opposition as regards the first aspect. Gandhiji himself has said that this education must be a kind of insurance against unemployment.[82] As regards the second sense, too, i.e., the school being able to meet its own expenses, Gandhiji is quite hopeful. He says:

> *"Every school can be made self-supporting, the condition being that the State takes over the manufactures of these schools."*
> *"Such education taken as a whole, can, must be self-supporting, in fact self-support is the acid test of its reality."*[83]

Above, we find two basic aspects a Gandhiji's *educational philosophy*--(1) education should centre around a suitable craft, and (2) the craft should be so chosen as to meet the expenses of the school, especially the teacher's salaries. It should be noted that Gandhiji does not want the economic independence of the student or of the school by means of a handicraft which is mechanically learnt. By introducing a craft as the centre of education he desires to introduce a sense of dignity of labour which has been so lacking in the school and college educated youths of the country. Gandhiji has also the support of John Dewey[84] when the latter says:

"In schools, occupations are not carried on for pecuniary gain but for their own content. Freed from extraneous associations and from the pressure of wage-earning, they supply modes of experience which are intrinsically valuable, they are truly liberalizing in quality."

In fact, Gandhiji does not want the craft to be carried on in the school only for pecuniary gain but for liberalizing influences. Sri Mahadev Desai says :

"The idea of self-supporting education cannot he divorced from the ideological background of non-violence, and unless we bear in mind that the new scheme is intended to bring into being a new age and from which communal hatred is eliminated and exploitation is eschewed, we cannot make a success of it."[85]

The creed of non-violence is another fundamental aspect of Gandhiji's philosophy of education. Gandhiji finds a kind of incompatability in education and violence. He cannot conceive of a society based on exploitation. He believes that all wealth is procured through exploitation of some kind or other and India cannot manage to spend millions on education as some countries are doing on the basis of exploitation.[86] Therefore he insists that "we have no alternative but this plan of education which is based on non-violence".[87]

A sense of social responsibility appears to be another fundamental aspect of Gandhiji's *philosophy of education*. When Gandhiji makes handicraft the basis of education he wants the child to learn through life situations in correlation with social and physical environment. He does not want that the child should indulge in passive absorption of information. By making the school activity-based he aspires to make it a place of work, experimentation and discovery.

Gandhiji's *philosophy of education* has some other features which may be regarded as secondary. They are as follows:

(1) Mother-tongue should be the medium of education. It

should be given the first place amongst languages to be taught in the school.

(2) The State should purchase the product made by the school children.

(3) The state should provide compulsory free education to children between 7 and 14 years of age.

Let us now see if Gandhiji's educational philosophy is psychologically, sociologically and biologically sound. The Zakir Husain Committee asserts that it is psychologically sound. It says:

> *"Psychologically, it is desirable, because it relieves the child from the tyranny of a purely academic and theoretical instruction against which its active mature is always making a healthy protest. It balances the intellectual and practical elements of experience, and may be made an instrument of educating the body and the mind in co-ordination. The child requires not the superficial literacy which implies, often without warrant, a capacity to read the printed pages, but the far more capacity of using hand and intelligence for some constructive purpose."*[88]

Gandhiji, too, is quite alive to this psychological feature of the scheme. He says:

> *"Our education has to be revolutionized. The brain must be educated through the hand ... why should you think that the mind is everything and the hands and feet nothing? Those who do not train their hands, who go through the ordinary rut of education, lack 'music' in their life ..."*[89]

Thus Gandhiji wants an integration in the training of the head and that of the hand through the medium of an activity based on a craft. It is hard to deny the fact that true education of the individual is best obtained through action. The learning by doing principle which is so much advocated today supports the above stand of Gandhiji.

Gandhiji says that education to be imparted to the child should be such as to make him a responsible citizen in society. The Zakir Husain Committee remarks that :

> *"Socially considered ... (the scheme) will tend to breakdown the existing barriers of prejudices between manual and intellectual workers, harmful alike for both. It will cultivate in the only possible way, a true sense of the dignity of labour and of human solidarity—and ethical and moral gain of incalculable significance."*[90]

In Indian society manual labour had long been considered as inferior, and workers like carpenters, pot-makers and blacksmiths are regarded as inferior 'castes.' Gandhiji's educational scheme based on a craft would raise the crafts to the status of honourable professions which would have their own independent status, equal to the status that learning enjoyed. As regards the social effects of his scheme Gandhiji makes the following observation:

> *"My plan to impart Primary Education through the medium of village handicrafts ... is conceived as spearhead of a silent social revolution fraught with the most far-reaching consequences. It will provide a health and moral basis of relationship between the city and the village and thus go a long way towards eradicating some of the worst evils of the present social insecurity and poisoned relationship between the classes ... And all this would be accomplished without the horrors of a bloody class war or a colossal capital expenditure such as would be involved in the mechanization of a vast country like India. Nor would it entail a helpless dependence on foreign imported machinery or technical skill... Lastly, by obviating the necessity for highly specialized talent, it would place the destiny of the masses, as it were, in their own hands."*[91]

Gandhiji believed that the craft would give real education to children because thereby they would bring thought into manual skill, and manual activity into thought. He did not regard the economic calculations involved in his scheme as out of place because he thought that they would produce ethical and social virtues in the students. His point of view is endorsed by Dewey :

> *"To charge that the various activities of gardening, weaving, construction in wood, manipulation of metals, cooking etc., which carry over these fundamental human concerns into school resources, have a merely bread and butter value is to miss their point. If the mass of mankind has usually found in its industrial occupations nothing but evils which had to be endured for the sake of maintaining existence, the fault is not in the occupations, but in the conditions under which they are carried on. The continually increasing importance of economic factors in contemporary life makes it the more needed that education should reveal their scientific content and their social value."*[92]

It must be noted that economic consideration was never the main consideration in Gandhiji's mind while he gave out his. scheme. However, he was not prepared to ignore whatever economic advantage might be forthcoming incidentally out of the education that the children received. He says:

> *"If such education is given, the direct result will be that it will be self-supporting. But the test of success is not its self-supporting character, but that the whole man has to be drawn out through the teaching of the handicraft in a scientific manner. In fact, I would reject a teacher who would promise to make it self-supporting under any circumstances. The self-supporting part will be the logical corollary of the fact that the pupil has learnt the use of everyone of his faculties. If a boy who works at a handicraft for three hours a day will surely earn his keep, much more a body who adds to the work a development of his mind and soul ."*[93]

Evidently, the self-supporting aspect of the scheme was only an expected result of the education that would be given to the boys, and it was never a primary condition. In fact, Gandhiji's primary aim was to draw out the whole person, that is, to further the maximum development of the personality of the child. However, it is wrong to believe that a vocational bias deprives education of its liberalizing influences. Jeffreys says:

> *"Vocational bias does not degrade education but gives it significance and that there is in fact no meaning or purpose in developing personal qualities and abilities unless they are used in the service of the community."*[94]

Whitehead supports this point of view in stronger terms when he says:

> *"There can be no adequate technical education which is not liberal, and no liberal education which is not technical; that is no education which does not impart both technique and vision."*[95]

It should be noted that Gandhiji developed his scheme of education for the atmosphere of village India. He realised that it was not possible to spread universal education in poor India during the present generation if the scheme depended on money. Therefore, he wanted to make it self-supporting in principle as far as possible.

Thus Gandhiji's *objective of education* is to develop the whole man through the medium of activity around some handicraft. Biologically that education is sound which enables man to lead a successful life under the conditions of a complex and ever-changing civilization. Thus the biological aim of education is to develop the whole individuality of man. Needless to remark that Gandhiji's *philosophy of education* is also biologically sound.

The Task of the Teacher

In order to put his ideals of education into practice Gandhiji wants a special type of teacher. He says that the teacher is:

> *"To teach his pupils discrimination. If we behave indiscriminately, we would be no better than machines. We are thinking, knowing beings and we must, in this period*

distinguish truth from untruth, sweet from bitter language, clean from unclean things, and so on."[96]

Evidently, the teacher must possess the virtues that he wants to inculcate in the students. The teacher must practise these virtues himself, otherwise his words will have no effect. The association of the teacher with the students should be a fine training in the fundamental virtues.[97] Gandhiji says:

"I have found that boys imbibe more from the teacher's own lives than they do from books they read to them, or the lectures that they deliver to them with their lips. I have discovered to my great joy that boys and girls have unconsciously a faculty of penetration whereby they read the thoughts of their teachers. Woe to the teacher who teaches one thing with his lips, and carries another in his breast."[98]

Therefore, Gandhiji wants that the teacher should be able to establish a heart to heart contact with the students.[99] He believes that the teacher can influence the life of the students more beyond the classroom than within. He says:

"I have felt that the teacher's work lies more outside than inside the lecture-room. In this work-a-day life where teachers and professors work for the wages they get, they have no time to give to the students outside the classroom, and that is the greatest stumbling block in the development of the life and character of the students today."[100]

Thus Gandhiji wants that the teacher and the taught should be in constant communion with each other. In fact, the teachers have to fashion the hearts of the students rather than their brains.[101] However, this does not imply that the teacher should expect blind obedience from the students. Gandhiji is against indoctrination. He wants to give full freedom to the student. He says:

"I can conceive of occasions when implicit obedience, without waiting for reasoning out causes, is a necessity ... But occasions

for such obedience are, and must be, rare in any well-ordered society. The worst thing that can happen to boys in school is to have to render obedience to everything that the teacher says. On the contrary, if the teachers are to stimulate the reasoning faculty of boys and girls under their care, they would continuously tax their reasons and make them think for themselves ... Teachers, of national schools will take note of the warning I have uttered and prevent their pupils from laxly basing their actions upon statements, without testing of men reputed to be great."[102]

Gandhiji, will not mind if the students protest against the immoral orders of the teacher.[103] He wants to guarantee to the students the greatest freedom of opinion and speech.[104] At best the teacher can give only his opinion about certain matters. He must never force anything on the students.

We shall understand now the aim of education as outlined by Gandhiji on the basis of his educational philosophy.

The Aim of Education

Gandhiji looks at education from different angles at different times. We shall see below the various aims of education as stated or pronounced by him at times.

Gandhiji wants that education should help one to become self-supporting in later life. He desires that each boy and girl should be self-supporting by finding an occupation after receiving the formal education. This means that he is not against the bread-and-butter aim of education. Expanding this idea further he says:

"The child at the age of 14, that is, after finishing a seven year course should be... an earning unit. Even now the poor people's children automatically lend a helping hand to their parents—the feeling at the back of their minds being: what shall my parents eat and what shall they give me to eat, if I do not also work with them? That is an education in itself.... You impart education and simultaneously cut at the root of unemployment."[105]

This should not lead one to believe that Gandhiji wants every child to be a wage earner. In fact, he wants him to learn while he earns and to earn while he learns. His labour should be a part of his learning and is to make him a worthy citizen.

Talking to the girls of the Kasturba Balikashram, New Delhi, on April 22, 1946, Gandhiji says:

> *"I attach far more importance to the cultural aspect of education than to the literary. Culture is the foundation, the primary thing which the girls ought to get from here. It should show itself in the smallest detail of your conduct and personal behaviour, how you sit, how you walk, how you dress, etc., ... Inner culture must be reflected in your speech ..."*[106]

Thus, according to Gandhiji, culture is not a product of intellectual work. It should be the quality of one's soul, pervading all aspects of human behaviour. To him this is a very important aim of education. Gandhiji says:

> *"By education I mean an all-round drawing out of the best in child and man-body, mind and spirit."*[107]

Again he says:

> *" True education is that which draws out and stimulates the spiritual, intellectual and physical faculties of the children."*[108]

Gandhiji has used the term "faculties" in the sense of "Powers", and it should not be thought that he was an advocate of faculty psychology which holds no water now. His conception of education appears to be in complete agreement with the aim of education formulated by many modern educational thinkers.

By education Gandhiji wants to train the hand, heart and head of the child. He lays greater emphasis on the education of three Hs than on the teaching of three Rs (Reading, Writing, and Arithmetic). In the education of hand, heart and head he foresees the all-round development of the child. We have already seen that he wants to bring out this all-round development through a craft. He says :

"You have to train the boys in one occupation or another. Round this special occupation you will train up his mind, his handwriting, his artistic sense and so on."[109]

Gandhiji considers good handwriting as a necessary part of education. Therefore, he wants that the child should be taught the art of drawing before he is taught to write.[110] He also wants that drawing and music should be taught to the child together."[111] He deplores that the modern system of education emphasises the training of the mind at the cost of utter neglect of training of the heart. To him training of the mind is useless if it is not accompanied by the training of the heart. He thinks that in the absence of proper education of the heart man is reduced to the level of lower animal. So to him culture of the heart must predominate any system of education. The education or culture of heart should be obtained by refining the emotions and impulses of the child and by awakening in him the deepest feelings of love, sympathy, fellowship and aesthetic sense. This awakening is possible through drawing, music and handicraft. Handicrafts will produce fellowship, aesthetic sense will be developed through drawing and love and sympathy through music. Thus Gandhiji emphasises the education of hand, heart and head.

It is worth noting that Gandhiji has not neglected the need for developing a healthy body. He is convinced that education of heart and head is possible only through a healthy body. For physical development he recommends "compulsory physical training through musical drill".[112]

In perfect conformity with his philosophy of life Gandhiji is not prepared to neglect the awakening of the soul. He regards a harmonious combination of body, mind and soul necessary for the making of the whole man. By an all-round education he means the education of heart, head, body and spirit. He believes that only such an education will enable an individual to solve all the problems of life.

Gandhiji says:

"I had always given the first place to the culture of the heart or the building of the character. I regarded character building as the proper foundation of education."[113]

He further says:

> *" ... Education should automatically serve to bring home to children the essential distinction between man and brute, to make them realize that it is man's special privilege and pride to be gifted with the faculties of head and heart both, that he is a thinking no less than a feeling animal as the very derivation of the word 'manushya' (that is, man) shows; and to renounce the sovereignty of reason over the blind instincts is, therefore, to renounce a man's estate. In man, reason quickens and guides the feeling; in brute, the soul lies ever dormant. To awaken the heart is to awaken the dormant soul, to awaken reason, and to inculcate discrimination between good and evil."*[114]

Gandhiji laid so much emphasis on character-building as an aim of education that he promptly answered the question—

> *"What is your goal of education when India obtains freedom"?*

> *"Character-building. I would try to develop courage, strength, virtue, the ability to forget oneself in working towards great aims. This is more important than literacy."*[115]

Gandhiji is prepared to accept the value of knowledge and of scholarship if they help in building good character. He observes, "The end of all knowledge must be the building up of character."[116]

While speaking to a gathering of college boys Gandhiji said:

> *"Your education is absolutely worthless, if it is not built on a solid foundation of truth and purity. If you, boys, are not careful about the personal purity of your lives, and if you are not careful about being pure in thought, speech and deeds then I tell you that you are lost, although you may become perfect finished scholars."*[117]

Gandhiji's *educational philosophy* has its roots in Indian life and culture. Those who are familiar with the history of Indian philosophy cannot regard "character building as the supreme aim of education" as unfamiliar.

Besides character-building, Gandhiji believes that education is that which liberates, that which initiates one into the higher life of the spirit. We have already seen in his philosophy of life that he is also conscious of the Ultimate Reality. He says to the student:

> *"Let all your work and play have the exalted objective of a life of restraint, let them take you nearer to God."*[118]

He again observes:

> *"In our languages, there is a beautiful word, equivalent for the word student, that is Brahmachari. It means searcher after God, one who conducts himself so as to bring himself nearest to God in the least possible time."*[119]

Gandhiji further remarks that:

> *"Modern education tends to turn our eyes away from the spirit. The possibilities of spirit force or soul force, therefore, do not appeal to us, and our eyes are consequently revetted on the evenescent transitory material force."*[120]

Therefore, he urges the students not to be led away by transitory things but to believe in the realization of the possibilities of the soul force. Therefore, he regards "the knowledge of God and self-realization" as the highest aim of education. To him self-realization is the Summum Bonum of life and education.

Thus, Gandhiji believes in two sets of educational aims, viz., immediate and ultimate. His immediate aims of education are many, because they touch life at different angles. Of all the aims advocated by him those of character-building and spiritual freedom are the most important, because they bridge the gulf between life here and life hereafter. His ultimate aim of education is the knowledge of God leading one to self-realization. In perfect conformity with his philosophy of life this is the most important aim of education for him.

As a great visionary, Gandhiji could see all the fundamentals of human life. Therefore his aim of education touches practically all the aspects of life. However, his ultimate aim of education, i.e., self-realization embraces all the immediate and subordinate aims of education because the aim of self-realization cannot be achieved unless man develops an all-round personality. Needless to remark that the ideal of self-realization is eminently suited to the genius of India and is quite consistent with our cultural heritage.

Gandhiji was a practical man, and so it was not possible for him to overlook the demands of modern human existence. He knew fully well that the aim of self-realization could not be attained unless the basic needs and requirements of man were fulfilled. Therefore, in later life he did not emphasize the goal of self-realization so much as preparation for life and the education of the whole man.

Gandhiji's Aim of Education : Both Individual and Social

Gandhiji advocates both individual and social aims of education at different times, because he knows that one implies the other, i.e., it is difficult to think of individual good without thinking of social good and the *vice versa*. He emphatically states that :

> *"The individual is the one supreme consideration"*[121] *and "I look upon an increase of the power of the State with the greater fear, because, although while apparently doing good by minimizing exploitation, it does the greatest harm to mankind by destroying individuality which lies at the root of all progress."*[122]

Thus, Gandhiji has the greatest respect for the individuality of man, because he believes that preservation of individuality is necessary both for material and spiritual advancement. He knows that a society is formed of individuals who have varying capacities, interests and characteristics. It means society constitutes of diverse elements. He wants unity in the diversity existing in the society. He believes that the individual should be so developed as to contribute the maximum towards the social good, but at the same time he must not lose his individuality. He seeks to achieve this goal by non-violent means. For this, he stresses the making of the individuals of which the society will be an outcome.

But it should be noted that Gandhiji believes in the good of the State as well. To him the good of individual and that of the State is mutually inclusive. On duty of the student, he says,

> *"He should ever keep before him the ideal of service ... never for making money ..."*[123]

Gandhiji's ideal of service knows no bound. He has remarked :

> *"I am a humble servant of India and in trying to serve India, I serve humanity at large."*[124]

He stands both for social service and individual development. He says:

> *"I value individual freedom, but you must not forget that man is essentially a social being. He has risen to his present state by learning to adjust his individualism to the requirements of social progress. Unrestricted individualism is the law of the beast of the jungle. We have learnt to strike the mean between individual freedom and social restraint. Willing submission to social restraint for the sake of the well-being of the whole society, enriches both the individual and the society of which one is a member."*[125]

Waterhouse supports the above stand of Gandhiji when he says:

> *"The relation of society to the individual is one of interaction, and in this relation egoism and altruism must find their balance... True altruism is a form of self-realization, and the true egoism is to find one's self in something greater than self ... In a perfect life there is neither egoism nor altruism, for the individual and the common good are one."*[126]

Gandhiji wants to raise a society in which the individuals will work for the common welfare of its citizens without losing their individuality. According to him, this society will not be built by the use of force, because he believes that the good that is brought about by force destroys individuality.[127] The social change that is created by love can alone preserve individuality.

Gandhiji believed that a good social structure could be the result of only well-integrated and rightly developed individuals. Therefore, the individual has always been his supreme consideration. Good individuals will always make good society. So through education Gandhiji wanted to create individuals who might imbibe co-operative attitude. He was prepared to entrust the welfare of the society to individuals so developed. This is clear when he says:

> *"I would feel that if we succeed in building the character of the individual, society will take care of itself. I would be quite willing to trust the organization of society of individuals so developed."*[128]

Moreover he wants to achieve a true synthesis between the individual and society by making self-realization possible only through social service. By his own example he has shown that in life and education there can be no conflict between self-realization and social service. He says:

> *"Man's ultimate aim is the realization of God, and all his activities—social, political, religious have to be guided by the ultimate aim of Vision of God. The immediate service of all human beings becomes a necessary part of the endeavour, simply because the only way to find God is to see Him in His creation and be one with it. This can only be done by service of all. I am a part and parcel of the whole, and I cannot find Him apart from the rest of humanity."*[129]

Therefore, the good of the State becomes an integral part of an individual's pursuit and education for a citizen inevitably becomes a necessary part of any good education. Varkey says :

> *"The present system of education has completely ignored this aspect ... a system of national education must produce a new generation with opportunities of understanding its own*

> *problems and rights and obligations. For this purpose we need a completely new system of education that will secure at least the minimum of education required for the intelligent exercise and duties of citizenship."*[130]

Therefore, Gandhiji's scheme of education regards citizenship as one of its main objectives, because everyone is to be a citizen and private individual. Speaking on Gandhiji's scheme of education Margaret Barr says :

> "*. . . Therefore, any scheme of education which truly sets before itself 'the balanced and harmonious development of all the faculties of the individual' cannot lose sight of the fact that every child is a citizen of tomorrow and that therefore it is at least as important to make him a competent earner of living."*[131]

The Wardha Scheme

After trials and experiments for over four decades Gandhiji on the basis of his educational philosophy finalized a, scheme of education in 1937 for its application throughout the whole country and published it in the *Harijan*. In a long inaugural speech at the All India National Educational Conference held at Wardha on the 22nd and 23rd October, 1937, he placed forth the salient features of his educational scheme. This scheme was discussed in the conference at great length. The conference appointed a committee under the chairmanship of Dr. Zakir Husain for preparing a detailed syllabus on the lines mainly indicated by Gandhiji. This Committee submitted its report on 2nd December, 1937. This report contains what is known as Wardha Scheme or Basic National Education. Its outstanding features which mainly embody some of Gandhiji's educational ideas were:

Free Compulsory Education

Between the ages of seven and fourteen, education should be free for all boys and girls. If parents desire the girls may be withdrawn from school at the age of twelve. During this period of seven years

Gandhiji wanted to include primary, middle and high school education,[132] because he thought that it was only 'so-called education' that was available to some people in the Indian villages. He was convinced that in order to improve the rural conditions, secondary and primary education must be combined. He wanted to leave higher education to private enterprises.[133] He believed that primary education was the minimum that must be available to all. He, however, did not mean to minimize the importance of higher education when once he remarked :

> *"I think we can postpone the question of higher education for some time; but the problem of primary education cannot be postponed even for a minute."*[134]

Craft as the Centre of Education

The Wardha Scheme provides that education should be given through the medium of some craft or productive work. It is around this craft that all other subjects in the school will be taught. The Zakir Husain Committee remarked:

> *"Modern educational thought is practically unanimous in commending the idea of educating children through some suitable form of productive work. This method is considered to be the most effective approach to the problem of providing an integral all-sided education."*[135]

The Committee thought certain conditions necessary for making a craft as the medium of instruction a success. So it recommended that the craft chosen should be rich in educational possibilities in such a way as to make correlation of subjects possible. In teaching through a craft the main emphasis should be on :

> *"the principles of co-operative activity, planning, accuracy, initiative and individual responsibility in learning ."*[136]

Thus the craft should not be learnt only for intellectual work or for economic self-efficiency. It should be used both as a means and an end.

Self-supporting Aspect

The self-supporting aspect of the scheme means that the products of the school should pay. Gandhiji has said :

> *"You have to start with the conviction that looking to needs of the villages of India our rural education ought to be made self-supporting if it is to be compulsory."*[137]

Gandhiji wants to make the child an earning member of society when he leaves school at the age of fourteen. We have already seen above that by his plan of education he seeks to banish unemployment from society. The Wardha Scheme depends upon the school efforts for covering a portion of the pay of the teacher. However, it wants that the State should pay for the rest of the expenses, such as for furnitures, books, tools and school-building, etc. It should be the responsibility of the state to provide for the marketing facilities for the goods produced in the school.

The Medium of Instruction

Gandhiji wants that all education must be given through the medium of mother-tongue. He thinks that a good knowledge of mother-tongue is necessary for developing precision of thought. Therefore in the Wardha Scheme mother-tongue has been recommended as the medium of instruction.

The Non-Violence Cult

The Wardha Scheme upholds Gandhiji's cardinal creed of non-violence. Mahadev Desai says:

> *"The idea of self-supporting education cannot he divorced*

> *from the ideological background of non-violence, and unless we bear in mind that the new scheme is intended to bring into being a new age from which class and communal hatred is eliminated and exploitation is eschewed, we cannot make* a success *of it.*"[138]

Ideal of Citizenship

The Zakir Husain Committee[139] says:

> "*... The new scheme ... will aim at giving the citizens of the future a keen sense of personal worth, dignity and efficiency, and will strengthen in them the desire for self-improvement and social service in a co-operative community.*"

The Idea of a Co-operative Community

The Wardha Scheme wants to promote the attitude of social service in all children. The Zakir Husain Committee expected that during the seven years of education the child would acquire the essential modicum of social and civic training.

The Syllabus of the Wardha Scheme

The Basic Crafts

The basic craft, such as, agriculture, spinning and weaving, cardboard work, woodwork and metalwork, gardening and leather work etc., as suitable to local conditions, should be chosen. The chosen craft must be rich in educational possibilities, and it should such as to permit natural correlation with important human activities and interests.

> *"The object of this new educational scheme is not primarily the production of craftsman able to practise some craft mechanically, but rather the exploitation for educative purposes of the resources implicit in craft-work. This demands the productive curriculum—its craft side—but it should also inspire the method of teaching all other subjects. Stress should*

> *be laid on the principles of cooperative activity, planning, accuracy, initiative and individual responsibility."*[140]

It is further expected that the craft should have some economic possibilities as well so that after seven years' education the child may be able to pursue it as an occupation. The inclusion of the craft should aim at making every student an intelligent and active member of society so that he may be able to contribute his share to the social growth. Thus the Basic Education aims at producing workers who will regard every work as honourable and they will be able to be self-reliant. Gandhiji wants that the craft chosen "should be a village craft and should be useful".[141] Thus to him what is learnt is more important. Therefore, the choice of just any craft will not serve the purpose. He desires that the choice be made in such a manner as to exploit the innate disposition of child nature so as to give it a definite form at the age of seven.

However, the pursuit of craft activities should be a play for the child in the beginning. Thus the child will find diverse fields of interesting activity within the same craft. He does not think that activities around a single craft will become boring. He says:

> *"... There will be newness in every lesson just as there can be new music on the same instrument. By changing over from one craft to another a child tends to become like a monkey jumping from branch to branch with abode nowhere."*[142]

Perhaps, Gandhiji stressed so much on a single craft, because the idea of self-supporting education was very dear to him and he wanted each child to give attention on one particular craft in order to acquire some resonable skill. The Secondary Education Commission (Government of India), too, supports Gandhiji's idea of a single craft with a self-supporting motive. It recommends that every high school student should offer one craft.

> *"We consider it necessary that every student devote some time to work with the hands and attain a reasonable high standard of proficiency in one particular craft, so that if necessary, he may support himself by pursuing it."*[143]

It is noteworthy that the Commission did not make the above recommendation on economic considerations alone. It was also alive to its educational possibilities. So it further says:

"By working with the hands the adolescent learns the dignity of labour and experiences the joy of doing constructive work. There is no greater educative medium than making, with efficiency and integrity, things of utility and beauty. It trains practical aptitudes, facilitates clarity of thinking gives chances for co-operative work and thus enriches the entire personality."[144]

It may be remarked that Gandhiji shows special fascination for the basic craft of spinning. He considers it as labouring for the country and a lesson in patriotism. He remarks:

"Moreover, to enable a person to clothe himself through his own effort, when the alternative is to be naked, is in itself an education. An intelligent pursuit of the various processes related to cotton spinning has, besides, a very high instructional value. In fact, it covers the whole education of man as no other craft does."[145]

Gandhiji regards spinning most useful as a basic craft. He sees great educational possibilities in this. He says:

"Some people ask me why agriculture could not be a basic craft. The answer is that it has not the educational possibilities of spinning. The function of Nai Talim (i.e. Basic Education) is not merely to teach an occupation but through it to develop the whole man."[146]

However, Gandhiji has admitted the possibilities of bringing in other crafts as basic ones in the school, but he has regarded spinning and weaving as supreme for this purpose and has remarked that:

"It must be treated seriously and must be taught in a proper and scientific manner like the other subjects."[147]

In the predominantly agricultural country India, Gandhiji wants that every youth should have a practical knowledge of agriculture and handweaving.[148] Therefore he has argued that "In any curriculum of the future, spinning must he a compulsory subject."[149]

The Mother-Tongue

In his scheme Gandhiji has recommended that the mother-tongue should be the medium of instruction. He thinks that the mother-tongue alone can acquaint the child with the social heritage, aspirations, ideas and ethical and moral values of his country and it alone can be the medium of his thoughts and emotions. Through his mother-tongue the child will be able to classify and clarify his experiences. Gandhiji did not agree with the suggestion that it would not be easy to impart technical education through the medium of mother-tongue. He believed that the dialects of the Indian villages were rich enough in expression and idioms. Therefore, he did not even feel the need to turn to Sanskrit or Persian for finding new expressions.[150] But he was not against the adoption of foreign terminologies for the purpose. He wanted to enrich the Indian languages in matter from whatever sources the new terms and words were taken. He approved of scholars devoting themselves to the learning of foreign languages in order to ultimately enrich the Indian languages. But he—

> *"would not have a single Indian to forget, neglect or be ashamed of his mother-tongue, or to feel that he or she cannot think or express the best thoughts in his or her own vernacular."*[151]

Keeping in line with this conviction of Gandhiji, the Zakir Husain Committee has emphasised the proper teaching of mother-tongue from the very beginning of education of the child. The Committee has specifically laid down that the student at the Basic Education stage should be able to converse freely, read loudly and silently, use the list of contents and index, consult dictionaries and reference books, write legibly and correctly about personal and village affairs, and use the library for acquiring further information on topics of his interest.[152]

Mathematics

In the Basic Scheme the aim of teaching mathematics is to enable the students to easily solve numerical and geometrical problems which crop up in connection with his learning of craft and in his home and social life. Therefore the Zakir Husain Committee suggested that the teaching of mathematics should not be limited to facts and operations of numbers alone. It was also felt that in learning mathematics the pupils would be required to measure quantities and values and thereby their reasoning capacities would also be developed.

Social Studies

Social Studies would consist of history, geography, economics and civics. It should be noted that the Wardha Scheme has not framed the syllabus of Social Studies as a fusion course. Through social studies the aim of Wardha Scheme is to enable the student to understand the nature, function and interrelationship of family, state and nation so that he may appreciate the various forces that influence modern life. Furthermore, the study of social studies should inculcate in the students the right attitudes and values which develop civic efficiency. It should also develop a sense of national patriotism and a love for international understanding. The Zakir Husain Committee explains the objectives of the study of social studies in following manner :

"(1) To develop a broad human interest in the progress of mankind in general and of India in particular.

(2) To develop in the pupil a proper understanding of his social and geographical environment, and to awaken the urge to improve it.

(3) To inculcate the love of the motherland, reverence for its part and belief in its future destiny as the home of a united co-operative society based on love, truth and justice.

(4) To develop a sense of the rights and responsibilities of citizenship.

(5) To develop the individual and social virtues which make a man a reliable associate and trusted neighbour.
(6) To develop mutual respect fot world religions".[153]

The above objectives clearly explain the Gandhian point of view. For the achievement of these objectives a judicious course has been outlined in history, geography, civics and current events together with a study of the essentials of various religions of the world with a view to show how there is perfect harmony between them. First of all, the child is acquainted with his immediate environment and problems and as his curiosity widens he is encouraged to take up the study of people in his own country and abroad.

General Science

The course in 'general science' consists of relevant and useful topics from such subjects as nature study, botany, zoology, chemistry, astronomy, physiology and hygiene. The Zakir Husain Committee has stated the following as the objectives of the general science course:

"(1) To give pupils an intelligent and appreciative outlook on nature.
(2) To form in the pupils the habit of accurate observation and of testing experience by experiment.
(3) To enable them to understand the important scientific principles exemplified (a) in the national phenomena around, and (b) in the application of science to the service of man.
(4) To introduce them to the more important incidents in the lives of great scientists whose sacrifices in the cause of truth make a powerful appeal to the growing mind."[154]

The Secondary Education Commission appears to be in perfect agreement with the above objectives. When speaking on the nature of general science course it lays down that:

"The teacher should aim at awakening in the pupils a lively

curiosity about the natural phenomena around them, at developing their capacity for the practical application of their knowledge, at appreciating the tremendous impact of modern science on all aspects of our life and at interesting them in the human side of scientific progress by introducing them to the lives of the great scientists. Such an approach will ensure that science becomes a part of "liberal" education and an instrument for the appreciation of the special characteristics of modern culture."[155]

Needless to say that the general science objectives as outlined by the Committee are quite comprehensive and inclusive and they really stand for liberal education which will enrich the whole personality of the child. It may be noted here that some people wanted to make the general science course so comprehensive as to include sex-education in it as well. Gandhiji would have raised no objection to it as he has said:

"I am strongly in favour of teaching young boys and girls significance and right use of their generative organs."[156]

But he says further that sexual science should be taught only by that person "... who has attained mastery over his passions".[157] Perhaps, it was because of this stipulation of Gandhiji that the Zakir Husain Committee did not include sex-education in the general science syllabus.

Drawing

Drawing, which has been a neglected subject in the Indian schools since long, occupies an important place in the Wardha Scheme. The Zakir Husain Committee states that the aim of teaching, drawing is to train the eyes to distinguish various kinds of forms and colours, to develop the faculty of appreciating the beautiful and to create an ability in the student to earn a living by drawing pictorial graphs.[158] During the first four years drawing is to be taught with a view to enable the students to give expression to their various activities. Hence during this period its teaching is to be correlated with the child's work in nature study, reading and the craft. But during the last three years drawing should be taught so as to enable the students to produce artistic designs and decorations.

Music

Gandhiji's remarks about the inclusion of music in the school syllabus are noteworthy. He says:

> *"The modulation of voice is as necessary as the training of the hand. Physical drill, handicrafts, drawing and music should go hand in hand in order to draw best out of the boys and girls and create in them a real interest in their tuition. That this means a revolution in the system is admitted. If the future citizens of the state are to build a sure foundation for lives' work, these four things are necessary. One has only to visit any primary school to have a striking demonstration of slovenliness acrd disorderliness and discordant speech."*[159]

For the modulation of voice the students should be taught a number of beautiful songs and in the curriculum national songs, folk songs and devotional songs should be included.[160] The Zakir Husain Committee has recommended that group and choral singing should also be included. It may be noted that the Committee has not envisaged the giving of comprehensive training in music at the basic stage. So it did not think necessary to draw a detailed syllabus of music consisting of 'ragas'[161] and 'tals'.[162]

Hindustani

Gandhiji believed that Hindustani was the 'resultant of Hindi and Urdu' and it should be a compulsory subject in the basic schools. He was against the Sanskritized or Persianized form of Hindustani.[163] He desired that Hindustani should be written both in Hindu and Urdu scripts. He wanted that this type of Hindustani should replace English and become the lingua franca of the country.[164]

A Criticism of the Wardha Scheme

Some critics say that the Wardha Scheme became famous because it originated from a universally loved person, Gandhiji. Had it come from a less important man, it would not have received the same support. Gandhiji himself said at the Wardha Conference:

> *"You should not accept anything out of your regard for me ... The Scheme should he accepted after full and mature consideration so that it may not have to be given up after a little while."*[165]

Gandhiji had a deep insight into the needs and requirements of the rural people and so he devised an educational scheme for them. Some critics remark that the scheme appears to be educationally sound except its "self-supporting" and "the craft as the core" aspects. The school cannot be made self-supporting because the products made by young children cannot compete with those made by experts in the line. Moreover, if the child has a motive of producing something which may fetch a higher price, the cultural side of education will be lost and the child will become a pure materialist. Then again, it is impossible to teach all subjects through a craft. But we see that Gandhiji had been prompt to modify his stand, he accepted the position that the knowledge to be given through a craft should be supplemented by other processes. He clearly emphasized that:

> *"During the first year everything should be taught through the takli,*[166] *in the second year other processes also can be taught side by side."*[167]

Lack of the type of teachers required, is another criticism against the Wardha Scheme. Any scheme, however good, ultimately depends upon teachers. Therefore, for making the scheme a success it is very important to devise ways and means for training the suitable persons as teachers and to raise the scale of pay for teachers in order to check frustration on their part. It is true that some State Governments have started Basic Training Colleges for training the type of teachers needed for Basic schools which are run these days basically on the lines indicated by the Wardha Scheme but it is, perhaps, premature to pass any judgement on the work that these colleges are trying to do.

Some critics remark that over-attention focused on the Wardha Scheme neglects the cause of secondary and higher education. But the supporters of the Scheme state that:

> *"This is a scheme of universal and compulsory basic education for all children, to be followed in due course by higher education for those who are qualified to receive it."*[168]

Some other critics contend that the Wardha Scheme is Utopian for it is produced by a philosopher who did not know much about education. But the supporters of the Scheme claim that those who are working out the scheme have no doubt about its successful operation. They argue that the Scheme must undergo a long experimentation on a nation-wide-scale over a sufficiently long period before any final shape is given to it. Only then, it will be proper to have any correct estimate of the Scheme.

Some people argue that the Wardha Scheme by recommending a craft as a core puts back the clock of civilization. In these days of scientific inventions it is wrong to popularise the medieval industries like spinning and weaving as the medium of education. The supporters of the scheme assert that such an argument betrays an utter lack of knowledge of rural conditions in the country. Promoting big industries in the rural areas at the cost of rural handicrafts would result in concentration of power in a few hands, exploitation of the poor by the rich, chronic unemployment and all such evils which modern industries bring in their train. Supporters of the Scheme believe that the handicrafts have been selected for their educative possibilities. In the name of civilization it is difficult to ignore the best treasures of art and industry inherited from the ancestors and which can still sustain the teeming millions in the country in this space age.

The chief purpose of this chapter is to understand Gandhiji as an educational philosopher. So we do not choose here to examine the working of those institutions (Private and Government) which have given the Wardha Scheme or National Basic Education a practical shape.

Gandhiji on Textbooks

Gandhiji does not want that the student should be loaded with too many books. He says, "I have always felt that the true text book for the pupil is his teacher."[169] He thinks that in the beginning the preliminary training of the child should be oral because the child learns much more through his ears than through his eyes.[170] So he observes:

> *"To impose on children of tender age a knowledge of the alphabet and the ability to reach before they can gain general knowledge is to deprive them, whilst they are fresh, of the power of assimilating instruction by word of mouth."*[171]

Gandhiji hates the dependence of instruction on a multiplicity of textbooks because he thinks that this multiplicity deprives the, poor village children of India of the means of instruction.[172] He deplores that most of the current textbooks in Indian schools do not have an Indian background and so they are not useful for Indian boys and girls. So he is of the opinion that no textbooks should be taught to children of lower classes. In these classes it is the teacher who should use the textbook and he "to do full justice to his pupils, will have to prepare the daily lesson from the material available to him".[173] Gandhiji further says :

> *"Almost from the commencement, textbooks deal, not with the things which the boys and girls have always to deal within their houses, but things to which they are perfect strangers. It is not through the textbooks that a lad learns what is right and what is wrong in the home life. He is never taught to have any pride of his surroundings. The higher he goes the further he is removed from his home, so that at the end of his education he becomes estranged from his surroundings. He feels no poetry about the home life. His own civilization is presented to him*

> *as imbecile, barbarous, superstitious and useless for all practical purposes.*"[174]

Thus Gandhiji is vehemently against the current textbook and he would not have hesitated to destroy all of them that do not deal with the immediate surroundings of the students in a useful manner.[175] He wants that the textbooks for Indian boys and girls must be written by patriotic India.[176]

It may be mentioned here that the aims and methods of the Basic education called for an entirely new approach in the preparation of textbooks. Therefore the Zakir Husain Committee recommended that the textbooks for Basic schools should be prepared by experts.[177]

The Place of Religion in Education

Gandhiji is deeply religious. He holds that life without religion is life without principles, and life without principles is like a rudderless ship. He does not agree with the notion that religion is opposed to material good. He says:

> *"In my opinion the author of the Gita has dispelled this delusion. He has drawn no line of demarcation between religious life and worldly pursuits. On the contrary he has shown that religion must rule even our worldly pursuits.*"[178]

We have already seen that Gandhiji conceives of a society which is casteless and classless. This society is to be based on cooperative human labour which will ultimately develop the ideas of love, peace, truth, justice and discipline. Such a society will not be interested in exploitation. Gandhiji thinks that education in this society should centre round a craft, because craft alone will be able to inculcate the virtues he cherished. So he recommends a type of religious education for young children which will help them to acquire "an inner relation to infinity".

To Gandhiji religion means one's own personal experience and not a set of creeds and dogmas. He regards religion as an abiding faith in the absolute values of truth, love and justice. He remarks :

> *"Religion is a very personal matter. We should be living the life according to our lights, share the best with one another, thus adding to the sum-total of human effort to reach God."*[179]

This brings us to consider the place of religion in education according to Gandhiji who was quite alive to the difficulties of religious education of India—a land of religions. He observed:

> *"Rank atheism cannot flourish in this land. The task is indeed difficult. My head begins to turn as, I think of religious education."*[180]

Hence, Gandhiji accepted instruction in the universal essentials of all religions and a training in the fundamental virtues of truth and non-violence as the fundamental basis of religious education. To him all the great religious of the world agree in fundamentals. Hence, these fundamentals should be made the basis of religious education. In spite of his firm faith in the need of religious education in the school, he deliberately omitted it from the Wardha Scheme. He says :

> *"We have left out the teaching of religions from the Wardha Scheme of education because we are afraid that religions, as they are taught and practised today, lead to conflict rather than unity. But on the other hand, I hold that truths, that are common to all religions can and should be taught to all children. These truths cannot be taught through words or through books. The children can learn these truths only through the daily life of the teacher. If the teacher himself lives up to the tenets of truth and justice, then alone can the children learn that truth and justice are the basis of all religions."*[181]

The Secondary Education Commission agrees with the above views of Gandhiji when it remarks that :

> *"Whether religious instruction or moral instruction is given,*

the benefit of such instruction will be derived not from its being treated more or less on the lines of class-room instruction but from the spirit of the school and the influence exercised by the teachers."[182]

The University Education Commission also supports the stand of Gandhiji, when it says:

"If we teach secterian creeds to our children in public schools, instead of developing in them the spirit of peace and brotherly love, we encourage the spirit of strife, as the children become conscious of their divisive creeds and group loyalties...If religion is a matter of realization it cannot be reached through a mere knowledge of the dogmas. It is attained through discipline, training, what we need is not formal religious education, but spiritual training."[183]

What Gandhiji omitted was the denominational religion, and not the spiritual education of the child. He wanted that every child in the school should be instructed to respect all religions and to show the spirit of religion in their conduct. He says:

"Fundamental principles of ethics are common to all religions. These should certainly be taught to the children and that should he regarded us adequate religious instruction so far as the schools under the Wardha Scheme are concerned."[184]

Gandhiji was in favour of such religious education. Therefore, the Zakir Husain Committee wrote that one of the aims of teaching social studies under the Wardha Scheme should be "to develop mutual respect for the world religions".[185] The Committee further laid down that :

"Emphasis should be given on the ideals of love, truth and justice, of co-operative endeavour, national solidarity and the equality and brotherhood of man. Emphasis should he laid on lessons drawn from life showing the superiority of truth and non-violence in all its phases and its concomitant virtues, over violence and deceit."[186]

Gandhiji was not in favour of a State religion. So he did not like that religious education should form a part of the school curriculum approved by the State. By this he did not mean that the State schools would give no ethical education. All religions advocate the same fundamental ethics, therefore, the teaching of such ethics should be a function of the State schools.[187]

Gandhiji on Women Education

Gandhiji says :

> *"Men and women are of equal rank, but they are not identical. They are a peerless pair being supplementary to one another; each helps the other; so that without the one the existence of the other cannot be conceived, and therefore it follows as a necessary corollary from these facts that anything that will impair the status of either of them will involve the equal ruin of them both."*[188]

Therefore, Gandhiji warned that in framing the curriculum of studies this basic truth must not be lost sight of. He desired that each should be given such an education as to make each one fit for the different tasks of life called for by their specific nature.

Basic education has been so designed as to fulfil this purpose. The general course upto the fifth grade in a Basic school is the same for both the sexes, but by the fourth grade General Science includes domestic science for girls and in the sixth and seven grades the girls are allowed to take an advanced course in domestic science in place of the basic craft.[189] The Wardha Scheme allows parents to withdraw their girls after the completion of the 12th grade, if they are not in favour of co-education; but this does not imply that the education of girls should end at that stage. The Second Kher Committee has recommended that if the compulsory education upto 14 is enforced that should be applicable for girls as well and such domestic subjects as laundry, homecrafts, cookery, needle work, first aid and care of children, etc. should be taught by correlating other subjects with these practical activities according to the general principles of Basic education.[190]

Gandhiji used to say that his greatest hope lay in women. He believed that they wanted a helping hand to come out of the well in which they had fallen. He felt strongly for the emancipation of women. He wanted to give them all education according to their particular aptitudes and life demands. He thought that education of young children could be more effectively handled by women than by men, and by mothers than by maidens.

In the Wardha Scheme Gandhiji made no differentiation between boys and girls. He permitted co-education upto the age of eight, but according to him, as far as possible boys and girls could be educated together upto the age of sixteen. However, in the Wardha Scheme co-education has not been made compulsory.

Gandhiji says :

> *"... The question of co-education has been left open. It will regulate itself according to the time-spirit. So far as I am aware the members of the Committee were not all of one mind. Personally I have an open mind. I think that there are just as valid reasons for as against co-education. And I would not oppose the experiment wherever it is made."*[191]

Gandhiji on University Education

On university education, Gandhiji observes :

> *"Today the youth educated in our universities either ran after Government jobs or fell into dubious ways and sought outlet for their frustration by fomenting unrest. They were not even ashamed to beg or sponge upon others. Such was their sad plight. The aim of university education should be to turn out true servants of the people who would live and die for the country's freedom."*[192]

Thus we note that Gandhiji is not against higher or university education. In fact, he is against the university education as prevailing today. Under his scheme of university education he wants better libraries, more and better laboratories, an army of chemists, engineers and other experts. He wants that all these experts should speak the language of the people and the knowledge acquired by them should be the common property of the nation and these experts will produce original work instead of mere imitation.

Gandhiji does not think it imperative for the State to establish universities. He believes that if the people want a university they will supply the necessary funds for it. But he says that "The State must pay for it wherever it has definite use for it".[193] He feels the necessity of reorienting the university education in the country. He thinks that the prevailing system of higher education has resulted unemployment. Therefore, he says that education in the university should also be given through vocational training, because such an education will give the youths economic independence and a sense of self-respect. Thus Gandhiji envisages a radical change in the existing pattern of university education in the country. He wants to run all educational institutions from the lowest to the highest stage on basic educational lines, i.e., through craft activity. This applies to university as well. He wants to scrap the existing university education completely and remodel it on new lines according to the material requirements of the country. On the reorganization of university education, he says :

> *"It must be organically related to the Indian scene. It must, therefore, be an extension and continuation of the basic education course."*[194]

He wants that the universities should have feeders in the form of schools and colleges imparting instruction through the medium of their respective provincial languages. He says that the university is at the top most rung and therefore it must have a solid foundation. On founding new universities Gandhiji remarks:

> *"Universities founded under foreign domination have run in the reverse direction. Any other result was perhaps impossible. Therefore, there is every reason for being cautious about founding new universities till India has digested the newly-acquired freedom."*[195]

Gandhiji : Adult Education

Gandhiji wants to extend the scope of basic education throughout the whole life of the individual, i.e., he wants to educate the adults or the parents of children. Consequently, the Third All India Basic Education Conference which opened at Sevagram in January, 1945 considered this problem. In the inaugural speech at this conference Gandhiji remarked:

> *"Up to the present, although our education was new, we have lined as it were in a bay ... in that our work was restricted in scope. Now we are being driven out of our bay and thrust into the open ocean. There, we have no guide except the pole-star. That pole-star is village handicrafts. Our field now is not merely the child of seven to fourteen years of age, the field of Nai Talim stretches from the hour of conception in the mother's womb to the hour of death ......"*[196]

Consequently the conference appointed a Committee which was entrusted with the task of finalising a scheme of education. Gandhiji considered the education of the parents as the first concern of the nation. He regarded the education of the adult as a necessary prelude to the growth of the new generation in new values. He says:

> *"The age of Basic Education includes the education of the whole of society beginning with the children and going up to adults and old men and women, It has to be imparted through the practice of handicrafts, village sanitation and medical relief, preventive and curative."*[197]

Thus we see that Gandhiji was quite conscious of the urgent necessity of adult education in the country. And the scheme of social education as formulated by the Government of India takes into consideration Gandhiji's approach—though goes a long way by including in it recreational aspects of education as well.

Today the concept of adult education has been revolutionized. Now adult education does not imply only the teaching of the Three

Rs., i.e., literacy. In fact, it means "literacy of the whole personality". So the term adult education has been replaced in India, as in many other countries, by 'Social Education' which means acquiring of knowledge for health and civic education, promotion of communal harmony, teaching of simple crafts and providing facilities for suitable cultural and recreational activities. Thus by social education, an attempt is made to raise the 'general level of the people life—material, moral, cultural and spiritual'. It is in the context of this concept of social education, that we shall now examine the place of Gandhiji as a social educationist. Gandhiji may be regarded as one of the greatest social educationists of all times. Wherever he went he disseminated knowledge and light for the education of countless men and women. His very life has been a sermon which can inspire one to sacrifice his all for selfless service of mankind.

Gandhiji advised students to spend their vacations in the service of the village people by conducting classes for them and teaching them rules of sanitation and healthy living.

> *"Gandhiji's teachings of Truth and Non-violence with all the corollaries attached to these two fundamentals and his own practice of the same form the most spectacular adult education experiment the world has ever witnessed. The Ashrams at Sabarmati and Sevagram that he established, his life in these historic places, the training that he imparted to hundreds and thousands there, the inspiration and learning that visitors to these places from all over country and also from abroad received are all brilliant achievements in the field of adult education."*[198]

K.G. Saiyidain calling him the greatest worker in the cause of adult education has remarked that :

> *"...His (Gandhiji's) voice has been calling the straying multitude back to the path of honour and rectitude and love."*[199]

NOTES

1. *In Mahatma Gandhi*, Ed. by S. Radhakrishnan, pp. 553-554.
2. *Harijan*, March 28,1936.
3. Lionel Curtis, in *Mahatma Gandhi*, Ed. by S. Radhakrishnan, p. 68.
4. Carl Heath; *Ibid.*, p. 92.
5. Ray, B.C., *Gandhian Ethics*, pp. 3-4.
6. *Young India*, Oct. 9,1921, p. 317.
7. Quoted by Romain Rolland in *Mahatma Gandhi*, p. 28.
8. *Young India*, Nov. 13,1924.
9. *My Experiments with Truth*, p. 6.
10. Andrews, C.F., *Mahatma Gandhi's Ideas*, p. 44.
11. Jeffrey's, M.V.C. Glancon, p.97.
12. *Young India*, March 3,1925.
13. *Ibid.*
14. *Young India*, November 11,1928.
15. *Ibid.*, December 31,1931.
16. St. John, 14:6.
17. Bose, *Selections from Gandhi*, p. 26.
18. *Ibid.*, pp. 26-27.
19. *Harijan*, May 14,1938, p. 109.
20. *Ibid.*, April 28,1946.
21. *Young India*, October 11,1928.
22. *Harijan*, June 3,1939, p. 151.
23. *Ibid.*, July 8,1933.
24. Shukla C, *Gandhi's View of Life*, p. 37.
25. *Ibid.*, p. 38.
26. *The Life of Vivekananda*, p. 234.
27. *Young India*, January, 1926.
28. Gandhi, M.K.: *Fellowship of Faiths and Unity of Religions*, p. 53.
29. Bose: *Selections from Gandhi*, p. 45.
30. *Ibid.*, p. 300.
31. *Ibid.*, 223.
32. *Young India*, II, p. 435.
33. *Ibid.*, p. 364.
34. *History of the Congress*, Quotation of Gandhiji, p. 979.
35. *Hind Swaraj*, p. 60.
36. *Young India*, II, p. 64.
37. *Harijan*, February 11, 1939, p. 8.
38. *Ibid.*, March 28,1936, p. 49.
39. Kriplani, J.B.: *Gandhi's Foreword to the Gandhian Way.*
40. *Autobiography*, II, p. 476.
41. *Harijan*, March 28,1936.
42. Groggy, R.B., *Power of Non-Violence*, p. 199.
43. *Speeches*, p. 503.
44. *Harijan*, June 23,1946, p. 199.
45. *Ibid.*, May 1,1937, p. 89.

46. *Ibid.* I, p. 734.
47. *Harijan*, September 5,1936, p. 237.
48. *Young India*, II, p. 984.
49. *Ibid.* III, p. 812.
50. *Harijan*, July 20,1935, p. 180.
51. *Young India*, Vol. II, p. 1204.
52. Romain Rolland, *Mahatma Gandhi*, p. 45.
53. *Harijan*, June 22,1935, p. 148.
54. *Young India*, Vol. II, p. 204.
55. *Ibid.*, April 3,1924.
56. *Harijan*, September 26,1936.
57. *Young India*, August 11,1920.
58. *Mahatma Gandhi*, p. 40.
59. *Yarvada Mandir*.
60. Srimati Sophia Wadia, *The Path of Satyagraha in Mahatma Gandhi*, p. 308, Edited by S. Radhakrishnan.
61. *Harijan*, October 14,1939, p. 303.
62. Speeches of Mahatma Gandhi, p. 301.
63. *Young India*, September 10,1931.
64. Bose, *Selections from Gandhi*, p. 233.
65. *Ibid.*, p. 284.
66. Bose : *Selections from Gandhi*, p. 66.
67. *Ibid.*, p. 67.
68. *Ibid.*, p. 72.
69. *Ibid.*, p. 240.
70. *Ibid.*, p. 246.
71. *Stages of Life*.
72. *Ibid.*
73. *Ibid.*, p. 242.
74. *Ibid.*, p. 241.
75. *Harijan*, July 31, 1937.
76. *The Year Book of Education*, 1940, p. 441.
77. Wilds, E.H., *The Foundations of Modern Education*, p. 469.
78. *Harijan*, September 11,1937.
79. Gandhi's Inaugural Speech at All India National Education Conference, Wardha, October 22,1937.
80. *Harijan*, July 31,1937.
81. *The Year Book of Education*, p. 441,1940.
82. *Harijan*, September 11,1937.
83. *Harijan*, October 2,1937.
84. Dewey, J., *Democracy and Education*, p. 235.
85. *Educational Reconstruction*, p. 94.
86. *Ibid.*, p. 66.
87. *Ibid.*
88. *Educational Reconstruction*, p.121.
89. *Ibid.*, p. 95.
90. *Basic National Education*, p. 9.
91. *Harijan*, October 9,1937.

92. Dewey, John: *Democracy and Education*, pp. 234-235.
93. *Harijan*, June 11,1938.
94. Jeffreys, Glancon, p. 86.
95. Whitehead, A.N, *Aims of Education and other Essays*, p. 74.
96. *Young India*, January 29,1925.
97. *Ibid.*, December 12, 1928.
98. Mahạdev Desai: *With Gandhiji in Ceylon*, p. 109.
99. *Young India*, April 4,1929.
100. *Ibid.*
101. *Ibid.*
102. *Young India*, June 24,1926.
103. *Harijan*, October 2,1937.
104. *Ibid.*
105. *Harijan*, September 18,1937.
106. *Mahatma Gandhi: To the Students*, p. 291.
107. *Harijan*, July 31,1937.
108. *Harijan*, September 11,1937.
109. *Harijan*, September 18,1937.
110. *Autobiography*, p. 28.
111. *Harijan*, September, 11,1937.
112. *Educational Reconstruction*, p. 63.
113. Gandhiji: *Autobiography*, p. 408.
114. *Harijan*, November 21,1936.
115. Carlton Washburne : *Remarkers of Mankind* (I 932), p. 105.
116. *Mahatma Gandhi : To the Students*, p. 107.
117. *Ibid.*, p. 122.
118. *Young India*, July 21,1927.
119. *Ibid.*, September 8,1927.
120. *Mahatma Gandhi: To the Students*, p. 190.
121. *Young India*, November 13,1924.
122. Bose, *Selections from Gandhi*, p. 27.
123. *Harijan*, March 10,1946.
124. *Ibid.*, November 17,1933.
125. *Young India*, March 26,1931.
126. Waterhouse, *Eric : Philosophical Approach to Religion*, p.121.
127. *Harijan*, March 9,1947.
128. Carlton, *Washburne: Remembers of Modern India*, p. 104.
129. *Harijan*, August 29,1934.
130. Varkey: *Wardha Scheme of Education*, pp. 30-40.
131. Margaret Barr: *Gandhiji and Peace Through Education*, p. 161.
132. *Ibid.*, October 21,1937.
133. *Ibid.*
134. *Ibid.*
135. *Ibid.*, p. 120.
136. *Ibid.*, p. 122.
137. *Harijan*, September 18, 1937.
138. *Educational Reconstruction*, p. 94.
139. *Ibid.*, p. 124.

140. *Basic National Education*, p. 11.
141. *Harijan*, October 9,1937.
142. *Harijan*, March 3,1939.
143. The Report of the Secondary Education Commission, Government of India, Ministry of Education, Delhi, 1953, p . 90.
144. *Ibid.*
145. *Harijan*, August 25,1946.
146. *Harijan*, November 9,1947.
147. *Young India*, October 15,1925.
148. *Speeches and Writings of Mahatma Gandhi*, p. 335.
149. *Young India*, January 19,1921.
150. *Harijan*, August 18,1946.
151. *Basic National Education*, pp. 17-18.
152. *Young India*, June 1,1921.
153. *Basic National Education*, pp. 19-20.
154. *Basic National Education*, p. 23.
155. The Secondary Education Commission, p. 94, Govt. of India, Ministry of Education, Delhi, 1953.
156. *Harijan*, November 2, 1936.
157. *Ibid.*
158. cf. *Basic National Education*, p. 25.
159. *Harijan*, September 11,1937.
160. *Basic National Education*, p. 26.
161. Tunes.
162. Measure of Time.
163. *Young India*, August 27,1925.
164. *Speeches and Writings of Mahatma Gandhi*, p. 396.
165. *Educational Reconstruction*, p. 74.
166. A Small Tool for spinning thread by hand.
167. *Educational Reconstruction*, p. 62.
168. *Ibid.*, p. 74.
169. *Autobiography*, II, p. 198.
170. *Ibid.*
171. *Young India*, September 16,1926.
172. *Ibid.*
173. *Harijan*, December 1,1933.
174. *Young India*, September 1,1921.
175. *Ibid.*
176. *Young India*, June 21,1928.
177. *Basic National Education*, p. 43.
178. Mahadev Desai : *The Gita According to Gandhi*, p. 126
179. *Harijan*, November 28, 1936.
180. *Hind Swaraj*, p. 67.
181. First Kher Report, p. 10, (cited by Zakir Husain).
182. *Op. cit.*, pp. 125-126.
183. University Education Commission Report, Government of India, Ministry of Education, pp. 294-295, Delhi, 1949.

184. *Harijan*, July 16, 1938.
185. *Educational Reconstruction*, p. 129.
186. *Ibid.*, p. 130.
187. *Harijan*, March 23, 1947.
188. *Speeches and Writings of Mahatma Gandhi*, p. 426.
189. *Basic National Education*, p. 27.
190. Reports, 1938-43, p. 13.
191. *Harijan*, July 16, 1938.
192. *Harijan*, August 25, 1946.
193. *Harijan*, July 9, 1938.
194. *Harijan*, August 25, 1946.
195. *Harijan*, Novermber 2, 1947.
196. Perianayickenpalayam Report, p. 27.
197. *Ibid.*, pp. 29-30.
198. *Journal of Education and Philosophy*, April, 1948—from an article by Prof. T.K.N. Menon.
199. From his Presidential Address to the All India Adult Education Conference held in December, 1947.

8

RABINDRANATH TAGORE (1861—1941)

His Life

Rabindranath Tagore was born on May 7,1861 in Calcutta. Maharshi Devendranath Tagore, the great Brahmo leader, was his father. Rabindranath Tagore was the youngest of his six brothers. He began to compose verses when he was only eight years old. His education had been very desultory. He had his education mostly at home through tutors and private readings. On his death in 1941, the Syndicate of the University of Calcutta thus placed on records his services to India:

> *"Through him India has given her message to mankind and his unique achievement in the fields of literature, philosophy, education and art have won imperishable fame for himself, and have raised the status of India in the estimation of the world."*

The world recognised the merit of Tagore by awarding him the Nobel prize for literature in 1913 for the English version of his Gitanjali. The University of Calcutta honoured him with the honorary degree of D.Lit. in December, 1913. The Government of India made him a Knight in 1915.

Tagore is a philosopher, poet, novelist, dramatist, actor, composer, educators, painter and prophet. By his writings he has enriched not only Bengali literature, but also English. Besides being a poet and artist of the highest order, he is also a prophet of humanity. Love of man is the very heart of his religion. Man, the divine, is the measure of all things to him. His love of humanity is the outcome of his spirituality. Throughout his work Tagore mirrors the ancient wisdom of India, though restated according to the needs of modern life.

But Tagore was not satisfied only with restating the sagacious message of the ancient India. He tried to lead the life of the poet prophets of old and wanted to create a community around him with the spirit of the ancient Ashramas. With this aim in view he established a school at Shantiniketan at great personal sacrifice, when he was almost forty years old. Here he surrounded himself with children to teach them to live in harmony with nature. He has described his educational experiment in this school and his educational ideologies into numerous articles. But before we come to understand his educational philosophy it is necessary to understand his philosophy in general, because it is from his philosophy that his educational ideas have originated.

Tagore's Philosophy

Tagore has a philosophy

Some people think that Tagore was a poet and an artist but not a philosopher. But we cannot agree with this point of view. Radhakrishnan says about Tagore's book entitled *Sadhana* that, "We feel that the atmosphere is charged with a particular vision of reality".[1] Dr. S.N. Das Gupta says:

> *"Although Rabindranath is no metaphysician, his property has gained in flesh and blood on account of his philosophic experience. Anyone who has read the works of Pringle Pattison, Bosanquet and Bergson will find striking similarities between many of the ideas of Rabindranath and those of the above mentioned authors."*[2]

In fact, no defence is necessary in writing about the philosophy of Tagore. The Indian tradition has been such that there is no incongruity in thinking about a poet's philosophy. We would in fact hesitate to call one a poet if he has no philosophy. Tagore had a vision. The Indian word for philosophy is *Darshana* or vision (of truth). Tagore certainly had a *Darshana*. The poetic and philosophic aspects of Tagore are not contradictory but complementary to each other.[3] It is true that Tagore does not give us a finished clear-cut theory of his philosophy but on the basis of his writing a theistic philosophy can be built up.

The General Nature of His Philosophy

Tagore has always depended upon personal experiences for arriving at a truth. He does not believe in a wholly impersonal method of looking at fundamental problems, because this method ignores the emotional side of human nature. Another essential feature of his philosophy has been his desire to reconcile all extremes and harmonize all contradictions. In his views about God and the relation of God to Man and Nature he has sought a reconciliation between the extremes of Transcendence and Immanence, Humanism and *Prapatti* (self-surrender), and one-sided Naturalism and extreme Spiritualism. In ethics, too, Tagore shows the same attitude. He condemns hedonism without losing his faith in the joy of life. He has tried to synthesize the one-sided tendencies of individualism and universalism in social life. He has shown the necessity of both freedom and determinism in human life. He is against both asceticism and egoistic ideal. He has shown a common ground between romanticism and realism. He has noted the proper limits of ugliness and beauty.

In his entire philosophic attitude Tagore has shown an attitude of softening the edges of intellectual preconceptions. He has tried to smoothen out the sectarian limits of thoughts. He has endeavoured to preserve the essential truths of each theory but has never accepted anyone in its totality. Thus Tagore has always sought a 'golden mean'. This search is clear in his poems. Any example of this search is evident in these lines from *Purabi* :

"In my heart is a stream of Darkness,
But a stream of light is in my eyes.
My song rises up to the Heavens,
But my dance is on this mortal Earth.
On my left, and on my right,
Are the two streams of Joy and Sorrow.

In the Ocean of Rest
The Wave of Movement doth merge."

His Views Regarding God

Tagore says :

"I have never looked at God, Man and Nature as problems which can be considered in isolation from each other. I could never conceive of their occupying watertight compartments."[4]

Therefore his philosophy presents an integral picture of God, Man and Nature. He says :

"My mind is used to look at reality as an integral whole, it being understood, of course, that I am referring to the wholeness of spirit, and not to material unity."[5]

Tagore regards God as a postulate, an axiomatic reality. Therefore, he has not considered necessary to give any traditional proof for the existence of God. He says, "We must feel God as we feel light."[6] He believes that the ceaseless activity going on in the universe cannot be accounted in the absence of an Infinite. "World movements are not then blind movements, they are related to the will of God".[7]

Man cannot feel satisfied merely by having his needs fulfilled. He often feels an unconscious recognition that there is something which he lacks. So he feels incomplete by himself. He wants to remedy this incompleteness by communion with Nature. But he does not get complete satisfaction.

"Our satisfaction in Nature, though real, is still incomplete. It is a satisfaction only of our empirical ego. But we have our higher self which finds contentment in the Infinite."[8]

Tagore says that:

"In this large life of social communion man feels the mystery of unity. From the sense of unity men come to their sense of God."[9]

Thus we find that like Kant, Tagore believed in the moral argument for the existence of God.

As regards the nature of God Tagore does not believe in the impersonal Absolute of Samskara-Vedanta, because he thinks that it does not meet the moral, religious or aesthetic requirements of mankind. So he accepts a God who is close to man. He does not like a God who is not interested in man's actions and thoughts. In fact, he believes that there can be some personal relation between God and man. No wonder then that he says:

> *"Dualistic philosophy in India has sought to supplement the idea of an impersonal Brahman by that of it personal Iswara."*[10]

However, he does not speak of the personality of God. He generally refers to a 'personal God'. By personality he does not mean a finite God. He regards God as the perfect person, whereas man is personal in an imperfect manner.

To Tagore the relation between God and man must be that of Love and Joy. He does not want to be devoted to a God to whom nothing can be attributed except that He exists. He does not like the impersonal existence of God, because he thinks that to do so is not to demand the existence of God but of the Indeterminate. He believes that the energy of the immortal Purusa urges us to be ethical.[11] He thinks that God must have a personality, otherwise we cannot account for our pursuit of the God.

However, it must be noted that Tagore does not overrule altogether the impersonal aspect of God. He has never stated that the idea of Personality of God exhausts His nature. Therefore, he does not dogmatically reject Advaita Vedanta. He regards Personality only an aspect of Reality, though the most important aspect. He says, "It will not do to reject the impersonal aspect of truth altogether".[12] In one of his lectures at Shantiniketan he says:

> *"Dualistic*[13] *philosophy in India proclaims a God who has his qualities and forms. Man's deliverance depends upon the fulfilment of his knowledge, love and strength. Such a fulfilment is precluded by a Nirguna Brahma."*

Thus we find that Tagore is naturally inclined towards the *Vaisnava* view of *Saguna Brahma*.

His Conception of Self

Tagore regards self as an independent reality. To him the independence of the self is necessary for Reality as a whole. In *Gitanjali*, Tagore describes God and man as two separate realities "floating at will".[14] It is true that the human self derives its contents from its affinity with the Infinite. But this affinity does not imply that it is not free to have its own individual experiences. Therefore, Tagore does not like to undermine the independence of the self by making it entirely subsequent to the Will of God. He believes that the self has the power to work on its own initiative as well. He says:

> *"The self must have complete freedom. Only a free entity can have relations with another entity. God has made this understanding with us. He has told us: 'Come to me as a free-self. Nothing that is bound can truly approach me'."*[15]

This freedom is necessary for union of self with God. It is because of this freedom that the human self has purpose and greatness.[16] Even in the highest stage of realisation the self must remain distinct from God. He does not think that the finite is lost in the absolute. Man may approach God, but he never merges into God. He believes that in his relation to God man finds himself more completely. In no way he loses himself. Tagore says :

> *"The difference between Atma and Brahma must always be there. He has become what we are ever striving to be. The difference is between 'being' and 'becoming.'*[17] *God is the Infinite ideal of 'perfection' and man 'the eternal process of its realisation'."*[18]

Necessity of Separation and Union

It is worth noting that Tagore strikes a balance between the two extremes of utter Dualism and absolute Monism. He recognises the existence of the 'many' and believes that this manyness does not affect the organic unity and coherence of the whole. According to him duality and unity are demands of creation. But a duality of unrelated realities is not acceptable to him. He believes that the separation and re-union should go hand in hand. He says:

> *"The universal is never seeking its consummation in the unique. The desire we have to keep our uniqueness intact is really the desire of the Universe acting in us."*[19]

He further says :

> *"In our physical existence, there is both separation and meeting between us and the world of things. The consciousness of this relationship takes a deeper line in our mental life where there is coutinual separation and reunion between the individual mind and the universal world of reason... It widens when there is separation and combination between the individual will and the universal world of personality."*[20]

Thus we find that Tagore emphatically asserts the dire necessity of separation and union in all our relations between physical, mental and spiritual.

Tagore does not choose to give a logical reason of the existence of both the Absolute and the Self as realities. To him this explanation is not possible at all. He has expressed this inability when he says:

> *"This I shall accept—How the One could become Two, I can not understand."*[21]

The Concept of Maya

We have seen that Tagore has been an exponent of theism, but he has never chosen to refute the *Maya*-theory. All through his writings he has tried to establish the reality of the world and to preserve the essential truth of the doctrine of *Maya*. He cannot accept an absolute separateness of Nature from God, nor can he agree with an utter identity of God with the world. We have already indicated above that he strikes a compromise between Transcendence and Immanence between Deism and Pantheism. This clearly means that he believes in the interdependence of God and the world and of God and the Self. He seems to adopt an extraordinary tolerant attitude towards the most extreme forms of the doctrine of *Maya* when he says:

> *"The world as an art is 'Maya'. It 'is' and 'is' 'not'. Its sole explanation is that it seems to be what it is. The ingredients are elusive; call them Maya, even disbelieve them, the Great Artist, the 'Mayavin' is not hurt."*[22]

Man and Nature

Tagore recognises a kinship between Man and Nature. He says:

> *"When a man does not realise his kinship with the world of nature, he lives in a prison-house whose walls are alien to him."*[23]

To Tagore Man and Nature are indispensable elements of the Reality. Both Man and Nature need each other in the same way as God and Man need each other. Nature and Spirit are complementary to each other. Nature derives its meaning from Spirit and Spirit express itself though Nature. According to Tagore whatever Nature possesses is not only, a storehouse of powers but a habitation of man's spirit as well'.[24] In a poem addressing Nature Tagore says:

In me, night and day, have your flowers bloomed
In me your seeds sprouted.
For me do your trees shower their
Perfume and foliage.[25]

It is the human mind that gives expression to the meaning of nature, by itself Nature is dumb. But this dependence of Nature on man is not one-sided. Spirit too needs Nature in the same manner. Man will lose his balance if he were to, "leave his resting place in universal nature and walk upon the single rope of humanity."[26]

Tagore goes further than saying that Man and Nature are independent. He suggests certain point where these two come in closer contact. He thinks that Man and Nature both possess '*Jiwan*

Shakti', i.e., 'Energy of Life'. It is because of this common possession that the union between the two becomes inevitable. Tagore finds a harmonious order in the phenomena of Nature in the same way as he finds it in the human life. To him both Nature and Man have "the rhythm of cosmic motion".[27] He believes that both Man and Nature are "held together in God". They are only spheres of the manifestation of the same God.

Tagore's Humanism

Thus we see that Tagore emphasises Man's intimate connection with Nature. But this emphasis must not lead one to think that he fails to see the advance of Spirit over nature. He admits the place of pride that Man occupies in the universe. He gives such a high status to man that he has declared that God himself may be considered in terms of humanity. He says, "Reality is human" and "Truth is human". Thus we can call Tagore a humanist par excellence because he gives man the highest place within the phenomena of the world, and he bestows even God with humanness and he depicts ultimate Reality in human terms. But this does not imply that he means to dethrone the Infinite and to glorify the finite man as 'finite'. He wants that man must outgrow himself and that the ideas of the "Human God must be supplemented by that of the divine Man".

Tagore accepts the idea of "degrees" in truth and reality. For example, to him both Man and Nature are real, but the former is more real than the latter. He says:

> *"The flower that has failed to bloom, the river that has lost its course in the desert, even these are not altogether devoid of meaning."*[28]

Thus to him the ultimate reality of an object is never lost. He believes that the Absolute is manifested in every object of creation, but

> *"Of all His manifestations, man is incomparable. The human self is unique, because in it God reveals himself in a special manner."*[29]

In *Sadhana*, Tagore is more explicit. He says:

> *"The revealment of the infinite is to be seen most fully not in the starry heavens, but in the soul of man."* [30]

Thus Tagore gives to man the loftiest position. He says:

> *"God has many strings to his 'sitar' (musical instrument), some are made of iron, others of copper and yet others are made of gold. Humanity is the golden string of God's lute."*[31]

To Tagore man is superior to nature. But in what does his superiority lie? It exists in his sense of freedom, magnificence and ethical and aesthetic consciousness which Nature lacks. In Nature there is Determinism. There is a certain internality in man due to which he "turns his vision inwards, and upsets Nature's scheme of balance".[32] Nature does not have this internality. Because of the freedom that man enjoys he becomes a creative being and looks beyond his minimum needs of survival. Man is not satisfied with the minimum. He wants more. "He is restless, he has a thirst for the distant and the far away".[33] There is no limit to man's progress. However great he becomes, he always aspires for higher goals.

Tagore's Views on Aesthetics

Tagore distinguishes the Beautiful from the *Ugly*, but he has not given us an exact definition of beauty. However, he has tried to state his concept of the beautiful. He does not regard anything as absolute evil. To him both good and evil are only aspects of the moral principle. In the same way, there is nothing like absolute death; life and death are only aspects of the life-principle. Similarly, Tagore believes that ugliness and beauty are aspects of the principle of beauty. Therefore, he does not want to exclude the ugly from art altogether. To him to do so would be:

> *"To admit that our sense of beauty creates a dissension in our universe, and sets up a wall of hindrance across the highway of communication."*[34]

But it must be noted that he has never given an independent reality to ugliness. Tagore believes that:

> *"The principle object of Art is the expression of personality, and that is why it uses the language of picture and music."*[35]

He further says that:

> *"Works of art are the signatures of beauty, in which the mingling of the personal touch leaves it memorial."*[36]

Thus he emphasises the personal element in art, because to him the art is personal and "personality is at the root of existence itself". For Tagore reality starts from a personal God and finds its ultimate significance in the relation that lies between this personal God and the personal self of man. To reveal the ties of beauty and love that make up this relation, is the real function of art. Tagore thinks that man creates beauty under diving inspiration, because man himself is God's art-work. He says:

> *"Our creations are only variations upon God's great theme of the universe.... Our freedom as creators finds its joy in contributing its own voice to the concrete of the world-music."*[37]

But from this one must not construe that Tagore brings in determinism in art and brings down the free creative activity of man, because his major stress is on human personality and even in his estimate of the divine and the human in art he obeys the principle of harmony and proportion. He says:

> *"The world of art even extends its frontiers to unexplored regions. Art is signalizing man's conquest of the world by its symbols of beauty, springing up in spots which were barren of all voice and colour ... Art is supplying man with his banners, under which he marches on to fight against the inane and the inert ... The encroachment of man's personality has no limit... The one effort of man's personality is to transform everything with which he has any true concern into the human. And art is*

like the spread of vegetation, to show how far man has reclaimed the desert for his own."[38]

Thus Tagore regards art as one of the unmistakable symbols of human progress. In art man 'transcends his finitude'.

Disinterested pleasure is the keynote of Tagore's aesthetics. To him utility may be an outcome of art, but it can never be its aim. The sole aim of art is delight. If the emphasis in the creation of art is placed on utility the artist will be diverted from the complete man to the merely useful man, and then the element of utility will be an impediment to the revelation of beauty. However, from this we must not infer that Tagore wants to maintain that art is purposeless. He believes that the excellence that the artist creates must have social worth for the common man. Thus he extends the boundaries of art. He does not regard as an escape from reality. He says:

"Art evokes in our mind the deep, rich sense of reality."[39]

Tagore's Views on Ethics

In his ethical doctrines Tagore desires to harmonise all extremes which have been noted in his metaphysical notions. To him the highest ethical ideal must satisfy the whole of human nature. Therefore, he regards moral discrimination as an essential part of human nature. He says:

"The life of an animal is unmoral, for it is aware only of an immediate present. The life of a man can be immoral but it cannot be unmoral; it must have a moral basis."[40]

Tagore believes that moral ideas must have influenced the course of civilization. That is why there is always a conflict in man with regard to "what is desired and what should be desired".[41] For his existence man depends upon the world of nature, but for his humanity he has to rely on the moral world. Because of this:

"Entry into the moral world, the dualism of the animal life and the moral makes us conscious of our personality as man."[42]

Tagore believes that the moral nature of man will never permit an extreme form of egoism. Goodness of man demands that a man must look beyond his own interests. Tagore says, "To live the life of goodness is to live the life of all".[43] Therefore he does not believe that "virtue is power", and "justice is the interest of the stronger." Anything that glorifies forces of violence is unacceptable to his moral temperament. Unlike Vietzche, Tagore believes that "that is not the power but love which is key to ethical value".[44] To him "love is not weakness but strength, egoism not strength but the weakness of the moral self."[45] Therefore to him God is God of love and tenderness.

Tagore says that egoism contradicts man's infinite ideal.

> *"The man who aims at his own aggrandisement underrates everything else. Thus in order to be conscious of the reality of all, man has to be free from bond of personal desires."*[46]

Thus an egoist cannot understand reality. He cannot even understand his self.

> *"The soul can only find its truth by unifying itself with others and only then it has its joy."*[47]

Thus according to Tagore, there must be some degree of altruism in thought and action of man. The man is aware of this altruism, therefore, he occupies the supreme position in creation.

Tagore does not accept hedonism as a basis of morality. He says:

> *"In sin we lust after pleasures not because they are truly desirable but because the red light of our passion makes them appear desirable."*[48]

Thus hedonistic ethics or pleasure depends upon the gratification of desire. The search after pleasure makes man fierce and aggressive. Pleasure is intimately connected with that part of man which is related with Nature. Man has to transcend Nature, therefore, the gratification of pleasure can never be the ideal of man. Tagore does not reject pleasure, but he does mean that it must be regulated by the higher spiritual nature of man. He says:

> *"In human nature, sexual passion is fiercely individual and destructive, but dominated by the ideal of love, it has been made to flow into a perfection of beauty."*[49]

Thus seeking of pleasure can never be the ideal of man, because it will degenerate him to the lowest level.

Tagore believes that man has the capacity to rise above utilitarian considerations. If man were to occupy himself only in the pursuit of utility, he would lose all charm and joy of life. Therefore, Tagore is opposed to utilitarianism. He says:

> *"There are sentiments in us which are creative, which do not clamour for gain, but overflow in gifts, in spontaneous generosity."*[50]

Hence Tagore is against the utilitarian tendencies of the modern age. He thinks that utilitarianism makes men mere "walking stomachs and brains."[51]

Tagore's views on hedonism and utilitarianism do not imply that he believes in rigorous asceticism. Therefore to him wordly life is not necessarily dangerous for the moral self. He does not regard body as the prison on the soul, or like Kant does he think that sensibility is necessarily irrational. He is against the overdose of asceticism contained in the ethics of Sankaracharya.[52] He says:

> *"Our knowledge in its vain endeavour to look at Absolute Reality in isolation from the world of things, has hardened like a stone. Our heart, in its effort to enjoy God by imprisoning Him within its feelings, faints of its own excess."*[53]

He further says :

> *"Heaven is here, in my body, my love and joy and sorrow. What greater fortune can there be than to have been born a human being."*[54]

Therefore Tagore has been regarded as a *Sadhaka* (a striver) and not an ascetic. He regards both acquisition and renunciation as the two real aspects of human life. To him both these aspects contribute equally to the dignity of man.[55]

Thus Tagore accepts the worldly values. Since he wants to live on amongst man, he believes in a life of action, and he wants to act in order to enjoy life and to transcend himself beyond worldly wants. The action that Tagore stands for is that which emerges from the fountain of spiritual joy. He says:

> *"Joy without the play of joy is no joy at tall, play without activity is no play. Activity is the play of joy."*[56]

Thus we see that Tagore does advise us to retire from the "fever and the fret" of active life.

Tagore does not think that Freedom is altogether opposed to Law or Restraint. To him freedom and restraint are mutually related parts of the Moral Order and they are complementary to each other. He says:

> *"Truth has freedom on one side and restraint on the other. Its one aspect declares: 'By fear to him fire burns'. Its other aspect proclaims: 'From joy are all things born'. To reject the law on the one side is to deny the possibility of making use of the freedom which is on the other side. The Absolute Himself is both free and not-free. He is bound by his Truth, and he is free in virtue of his joy. We too can gain the enjoyment of freedom fully only if we accept the bounds of truth."*[57]

Thus freedom from all restraint cannot be Tagore's ideal. He does not recognise anything as absolute freedom. He finds even "God bound in the very process of creating the world."[58]

It is from Tagore's idea of freedom that we can infer what he means by immortality. He thinks that only that can be immortal, deathless and eternal who is free. The perishable or the mortal is bound. Thus we find that Tagore connects immortality with freedom.

Tagore recognises the boundless worth of the human individual. To him the highest conception of human progress is the fullest development of each human personality. Therefore, he recognises the self as the highest human reality.

Tagore says :

> *"Man's moral history is the history of his journey to the unknown in quest of the realisation of his immortal self— his Soul... Man is marching from epoch to epoch towards the fullest realisation of his Self, the Self that is greater than the things he accumulates, the deeds he accomplishes, the theories he builds ...the soul whose onward course is never checked by death of dissolution."*[59]

This onward course of the soul is full of difficulties. Hence at times there is stagnation which again is followed by periods of great moral effort. Tagore is conscious of the wholeness of the moral ideal. Therefore to him progress means the development of all the sides of human nature.

> *"Man must realise the wholeness of his existence... He must know that hard as he may strive he can never create his honey within the cells of a single hive, for the perennial supply is outside."*[60]

This emphasis on 'wholeness' indicates Tagore's loyalty to the traditions of Indian philosophy. Therefore, he pleads that moral development must not exclude intellectual development. True spirituality means a correlation of the within and the without. To him this type of wholeness is the criterion of morality.

Tagore's Educational Philosophy

'Harmony with all thing' is the basic principle of Tagore's philosophy. He interprets this harmony in three contexts—with nature, with human surroundings and with international relations. To him the real education is that which teaches one to live in harmony with all that exists around him. During early childhood he left his school and rebelled against the prevailing system of education, because he found that it did not teach harmony with existing things. According to Tagore the primary object of an educational institution should be to bring the educated in perfect tune with the symphony of response between life and world. Tagore realised this idea in his Bolpur school which has now been developed in Visva Bharati. We find four fundamentals in Tagore's educational philosophy: Naturalism, Humanism, Internationalism and Idealism.

Tagore's Naturalism

Nature in Indian Civilization

Indian civilization was born in forest near which the early Aryans made their abode. The forest supplied them with all their necessities. This feature in the beginning gave the civilization a distinct character. It was surrounded by nature on all sides, it was clothed and fed by her and had the most intimate intercourse with her varying aspects.[61] This distinctive feature of Indian civilization is of great importance in Tagore's thinking. Tagore says, "All the modern civilizations have their cradles of brick and mortar".[62] This feature of modern civilization creates a barrier between man and nature and results a lack of harmony between the two. But in India civilization has its roots in nature. So there grew a relationship between man and his natural environment. Tagore gives expression to his experience with nature in the following words:

> *"Some shadow-haunted living reminiscence in me seemed to ache for the pre-natal cradle and playground it once shared with the primal life in the illimitable magic of land, water and air. The thin shrill cry of the high flying kite in the blasing sun of a dazed Indian midday sent to a solitary boy the signal of a dumb distant kinship. The few coconut palms growing by the boundary wall of our house, like some war captives from an older army of invaders of this earth, spoke to me of the eternal companionship which the great brotherhood of trees has ever offered to man. They made my heart wistful with the invitation of the forest."*[63]

In his conception of natural life Tagore includes the idea of living in the natural surroundings, because he believes in the unity of all creation. That is why he was immensely interested in the researches of Sir Jagadish Chandra Bose. He says :

> *"Life lies invisible in some hidden recess in the depths of matter. The hope that the researches of Jagdish would some day place this truth on a scientific foundation intoxicated me with joyful anticipations, for I had from childhood been familiar with the teaching of our Rishis : All these which are the process of creation flow, from and are vibrant with life of that all-pervading vibration science was becoming more and more cognisant, but it had not been able to gather into its storehouses of fact any proofs of its identity with Life. So when the experiments of Jagadish began to disclose the life-like responses of matter, I felt that the day of the recognition of this truth by science could not be far distant."*[64]

Natural Life and Education

Tagore carries the principle of natural life in education and gives us his first impression of his school in the following words:

> *"All of a sudden I found my world vanishing from around me, giving place to wooden benches and straight walls staring at me with the blank stare at the blind."*[65]

Tagore elaborates his ideas again in the answer to a question put in Moscow as to how his school combined its life work with its surroundings:

> *"I have my natural love for life, for nature, and for my surroundings where I have in dear ones; and to be snatched away from these natural surroundings with which I had all my inner deeper life of relationship, and to send me an exile to the school, to the class with its bare white walls, its stare of dead eyes, frightened the everyday. When I was once inside these walls, I did not feel natural. I was absolutely a fragment torn away from life and this gave me intense misery because I was uprooted from my own world and sent to surroundings*

> *which were dead and unsympathetic, disharmonious and monotonously dull.*"[66]

Thus, Tagore tells us as to how the children should grow into knowledge. He does not want that the children should acquire knowledge by conquering nature. In fact, the question of 'conquest of nature' must not arise, because according to Tagore our attitude to the world should be that of acceptance. He does not want that the child's life should be gradually weaned away from nature in such a way as to form in him certain fixed habits which bring him in opposition to the world. Tagore says:

> "*We rob the child of his earth to teach him geography, of language to teach him grammar. His hunger is for the Epic, but he is supplied with chronicles of facts and dates.*"[67]

Thus Tagore wants that the child's life should be surrounded with things of nature and he must be kept away from the sophistication of the so-called modern civilization.

After nature Tagore wants the child to pass through the stream of social behaviour. The child must be socialized. Hence the necessary opportunities should be given to him for promoting his socialization. Co-operative activities will help him in this respect, and such activities should find an important place in all the educational activities carried out in the school. In such co-operative activities the child will enjoy freedom, because whatever restraint he will have to abide by will be an outcome of self-restraint and not from an imposition placed from without.

To Tagore education must provide for creative self-expression on the part of the child. This expression may be promoted through various forms of handiworks and through music and arts because these are a spontaneous outflow of our deeper nature and spiritual self. Tagore compares the growth of the child with that of a tree. Thus he shows the relation between childhood and Nature. He says:

> "*Children have their active subconscious mind which like a tree, has the power to gather its food from the surrounding atmosphere. For them the atmosphere is a great deal more*

important than rules and methods, buildings, appliances, class-teachings and textbooks."[68]

Tagore wants a communion between Man and Nature, because he regards nature as a great co-ordinating factor.

"For the young child, nature will become an unconscious symbol of super-personal growth and evolution, something that need background for its dreams and its play. For the adolescents. Nature will become an object of either scientific or lyrical curiosity; and both these aspects were always encouraged by Rabindranath. The adult who was passed through all these stages will see in the soil on which his country and his people grow, the cultural and economic background of human existence."[69]

Thus Tagore regards Nature as the focus where the aspirations of human beings meet. But he wants that knowledge of nature should be acquired not in the laboratories alone, but by living nature.

To the field of education Tagore seems to bring the concept of joy, freedom, play, creative self-expression, the activity-principle, the integration and co-ordination of all knowledge. Aronson says that like Froebel, Tagore recognises stages through which the child passes for reaching maturity. He says:

"First the emotional adaptation to his environment, then the learning and training of intelligence and lastly the fruitful co-operation among human beings based upon the awareness of ones own individual separateness and of one's responsibility towards the society in which one happens to live and towards all the other societies that constitute humanity."[70]

Tie Child's Love for Nature

The child wants a personal experience of things. He can have no hesitation to accept the world naked and simple. He desires to be natural with nature. Tagore believes that children's personal experiences of nature help them to obtain useful knowledge. He says:

> *"The boys of my school have acquired instinctive knowledge of the physiognomy of the tree. By the least touch they know where they can find a .foothold upon an apparently inhospitable trunk; they know how far they can take liberty with the branches; how to distribute their bodies' weight so as to make themselves least burdensome to branchlets. My boys are able to make the best possible use of the tree in the matter of gathering fruits, taking rest and hiding from undesirable pursuers. I myself was brought up in a cultured home in a town, and as far as my personal behaviour goes. I have been obliged to act all through my life as if I were born in a world where there are no trees. Therefore, I consider it as a part of education of my boys to let them fully realise that they are in a scheme of existence where trees are a substantial fact."*[71]

Thus Tagore wants that the children should be brought into direct contact with nature, because by doing so, they will appreciate the 'scientific' facts about nature with great interest. This indicates that the teaching of natural sciences in most of our schools is not natural.

Tagore wants that "Men should have some limited period of their life specially reserved for the life of the primitive man".[72] He further says that "for our perfection we have to be vitally savage and mentally civilized".[73] Even a young child has go grow under imposed social conventions and he loses the freshness and naturalness of his life. Tagore recognises the place of social conventions in life, but he believes that they have a place during the course of a man's career and not at the beginning and at the end of it, during childhood and old age. Therefore, he stands for complete freedom for the child. The child should not be subjected to "the necessity of specialization onto the narrow bounds of social and professional conventionalism". He must not be forced to form any habit. His life should not be dissociated from nature. Tagore does not like to equip his school with the paraphernalia of modern furnitues, because they keep the children away from reality. He wants that the children be brought into naked contact with the dust. It is in the responding to the naked nature that they should live their life at first, because their physical and mental powers will grow by their spontaneous activities which are free from artificial stimulations. Children love natural life. Therefore, they should be encouraged to acquire knowledge through their love of natural life, and then they will devote their lives to gain knowledge. After gaining knowledge they will realise their lives with ripened wisdom.

Education in Co-operation with Nature

Tagore believes that the school which is generally based on the conventions of society does not allow the free development of the mind of the child. The society tries to fashion the mind of the child through the instrumentality of the school. The arrangements of the schools are too inconducive to communication with nature. So Tagore wants to conduct the education of the child close to nature. This is clear from the following account that he gives about the education of his own son:

> *"This is why when I had to face the problem of my own sons education I was at a loss to give it a practical solution. The first thing that I did was to take him away from the town surroundings into a village and allow him the freedom of primeval nature as far as it is available in modern days. He had a river noted for its danger, where he swam and rowed without check from anxiety of his elders. He spent his time in the fields and on the trackless sandbanks coming late for his meals without being questioned. He had none of the luxuries that are not only customary but are held as proper for boys of his circumstance. For which privations, I am sure, he was pitied and his parents blamed by the people for whom society has blotted out the whole world. But I was certain that luxuries are a burden to boys. They are the burdens of other people's habits, the burdens of the vicarious pride and pleasure which parents enjoy through their children."*[74]

Thus, Tagore stands for education through, "an institution

where the first great lesson in the perfect union of man and nature, not only through love but through active communication, can be had unobstructed."[75] He wants to take away the children from the artificial life of the adults. He writes that in his school:

> *"Much to the disgust of people of expensive habits, I had to provide for this great teacher, the barrenness of furniture and materials, not because it is poverty, but because it leads to a personal experience of the world."*[76]

Tagore regards the atmosphere more important in its effect and results than rules and methods, buildings, textbooks, instruments and class-teachings. He says:

> *"The earth has her mass of substance in her hand and water. But, if I may be allowed figurative language, she finds her inspiration of freedom, the stipulation of her life, from her atmosphere. It is, as it were, the envelopment of her perpetual education. It brings from her depth responses in colour and perfume, music and movement, her incessant self-revelation, continual wonders of the unexpected."*[77]

No wonder then that Tagore's Shantiniketan is surrounded by natural settings. There classes are held in the open in the groves and under the trees as far as possible. The natural beauty of the atmosphere leads the students to love all that is peaceful and beautiful. Tagore believes that natural atmosphere of his school will enable the children "to respond to the deeper call of reality" and so to be "weaned away from the lure of the fictitious value of things".[78] About the influence of nature he speaks to his students thus:

> *"We must not, however, forget the part that the environment played in our life. The surrounding Nature was a greater teacher to us. She moulded our daily life in the spirit of beauty and delight, harmony and colour, and caused us to meditate upon our inner being. It was nature that inspired me to write*

songs, dramas and poem dedicated to her. We had our dances and seasonal festivals and the whole place actually rang with the students' happy voices and music. Surely Nature helped them and us in forming our outlook and creating an atmosphere."[79]

We have noted above that Tagore finds a fundamental unity between man and nature. Therefore, he wants that "the child's education must be organized in natural surroundings". He believes that education given in natural surroundings develops intimacy with the world. Because of this intimacy the child may develop on his own accord the power of communication with it. Tagore says:

"Children with the freshness of their senses come directly to intimacy of this world. This is the first gift they have. They must never again lose their power of immediate communication with it."[80]

Therefore, Tagore does not want that the natural senses of children should be debased in urban atmosphere. He is in full accord with the *Gurukula Ashrama*[81] idea of ancient India. He is of the opinion that the Ashrama idea of ancient India did not imply one-sided development. The moral life of the forest civilization aimed at "bridging the chasm between man and nature and helped us to obtain a more balanced view of life."

Like a naturalist Tagore was very much influenced by Robinson Crusoe. He writes:

"I shall believe that it is the best book for boys that has ever been written. There was a longing in me, when young, to run way my ownself and be one with everything in nature."[82]

He further says:

"I believe that children be surrounded with the things of Nature which have their own educational value. Their minds should be allowed to stumble on and be surprised at everything that happens in the life of today. The new tomorrow will stimulate

> *their attention with new facts of life. This is the best method for the child. But what happens in school is, that everyday, at the same hour, the same book is brought and poured out for him. His attention is never hit by the chance surprises which come from learning from Nature."*[83]

It is remarkable that Tagore's naturalism paves the way to spiritualism. He finds music as an aid to the development of spiritualism. He emphatically states that while starting the school in the natural surrounding of Bolpur his principal object was to give spiritual culture to the students.

Like a naturalist Tagore is a staunch advocate of individualism. So he puts more faith in an individual than in any institution. He supports individualism in education. He does not want that the child should be crushed by the heavy traditional methods of instruction. The individual child is more important to him than the books, methods and the teacher. Self-realisation, self-salvation, self-perfection and self-expression—all these are individual problems and these can be achieved through individual efforts alone. Hence the individual is of supreme importance in any scheme of education. Tagore believes that it is the inalienable right of the individual to carve out his own destiny. So he stands for maximum freedom to the child in education. Freedom of mind becomes the object of education to him.

We have already seen that Tagore's naturalism stands for love and harmony with all that exists in nature. Therefore his naturalism is different from that of Rousseau's. His naturalism stands for a kinship with the world. To him, "When a man does not realise his kinship with the world, he lives in a prison-house whose walls are alien to him". The city life will not develop this kinship in the child. Therefore, the child's education should be carried on in natural surroundings. The freshness, beauty of form and colours existing in nature attract the child and develop in him a love for freedom. This freedom fosters self-activity in the child and suggests to him the idea of union between Man and Nature through love and active communication. Quite naturally then Tagore, like a true naturalist, regards nature as a great educational agency. The natural surroundings of the Visva Bharati are a testimony to this.

Tagore believes that the subconscious mind of children is more active than their conscious intelligence. Therefore children learn many things through their subconscious mind without feeling any fatigue. Tagore regards this subconscious faculty of knowledge as completely one with one's life. In order to enable children to learn good things through their subconscious mind, it is necessary to maintain an educative atmosphere, and an atmosphere where children are not compelled to learn things from textbooks, but from the natural surroundings, which are most educative. Like Rousseau, Tagore thinks that books come between children and their world. So during the early period of education children should receive their lessons through natural processes—directly through persons and things; and they must not depend upon books. Tagore was so convinced of this point of view that he tried to create an atmosphere of ideas in his school. He made this school his home and lived there. In order to make it an atmosphere of ideas he decided to carry on his literary activities there. He composed most of his songs there and latter-day dramas were also written there and were enacted by the children of the school. It was there that he established his international university, Visva Bharati, where he tried to encourage the study of the cultures of All Asian countries in order to reveal the Eastern mind to the world and promote a mutual understanding between the East and the West.

Tagore's Humanism

While discussing Tagore's philosophy we have seen that because of his humanism Tagore has immense faith in man. When his faith in European civilization was shattered because of the Second World War he did not lose his faith in humanity as he remarks:

> *"I shall not commit the grievous sin of losing faith in man. I would rather look forward to the opening of a new chapter in his history, after the cataclysm is over and the atmosphere rendered clean with the spirit of service and sacrifice. Perhaps that dawn will come from this horizon, from the East where the sun rises."*[84]

Thus to Tagore man is the measure of everything. Throughout his whole life he has been striving to make the people of the world conscious of this supreme truth. So according to him all values and virtues are to be realised through man.

He believes that "The decay and fall of a civilization is due to the causes which produce callousness of heart and lead to the cheapening of man's worth." It is this love for man that stimulated Tagore to turn to the education of children and he founded a school at Bolpur. Because of his humanism, he has great love for children and he advises the teacher to be like children and not to think himself their superior.

Two prominent trends may be sensed in Tagore's humanism. In the first place, he seems to emphasise the creative activity of man through art; and secondly, he lays stress on the ideal that man must achieve a unity higher than ever before.

The Ideal of Creative Activity and a Higher Unity

Tagore was quite conscious of the spiritual culture under which the forest schools of ancient India were nurtured and he had such a great reverence for the same that he tried his best to bring in the same culture in his Shantiniketan. But at the same time it is quite remarkable that he was very much alive to all that is best and noble in the ideals that govern the modern society. This feeling led him to the ideal action of creative-activity. He is of the conviction that man must realise himself in action also and not only in thought.

Tagore believes that it is man's right to feel the joy of the universe and of life. So he makes this one of the important features of the students' life at his school:

> *"Where they are bidden to realise man's world as God's kingdom to whose citizenship they have aspire; where the sunrise and sunset and the silent glory of stars are not daily ignored; where nature's festivities of flowers and fruits and their joyous burst receive recognition from man."*[85]

This attitude to life led Tagore to appreciate all the highest expressions of life as manifested in art which he considered as fundamental to human life. He endeavoured to promote this idea in children of his school. Consequently, Shantiniketan is not only a home of spiritual culture, a place of intellectual advancement, but it is also a centre of art and aesthetic development. Therefore Shantiniketan grew up as a revolt against the prevailing educational system which had reduced education to "a mere mechanical contrivance to spread literacy or a commercial investment in the name of enlightenment."[86] Tagore wanted to stimulate the human spirit in all essentials and he never liked to insist upon the clockwork precision of efficiency. Therefore he says:

> *"I had made provision not only for academic course of teaching but also for other elements of culture; music and art and dancing, seasonal festivities and opportunities of helping the neighbouring villages."*[87]

Tagore believed in the fundamental unity of mankind. Therefore, he used to say to his students at Shantiniketan to:

> *"Make friends with strangers and offer your hearts to one another .... You come here with the mission of realising the fundamental unity of humanity through co-operation and love."*[88]

He tells his students about the great welcome that he received from people in Sweden when he went there to receive the Nobel Prize. He was told by the people there that the reason of that welcome was because they realised that he did not belong to a particular country but to the whole world. Tagore comments on this fact thus:

> *"When I received human kindness from such strangers, I said to myself that I would throw open my doors to all, let my Ashrama become the guest-house of India, a centre of culture and maitri (friendship)."*[89]

Tagore remarks that science has removed the geographical barrier which in the past separated people of one land with those of another, but he feels sad that now artificial barriers of national politics and diplomacies exclude one race from another. He regards this moral disunity as alarming. So he writes:

> *"The mentality of the world has to be changed in order to meet the new environment of the modern age. To accept the truth of our own age it will be necessary to establish a new education on the basis, not nationalism, but of a wider relationship of humanity."*[90]

Needless to say that the Visva Bharati is an illustration of the 'new education' that Tagore has expressed here. In his own words the aim of Visva Bharati:

> *"Lies in imparting life-breath to the complete man, who is intellectual as well as economic, bound by social bonds, but aspiring towards spiritual freedom and final perfections."*[91]

We can clearly sense that in this endeavour towards perfection there is a humanistic emphasis. Thus, we note that there are two outstanding trends in Tagore's humanism, namely: (1) the emphasis on the creative activity of man as displayed in works of art, and (2) the emphasis on the ideal that "mankind must realise a unity, wider in range, deeper in sentiment, stronger in power than ever before."[92]

For the fulfilment of the first ideal he allows in Shantiniketan free scope for the manifestation of creative faculty in various forms. For the second ideal he suggests three ways. The first is to give full freedom for the expression of the creative aspect of the Indian mind, because he is of the conviction that:

> *"India ...has its own mind, which has deeply thought and felt and tried to solve according to its light the problems of human existence."*[93]

The second is his desire:

> *"To extend by degrees the scope of this university on simple*

> *lines until it comprehends the whole range of Eastern cultures—the Aryan, Semitic, Mongolian and others.*"[94]

So that it may be able to express the Eastern mind to the world. And the third is for the East to enrich itself judiciously from the essentials of the European culture. Tagore remarks that in doing so the East must see that it does not:

> *"Allow her priceless inheritance to crumble into dust, and trying to replace its clumsity with feeble invitations of the West, make herself superfluous, cheap and ludicrous."*[95]

Thus Tagore wants that the East must not lose its individuality. Therefore, we find in the realm of education the highest humanistic thought of India in the objectives of the Visva Bharati which are thus stated:

- To study the Mind of Man in its realisation of different aspects of truth from diverse points of view.
- To bring into more intimate relation with one another, through patient study and research, the different cultures of the East on the basis of their underlying unity.
- To approach the West from the standpoint of such a unity of the life and thought of Asia.
- To seek to realise in a common fellowship of study the meeting of the East and the West, and thus ultimately to strengthen the fundamental conditions of world peace through establishment of free communication of ideas between the two hemispheres.[96]

Tagore's Internationalism

Tagore's humanism knows no bound. He is an ardent prophet of world unity. All through his strenuous life he has worked for a closer contact between the East and the West. He wanted that the East should give its best to the West and in turn it should assimilate the best that the West had to offer. He felt indebted to both the East and the West and believed that the problem of the world could be solved only if a judicious synthesis was attained between the contributions of the East and the West. He wanted to achieve this synthesis in his Visva Bharati as we have already indicated above.

Tagore's Idealism

Tagore's educational theories are idealistic in conception. Therefore, in his various educational writings and pronouncements an idealistic note is always present. We can easily sense this note when we study his views on education in different contexts.

Tagore's Homesickness and Quest for Harmony

Tagore felt the lack of harmony in the world and the individual. He found the spirit of man at cross-purposes by being engrossed in material things. Tagore regards man a finite-infinite being who combines in himself nature and spirit. "Man is earth's child but heaven's heir. At one end of his being man is one with stocks and stones but at the other he is separate from all".[97] Hence there is a restlessness and yearning in his spirit for the things that exceed his grasp:

> *"I am restless, I am athirst for far-away things,*
> *My Soul goes out in a longing to touch the skirt of the dim distance.*
> *O Great Beyond. O the keen call of they flute.*
> *I forget, I ever forget, that I have no wings to fly, that*
> *I am bound in this spot evermore."*[98]

Thus Tagore finds himself an exile in the world, and he feels restless and homesick. So he sets out to find his home. This was not far to find out. Firstly, there was before him the tradition of ancient Gurukul of India (the forest colonies of the ancient teachers in India). Secondly, his father, Maharshi Devendranath Tagore, in the course of his efforts to realise God had established an Ashrama which he called *Shantiniketan* or the Abode of Peace. This modern revival of the ancient tradition caught the imagination of Tagore. He says:

"In India we still cherish in our memory the tradition of the forest colonies of great teachers. These places were neither schools nor Montessories in the modern sense of the word. They consisted of homes where with their families lived—men whose purpose was to see the world in God and to realise their own life in Him. Though they lived outside society, yet they were to society, what the sun is to planets, the centre from which it received its life and light. And here boys grew up in an intimate vision of eternal life before they were thought fit to enter the state of the householder."[99]

Quite naturally, homesick as he was, it was a home-coming to him and to the children he gathered around him when he started schools the old tradition at his father's Ashrama. At this school the souls of men would find the harmony that was absent in the world outside. Thus Tagore's school had the background of a forest as the ancient *Ashrama* used to have. This forest occupied an important role in one's life and education:

"The forest, unlike the desert or rock or sea, is living; it gives shelter and nourishment to life. In such surroundings the ancient forest dwellers of India realised the spirit of harmony with the universe and emphasised in their minds the monistic aspect of truth. They sought the realisation of their soul through union with all."[100]

Harmony with the Universe Necessary for Self-realisation

Tagore regards realisation of the self as the end and harmony with the universe, the means. In his school he endeavoured to produce this harmony by living a life in the forest, in the open air. He says:

"The young mind should be saturated with the idea that it has been born in a human world which is in harmony with the world around it."[101]

He further remarks that the ordinary school does not at all care for such a harmony; on the other hand it:

"Forcibly snatches away children from a world full of the mystery of God's own handwork, full of the suggestiveness of personality."[102]

In ancient India the greatest teachers aimed, "To grow in sympathy with all creation and in communion with the Supreme Being".[103] Therefore, Tagore too, in his Ashrama school (at *Shantiniketan*) endeavoured to realise the ideal of securing a harmony between man and nature and so realising one's self in God. He thinks that nature has soul which helps man towards a union of his soul with God. India and the ancient forest schools have a special mission in this respect:

"India's climate has brought to us the invitation of the open air; the language of her mighty rivers is solemn in their chants; the limitless expanse of her plains encircles our homes with the silence of the world beyond; there the sun rises from the margin of the green earth like an offering of the unseen to the altar of the Unknown, and it goes down to the west and the end of the day like a gorgeous ceremony of nature's salutation of the Eternal. In India the shades of the trees are hospitable, the dust of the earth stretches its brown arms to us, the air with its embraces clothes us with warmth. These are the unchanging facts that even carry their suggestions to our minds, and therefore, we feel it is India's mission to realise the truth of the human soul in the Supreme Soul through its union with the soul of the world. This mission had taken its natural form in the forest schools in the ancient time."[104]

Harmony and Love between Man and Nature

Tagore feels a need for harmony between man and nature. This relation between man and nature is, "That of personal love and not that of mechanical law of causation."[105] Tagore finds nature plays the role of mother. Just as the mother nurtures the child, similarly in nature one may find complete nourishment both for the body and for the soul. The individual finds the emotional, moral and spiritual nourishment from the world. Thus the relationship between man and the world around him is characterised by love. It is not merely the mechanical law of causation that governs this relationship.

A Love of Spiritual Culture

Tagore is not prepared to tolerate the neglect of the spiritual development of the child. He is very much pained at the over-emphasis placed on the intellectual and physical development in the schools at the cost of the spiritual. Earlier, when the life was simple, the various aspects of development of the individual could be easily harmonised. But today human life has become so complex that the physical, intellectual and spiritual developments of the individual become so isolated that in attending to one the other is excluded. It is the spiritual life which is neglected most. It was the realisation of this singular defect that encouraged Tagore to start his new school.

> *"To give spiritual culture to our boys was my principal object in starting my school in Shantiniketan."*[106]

To Tagore the man whose mental and physical strength outgrows his spiritual force is like:

> *"An exaggerated giraffe whose head has suddenly shot up miles away from the rest of him, making normal communication difficult to establish."*[107]

The Belief in the Immanence of the Infinite in Nature

It is noteworthy that Tagore's spiritual world belongs to this world of ours. "With the breath we draw we must always feel this truth that we are living in God."[108] Thus Tagore finds spiritual significance in natural elements. If man penetrates deep beyond the externals of natural phenomena he will have spiritual vision. For example, he will realise that water does not merely cleans his body but purifies his heart as well, because it touches his soul; the earth does not merely support the body, but it also makes the mind happy because its contact is more than physical—it is that of a living presence. In this way man will realise the eternal spirit in all object and will ultimately find the perfect truth. So the man must find himself in the closest relation with all the things around him and he should regard the sun, the moon, water, earth as the manifestations of the same living truth that holds them together.[109] Thus Tagore has an intense belief in the immanence of the infinite in nature. This conviction leads him to stand for :

> *"Life in nature and in the open air is the best means of spiritual progress, for in nature the religious eye will see the infinite lying stretched, in silent smiling repose."*[110]

The Child to have full Measure of Life

Tagore believes that, "Man's introduction to this world is his introduction to his final truth in a simple form". He is born into a world where he is conscious of others and others are conscious about him. He enjoys the attention and care of others. Gradually, he begins to doubt his personal relations with others. He finds himself caught in a "civil war between his personality and his outer world". Again in order to realise the truth of his life he has to unite himself with all in an infinite bond of love. Therefore, Tagore believes that a child should be allowed to have the full measure of life's draught. He thinks that the child has an endless thirst for leading his full life. So he vehemently criticise the current schools which snatch away children from the natural surroundings and rear them up in an atmosphere which is full of artificialities and sophistications of the civilized society. The individuality of the child is totally ignored in these schools which try to produce uniform individuals as a machine produces uniform pins.

Tagore deplores that the education that is given to the youth in India is not that of the whole man. The modern school is a factory, "Specially designed for grinding out uniform results".[111] Tagore feels sad that Indian children are forgetting their own past and are unable to understand their own nature. He regards the Indian educated youth, "as barriers choking the stream that flows from the mountain, peak of their ancient history", and therefore, India's future will not get the nourishing water "that has made her culture so fertile with richness of beauty and strength."[112] Therefore, Tagore wants that the ancient ideal of Indian education should come back in its essence, though not in its entirety. He says :

> *"The object of education is to give man the unity of truth. Formerly, when life was simple, all the different elements of man were in complete harmony. But when there came the separation of the intellect from the spiritual and the physical, the school education put entire emphasis on intellect and the physical side of man. We devote our sole attention to giving children information, not knowing that by this emphasis we are accentuating a break between the intellectual, physical and the spiritual life ..."*[113]

But can this spiritual life be cultivated? Tagore says that it can be done by allowing the souls to express themselves freely and spontaneously. He believes in the instinct of the student and the atmosphere of the Ashrama for developing spiritual life. He says:

> *"... With the breath we draw, we always feel this truth that we are living in God ...."*[114]

In his school at Bolpur Tagore strives towards this soul culture. The ideal school, Tagore says:

> *"Must be an Ashrama where man have gathered together for the highest end of life, in the peace of nature; where life is not merely meditative but fully awake in its activities, where boys' minds are not perpetually drilled into believing that the ideal of the self-idolatry of the nation is the truest ideal for them to accept, where they are bidden to realise; man's world as God's kingdom to whose citizenship they have to aspire; where the sunrise and sunset and the silent glory of the stars are not daily ignored; where nature's festivities of powers and fruit have their joyous recognition from man; and where the young and the old, the teacher and the student, sit at the same table to partake of their daily food and the food of their eternal life..."*[115]

Tagore does not believe in an average individual. To him every child has a unique personality and he should be treated as such. He believes that, "God's intention as to how children should grow into knowledge", is being neglected in the modern schools.

Tagore believed that highest education is that which not only gives knowledge, but which makes the individual live in harmony with all existence. Thus there is a need of this education of sympathy. Tagore very much deplores the neglect of this education of sympathy in the modern schools.

Education to be a Part of Life

Since Tagore wants to give to the child full measure of life, he is of the conviction that, "Education should be a part of life itself and must not be detached from it and be made into something abstract."[116] He develops this idea further in the following words:

> *"Or education should be in full touch with our complete life, economic, intellectual, aesthetic, social and spiritual; and our educational institutions should be in the very heart of our society—connected with it by the living bonds of varied co-operations. For, true education is to realise at every step how our training and knowledge have organic connection without surroundings ..."*[117]

Thus in Tagore we find an idealist who never ignores the hard realities of life. According to him:

> *"The school must be a laboratory not merely for absorbing knowledge, or for producing sheltered hot houses growth, but for giving cut, for adventure into the realm of practical economics and self-government, of self-discipline and self-government, of self-expression in the world of spiritual abstraction and human welfare....."*[118]

Evidently, Tagore wants to acquaint the child with the world of human life at large. Education which cuts off the children from currents of life is meaningless. If education is to be meaningful, the children must be given the experience of every phase of adult life.

Realisation of the Essential Unity

To Tagore, the idealist, education must promote the fullest growth and freedom of the soul. He finds an essential unity in the whole universe. So the objective of education should be the realisation of this unity. This unity cannot be realised unless the different elements of man are harmonised with each other. The physical, the intellectual and spiritual are connected with each other. So in any scheme of education all these three must be attended to adequately. The neglect of any will hamper the growth of the personality and will check the realisation of the pervading unity in the universe. Tagore feels sad that the prevalent system of education does not meet this demand and it enters only to the intellectual aspect of a man's growth, and the physical, moral and spiritual are neglected. Therefore, the curriculum must be enriched in order to foster the growth of all the aspects of an individual's personality. Tagore's emphasis on an all-round development led him to make his school train both the hand and heart of the child. For the training of the hand he included some compulsory handwork for the students of his Bolpur school and for the spiritual development, religion. But Tagore thought that religion could not be taught life a school subject.

> *"It cannot be doled out in regulated measure, not administered through the academic machinery of education. It must come immediately from the burning flame of spiritual life, in surroundings suitable for such life ..."*[119]

The Ancient Indian Ideal

Tagore regarded the *Tapovana Ashrama* (forest school based on rigorous discipline) of the ancient India as the ideal for solving the educational problem of the country. "The simple living and high thinking" motto of the ancient Ashrama appealed to him very much as it provided the right atmosphere for the development of life in its purity. He thinks that :

"It is idle to try to educate the children in the midst of much that tend to lead the learners away from the path of truth. There the field is full of struggles for the self and thoughts centre round the self, and human nature purifies and looks for enjoyment in artificial ways... They must, therefore, be removed from the field where men struggle for the satisfaction of their baser propensities, and should be placed where conditions are favourable for their vast possibilities to develop, where their lives could move peacefully along the path of accumulated human experience, and where for them waits ready garnered man's spiritual heritage ..."[120]

Here, too, we find that Tagore believed in the ancient Indian educational ideals and practices. He has so much regard for *Brahmacharya* that he considered education as a *Brahmacharya-Vrata* (a vow of celibacy), a *Dharma-Vrata* (a vow of religion). To him education is not information, nor does it consist in passing examinations. He regards education as a preparation for a living in the world with a view to seek communion with the Divine Power. He thinks that education can fulfil this task only if the schools follow the cardinal educational ideals of the ancient Indian *Gurukul*.

On Freedom and Discipline

According to Tagore the child desires:

"The fullest freedom to satisfy the fertile imagining of his brain, imaginings which like the tender plants call so easily be crushed and mutilated, revolting against the bonds of what seems so often an unreasoned disciplines ... "[121]

Thus freedom is the very nature of the child, but he would accept restrictions of discipline if these are coloured with sympathy and love. Tagore has great sympathy for the child. So he does not want that the child should be suppressed by an authority. He thus defends the child that has been scolded:

"Why are those tears in your eyes, my child? How horrid of them to be always scolding you for nothing! You have stained

your fingers and face with ink while writing—Is that why they call you dirty?
O lie! would they dare to call the full moon dirty because it has smudged its face with ink?"[122]

Tagore has a capacity to understand the child and he says that the child regards the school studies as a interference with his freedom. He himself had to suffer from such an interference as a boy. So he has developed an insight to find out a solution of the conflict:

"In talking of his own school days, Rabindranath Tagore spoke with the feeling of a man who had suffered much and needlessly in his own boyish experience, and had sought a cure for so deterrent and mortifying a discipline in the case and for the sake of others. To some it may seem that the trouble which we recognise in our schools is due in part to the obstinate great ailment of youth itself. To him it seemed possible to find a more natural way of education, by going back to instinct and going on to a new understanding of the imaginative and the humane needs of the growing boy..."[123]

Hence Tagore decided to give the maximum amount of freedom to children in his school. He deliberately made the environment of the school such as to permit maximum amount of physical and mental freedom. He says:

"I know that the mind has its hunger for the ministrations of nature, mother nature, and, so I selected this spot where the sky is unobstructed to the verge of the horizon. There the mind could have its fearless freedom to create its own dreams and the seasons could come with all their colours and movement and beauty into the very heart of the human dwelling ... "[124]

Tagore is convinced that:

"The object of education is the freedom of mind which can only be achieved through the path of freedom—though freedom has its risk and responsibility as life has ... "[125]

About the nature of school, he says:

> *"It is not a school which is imposed upon the boys by authorities. I always try, to impress upon their minds that it is their own world, upon which their life ought fully and freely to react ..."*[126]

Accordingly, he gave much freedom to children in his school. He tried to arouse their interest in the various aspects of the universe in a natural manner, and not only through class teaching. The teacher is present only to stimulate and guide but it is the child who is to choose and react according to his natural inclinations.

Tagore is against the so called traditional school-discipline because it does not take into account the individual interests and abilities. About the traditional school, he says:

> *"It is a factory specially designed for grinding out uniform results. It follows all imaginary straight line of the average in digging its channel of education. But life's line is not the straight line ..."*[127]

Therefore social traditions must not be imposed upon children, because they interfere with their natural freedom. Once an experienced and successful disciplinarian headmaster visited Tagore's school and expressed his disapproval when he saw a boy climb a tree for choosing a fork of the branches for setting down to his studies. In explanation Tagore told him that:

> *"Childhood is the only period of life when a civilized man can exercise his choice between the branches of a tree and his drawing-room chair, and should I deprive this boy of that privilege because I, as a grown-up man, am barred from it?"*[128]

Tagore regrets that the adults generally ignore the natural inclination of the imaginative power in the child. They want to make the child a practical person. So they crush the imagination of the child. Tagore reminds us that we owe our present progress to the fertile imagination of dreamers. He says:

> *"Steering by the light of an anarchic discontent, man has explored and is still, exploring every sea of human knowledge, driven forward by the breezes of his fertile imagination. But with the child we insist that he shall not start out his voyage until he has learnt off by heart the chart we have drawn for him out of our own experience whilst his little ship of life, anchored within the school-room, wallows in the untroubled calm of the conventional, the artificial and unimaginative ..."*[129]

Quite naturally then, Tagore disapproves school curriculums which do not give full freedom to the child for the exercise of his imagination.

Tagore believes in a self-imposed discipline. Therefore, in Shantiniketan a provision has been made for the boys' own court of justice which deals with all the branches of conduct on the part of the boys. It is only the serious cases that teachers themselves have to deal with. Thus Shantiniketan is, "not a school which is imposed upon the boys by autocratic authorities..."[130]

Tagore says the purpose of education is the freedom of soul, "For that ultimate truth which emanicipates us from the bondage of the dust and gives us the wealth, out of things but of inner light, not to power but of love."[131] In the educational activities of Shantiniketan we find two aspects of the higher freedom. One aspect equips the child with all the skills that he needs for earning a livelihood. After this he would widen his sympathies. Thus he becomes an efficient and useful citizen and he also finds opportunities for creative expression of his various natural capacities and at the same time discovers, "The best means of self-preservation as an individual, as a citizen and a creative agent, and to experience daily the delights and difficulties of perpetual growth—this is true freedom ...".[132]

According to Tagore other aspect is related to the world of emotion and of abstraction.

> *"Having attained self-confidence as to his power to subsist by the labour of his own hands and thus to survive within the human family, both adult and child are free to pass into this*

other religion where there is no grammar except that which the adventurer makes for his own convenience, nor any rules or regulations ..."[133]

Almost all children share this world of emotion, and in this realm they have no ulterior motive to fulfil. Therefore, adventures into this realm must be encouraged, but they must never be imposed. The children must be given complete freedom in this matter. "This spirit childhood, like the gift of imagination, bloweth where it listeth, and like the wind it comes and goes, and knows no man-made law".[134] Shantiniketan is an excellent example of this freedom in the world of emotion and abstraction. The entire educational effort of the school is to lead children towards this freedom.

On Religious Education

We have seen that Tagore was God-conscious. He believed in the imminences of the infinite in nature. Therefore, he had a deep feeling of adoration for the universe. Everywhere in the universe be found his object of worship. To him knowledge and devotion—the intellectual and the spiritual—are only two aspects of reaching truth. In Shantiniketan he has provided opportunities for both these aspects. But we must note that he has provided very little formal religion in Shantiniketan, because:

"According to him, the best way to derive divine inspiration is to lose oneself in the contemplation of nature. In silence and in solitude we have to enjoy the presence of the divine in nature ..."[135]

Tagore believes that religious feeling and piety will usher in if the environment is pure and noble. He says:

"We do not want now-a-days temples of worship and outward rites and ceremonies. What we really want is an Ashrama. We want a place here the beauty of nature and the noblest pursuits

of man are in a sweet harmony. Our temple of worship is there where outward nature and human soul meet in union."[136]

Thus Tagore relies almost entirely on the atmosphere of the place of learning for religious education. He believed in the ideal of depending upon the natural instinct of each boy for the development of his spiritual side of nature.

Tagore has great faith in the efficacy of meditation and prayer as an exercise for spiritual consciousness. In Shantiniketan fifteen minutes are usually given both in the morning and evening for prayers. He regards meditation as a method of reaching truth which is opposite to methods such as observation and reasoning, etc. He says:

> *"There are things that we get from outside and take to ourselves as possessions. But with meditation, it is just the opposite. It is entering into the very midst of some great truth, so that, in the end, we are possessed by it ..."*[137]

Tagore is convinced that the highest kind of truth can be realised by this method of meditation, that is, merging one's consciousness in the truth.

But we must note that Tagore does not want to attach undue importance to contemplation. He thus points out the danger in it.

> *"Our partiality is for the internal world. We would cast aside with contumely the field of power and of extension. We would realise Brahma in meditation only in his aspect of completeness, we have determined not to see him in the commerce of the universe in his aspect of evolution. That is why in our seekers we so often find the intoxication of the spirit and its consequent degradation ..."*[138]

Thus Tagore's emphasis is on the world of action. Therefore, he provides for ample opportunities in Shantiniketan for social service of various kinds in the execution of which the students and teachers find innumerable occasions for "self-sacrificing good works". If this attitude of Tagore appears to be more humanitarianism than religion, let us remember that in this materialistic and self-speaking world of ours this attitude is of inestimable value and in no way less important than rites and ceremonies and worship as parts of religion.

On Individual and Social Aims

Tagore believes that the child should grow amidst community life. To him self-realisation can be achieved in communion with others and not in isolation. He wants that the individual must be conscious of the universe of which he is only a part. Without this consciousness, no self-realisation is possible. Tagore says, "When we become merely man, not man-in-the-universe, we create bewildering problems".[139] Therefore, he regards society as a means of self-realisation. He further remarks:

> *"It is best for the commerce of the spirit that people differently situated should bring their different products into the market of humanity, each of which is complementary and necessary to the others..."*[140]

At the same time Tagore is not at all prepared to lose his individuality, that is to him the individual is separate from all. He observes:

> *"There I have broken through the cordon of equality and stand alone as an individual. I am absolutely unique, I am I, I am incomparable. The whole weight of the universe cannot crush out this individuality of mine. I maintain it in spite of the tremendous gravitation of all things. It is small in appearance but great in reality. For it holds its own against the forces that would rob it of its distinction and make it one with the dust..."*[141]

Thus Tagore considers individuality of supreme importance and the most precious possession of man who must uphold and preserve it against all odds. In preserving it man will be acting according to the plan and purpose of the universe. Tagore says:

"If this individuality he demolished, then though no material be lost, not an atom destroyed, the creative joy which was crystalised therein is gone. We are absolutely bankrupt if we are deprived of this speciality, this individuality, which is the only thing we can call our own; and which, if lost, is also a loss to the whole world. It is most valuable, because it is not universal. And, therefore, only through it can we gain the universe more truly than if we were lying within its breast unconscious of our distinctiveness. The universal is ever seeking its consummation in the unique. And the desire we have to keep our uniqueness intact is really the desire of the universe acting in us. It is our joy of the infinite in us that gives us our joy in ourselves..."[142]

But from the above it will be wrong to infer that self is all and it has its complete meaning in itself. By its very nature the self tries to transcend its limits, and if we try to make the self as the end of life, we shall be obstructing it from revealing itself. It must be remembered that it is in revealing itself that the true value of the self lies. Its revelation is dependent upon the existence of other objects in society. Self and society are thus so closely bound up that a line of demarcation can hardly be drawn between the two. Hence there is a need of reconciliation and harmony between the two. Tagore says:

"He who is wise tries to harmonise the wishes that seek for self-gratification with the wish for the social good, and only thus can we realise his higher self.
In its finite aspect the self is conscious of its separateness, and there it is ruthless in its attempt to have more distinction than all others. But in its infinite aspect its wish is to gain that harmony which leads to its perfection and not its mere aggrandisement.."[143]

Thus Tagore stands for a harmony between the individual and the society. And it is the ideal which guides the various activities at Shantiniketan as is clear from his own words when he speaks about the prevailing atmosphere of his school, thus:

"The spirit of sacrifice and comradeship, the disinterested desire to help others, which these boys have developed are rare even in children who have had better opportunities ... The logic of facts showed to them the reality of moral principles in life, and now they feel astonished at instances when other boys do not understand ..."[144]

Just as an individual can attain his full self only in society, similarly a nation must grow among the nations of the world. Narrow nationalism of the individualistic type had no place in Tagore's thinking. Therefore, he had an intense desire to make his school at Shantiniketan an international centre of learning. In the year 1913 he wrote thus:

"All our vagueness will disappear if we can place our institution in the light of the whole world. If we confine our institution within the local limits of the time and space of our country, it will lose its parity. The development of a complete manhood is our object, and we must not aim at anything less than this ..."[145]

The above international outlook of Tagore has certainly been a new note to his countrymen, and it made Shantiniketan a place where came scholars and professors from various countries of the world fulfilling his idea for his school, *viz.*

"Visva Bharati represents India where she has her wealth of mind which is for all. Visva Bharati acknowledges India's obligations to offer to others the hospitality of her best culture and India's right to accept from others their best ... "[146]

Thus Tagore has established at Shantiniketan a school for the whole world with the purpose of promoting individual development and social service, especially in the area of cultural life. Hence the motto of the school that here "The whole world finds its shelter..."

On the Duty of a Teacher

Like a staunch idealist, Tagore says:

> *"A teacher can never truly teach unless he is still learning himself. A lamp can never light another lamp unless it continues to burn its own flame. The teacher who has came to an end of his subject, who has no living traffic with his knowledge, but merely repeats his lessons to his students, can only load their minds, he cannot quicken them. Truth not only, must inform but also inspire. If the inspiration dies out, and the information only accumulates, then truth loses its infinity. The greater part of our learning in the schools has been wasted because, for most of our teachers, their subjects are like dead specimens of one liking things, with which they have a learned acquaintance, but no communication of life and love..."*

Thus Tagore wants that the teacher should try to understand the relationship between their subjects and human life and the same should be brought home to the students as well. This can be possible only when the teacher continues learning and does not stop his growth by stuffing their minds with dead matter. Thus Tagore makes the duty of the teacher and class procedures clear.

Tagore's Visva Bharati

To Tagore a university should not be a mechanical organization, for collecting and distributing knowledge. A university should be a medium of enabling people to offer their wealth of mind to others. The conception of his Visva Bharati is in accordance with his notion of Greater India where the humanity will strive to reach a reconciliation of different races with different religions and civilizations. Tagore believes that this Greater India or New India will not belong to this race or that race, this religion or that religion, but to humanity. His Visva Bharati is a symbol of his passionate faith in the brotherhood of nations. In the year 1934 while responding to Professor Gulbert Marry's invitation to help in bridging the gulf between various nations through international cooperation of thinkers in all countries, Tagore wrote:

"Willingly, therefore, I harness myself in my advanced age to the arduous responsibility of creating in our educational colony at Shantiniketan a spirit of genuine international collaboration based on a definite pursuit of knowledge, a pursuit carried on in an atmosphere of friendly community life, harmonized with Nature and offering freedom of individual self-expression."[147]

This is the ideal on which Tagore has based his Visva Bharati. Tagore had three main purposes in establishing the Visva Bharati. He has described them as follows:[148]

1. To teach the different cultures of the East, specially, those that originated in India or found shelter within her shores.
2. To establish 'The institute of Rural Reconstruction' in order to lay the foundation of a happy, contented and humane life in the villages, and lastly.
3. To seek to establish a living relationship between East and West, to promote inter-cultural, inter-racial amity and understanding, and fulfil the highest mission of the present age—the unification of mankind.

"And with such ideas in view to provide at Shantiniketan aforesaid a centre of culture where research into the study of religion, literature, history, science and art of Hindu, Buddhist, Jain, Islamic, Sikh, Christian and other civilizations may be pursued along with the culture of the West, with that simplicity in externals which is necessary for true spiritual realisation, in amity, a good-fellowship and co-operation between the thinkers and scholars of both Eastern and Western countries, free from all antagonism of race, nationality, creed or caste and in the name of One Supreme Being. Who is Shantam, Shivam, Advaitam..."[149]

The Visva Bharati has been now recognised as a full-fledged central university by the Government of India by a special Act passed by the Indian Parliament. *Vidya Bhavan* (School of Research); *Siksha Bhavan* (College); *Patha Bhavan* (School); *Kala Bhavan* (School of Music and Dancing); *Sri Niketan* (Institute of

Rural Reconstructions); *Shilpa Bhavan* (School of Industries); *Vinaya Bhavan* (Teachers' College), *China Bhavan*, *Hindi Bhavan*, and the Islamic Research Section are the various constituent departments of the Visva Bharati.

Many of the classes at the Visva Bharati are held in the open air. The development of individuality in all its aspects is the aim of this unique institution. Every student is free to give expression to his tastes and aptitudes. The curriculum is so broad as to provide for the various aptitudes of the students. The social side of the students is not ignored. The institution tries to keep itself in touch with the poor, unhappy and downtrodden masses of the neighbourhood. Thus Tagore has tried to make the Visva Bharati a centre of Indian renaissance. He has made it a centre of international learning. He also made it a place from where solid work may be done for social and economic reform of the nation. Above all, he made it a place from where India may give the message of humanity to the whole world. Tagore is no more, but his personality still pervades the Visva Bharati.

NOTES

1. Radhakrishnan, *The Philosophy of Rabindranath Tagore*, p. 7.
2. Dr. S.N. Das Gupta, *Rabi Dipika*, p. 112.
3. *Modern Review*, Vol. 49, p. 639.
4. Amar Dharma.
5. Address at Shantiniketan, 1931.
6. *Religion of Man*.
7. Personality, pp. 61-62.
8. *Atmaparichaya*, p. 48.
9. Creative Unity, p. 22.
10. *Shantiniketan*, Fourth Series.
11. Man, p. 56.
12. Religion of Man, p. 19.
13. *Shantiniketan*, Fourth Series.
14. Gitanjali, Poem, No. 84.
15. *Shantiniketan*, Thirteenth Series.
16. *Ibid*. Twelth Series.
17. *Ibid*. Eighth Series.
18. Creative Unity, p. 15.
19. *Sadhana*, p. 70. -
20. Personality, p. 84.

21. Naibaedya, No. 88.
22. *The Religion of an Artist*.
23. *Sadhana*, p. 8.
24. Creative Unity, p. 27.
25. From the Poem, *Basundhara*.
26. *Sadhana*, p. 10.
27. *Creative Unity*, p. 10.
28. *Gitanjali*, Poem No. 147.
29. *Shantiniketan*, Third Series.
30. *Sadhna*, p. 4.
31. Address to *Shantiniketan*, 1931.
32. *Religion of Man*, p. 162.
33. From Kheya.
34. *Sadhana*, p. 138.
35. *Personality*, p. 138.
36. Creative Unity, p. 115.
37. *Personality*, p. 55.
38. *Ibid.*, pp. 28-29.
39. *The Religion of Man*, p. 141.
40. *Sadhana*, p. 56.
41. *Personality*, p. 80.
42. *Ibid.*, p. 81.
43. *Sadhana*, p. 77.
44. *Ibid.*, p. 259.
45. *Gitanjali*, Poem No. 89.
46. *Sadhana*, p. 19.
47. *Ibid.*, p. 27.
48. *Sadhana*, p. 19.
49. *Creative Unity*, p. 8.
50. *Ibid.*, p. 117.
51. *Creative Unity*, p. 24.
52. Das Gupta, *History of Indian Philosophy*, Vol. I, p. 490.
53. *Shantiniketan,* Fourteenth Series.
54. *Balaka*, Poem No. 24.
55. *Ibid.*, 177.
56. *Sadhana*, p. 131.
57. *Shantiniketan*, Fourteenth Series.
58. *Gitanjali*, Poem No. 119.
59. *Ibid.*, 141.
60. *Sadhana*, p. 33.
61. Rabindranath Tagore, *Sadhana*, p. 4.
62. *Ibid.*, p. 3.
63. Rabindranath Tagore : A *Poet's School, Visva Bharati Bulletin*, p. 95.
64. Rabindranath Tagore: 'Jagadish Chandra Bose', *The Modern Review*, January, 1938.
65. *Rabindranath Tagore, Personality,* p. 114.
66. *Rabindranath Tagore, My School, The Modern Review*, January, 1931.

67. *Rabindranath Tagore: Personality*, p. 116.
68. *Rabindranath Tagore: A Poet's School.*
69. Aronson, Alex, Rabindranath's *Educational Ideals and the West,* pp. 36-37.
70. *Ibid.*, p. 31.
71. *Rabindranath Tagore : Personality,* pp. 118-119.
72. *Ibid.*, p. 122.
73. *Rabindranath Tagore: A Poet's School, Visva Bharati,* No. 9, p. 6.
74. *Rabindranath Tagore : Personality*, pp. 124-125.
75. *Rabindranath Tagore : A Poet's School,* Visva Bharati Bulletin No. 9, p. 8.
76. *Ibid.*
77. *Ibid.*, p. 12.
78. *Ibid.*
79. An Address : *The Visva Bharati Quarterly,* August 1938.
80. Tagore: *Religion of Man*, 1931, p. 172.
81. The Forest School.
82. *Ibid.*, p. 174.
83. Macmillan, 1929, *Thoughts from Rabindranath Tagore,* p. 196.
84. From his address on *"The Crises of Civilization"*, April 14,1941.
85. *Rabindranath Tagore: Personality,* p. 148
86. Rabindranath Tagore : An Address, *Visva Bharati Quarterly,* August 1938, p. 135.
87. *Op. Cit.*
88. *Op. Cit.*
89 *Ibid.*, p. 135.
90 Shantiniketan and the Educational Institutions, *Visva Bharati Bulletin* No. 12, p. 23.
91. Rabindranath Tagore : An Eastern University, *Visva Bharati Bulletin.*
92. *Ibid.*, p. 2.
93. *Rabindranath Tagore : The Centre of Indian Culture,* p. 1.
94. *Rabindranath Tagore : An Eastern University,* Visva Bharati Bulletin No. 7, p. 3.
95. *Ibid.*, No. 12, p. 1.
96. Memorandum of Association, Statutes, Regulations and Rules, *Visva Bharati Bulletin* No. 5. p. 1.
97. *Rabindranath Tagore : Sadhana*, p. 69.
98. *Rabindranath Tagore: The Gardner,* p. 5.
99. *Rabindranath Tagore: Personality,* p. 128.
100. Tagore quoted in P.C. Mahalanobis, The Growth of Visva Bharati, 1901-1921, *Visva Bharati Bulletin*, No. 8, p. 2.
101. *Rabindranath Tagore: Personality,* p. 114.
102. *Op. Cit.*
103. Pearson, W.W. Shantiniketan, p. 17.
104. *Rabindranath Tagore: Personality,* p. 138.
105. *Ibid.*, p. 13.
106. Quoted in Shantiniketan and the Educational Institutions, Visva Bharati, No. 12, p. 6.
107. *Rabindranath Tagore, Nationalism*, pp. 35-36.
108. *Rabindranath Tagore, Personality,* p. 187.

109. *Rabindranath Tagore: Sadhana,* pp. 8-9.
110. Radhakrishnan : *The Philosophy, of Rabindranath Tagore,* p. 21.
111. Personality, p. 114.
112. *The Spirit of Japan.*
113. *Ibid.,* p. 126.
114. *Ibid.*
115. *Ibid.,* p. 148.
116. Rabindranath Tagore : *My School, The Modern Review, January,* 1931.
117. Rabindranath Tagore : *The Centre of Indian Culture,* p. 2.
118. Rabindranath Tagore : A Poet's School, *Visva Bharati Bulletin,* No. 9. p. 24.
119. Ghose, T., Rabindranath's *Contribution to Education in India,* pp. 18-19.
120. Chattopadhya, J. : *Rabindranath and His Ashrama School,* p. 12.
121. Rabindranath Tagore : A Poet's School, *Visva Bharati Bulletin,* No. 9, p. 25.
122. Rabindranath Tagore : Crescent Moon, the Poem called "Defamation".
123. Ernst Rhys : *Rabindranath Tagore,* pp. 135-136.
124. Rabindranath Tagore : My School, *The Modern Review,* January, 1931.
125. Rabindranath Tagore: *Personality,* p. 157.
126. *Ibid.,* p. 146.
127. *Ibid.,* p. 114.
128. *Ibid.,* pp. 117-118.
129. Rabindranath Tagore : A Poet's School, *Visva Bharati Bulletin,* No. 9, p. 25.
130. Rabindranath Tagore: *Personality,* p. 146.
131. *Op. Cit.*
132. Rabindranath Tagore : A Poet's School, *Visva Bharati Bulletin,* No. 9, p. 27.
133. *Op. Cit.*
134. *Op. Cit.*
135. Radhakrishnan : *The Philosophy of Rabindranath Tagore,* p. 121.
136. *Ibid.,* p. 22.
137. Rabindranath Tagore: *Personality,* p. 51.
138. Rabindranath Tagore, *Sadhana,* pp. 126-127.
139. Rabindranath Tagore : *Sadhana,* p. 10.
140. *Ibid.,* p. 12.
141. *Ibid.,* p. 69.
142. *Ibid.,* p. 70.
143. *Ibid.,* p. 83.
144. Rabindranath Tagore : A Poet's School, *Visva Bharati Bulletin* No. 9, p. 11.
145. Mahalanobis, P.C. : The Growth of the Viswa Bharati, 1901-1921, *Visva Bharati, Bulletin* No. 8, p. 7.
146. Shantiniketan and the Educational Institutions, *Visva Bharati Bulletin,* No. 12, p. 1.
147. Quoted by D.S. Sharma in *The Renaissance of Hinduism,* p. 349.
148. Dayal Bhagwan *The Development of Modern Indian Education,* p. 495.
149. *Ibid.*

9

WHAT WE CAN IMBIBE

In the preceding chapters an attempt has been made to understand, amongst other things, the standpoints of some major educational philosophers of India. In the present chapter, by way of conclusion, it is proposed to indicate as to what we can basically imbibe from the teachings of these educational philosophers in order to make our educational system what it should be. Herein, therefore, we shall focus our attention only on those aspects of their teachings which appear to us as pointers for correcting the inadequacies existing in the prevailing system of education in the country.

In this Chapter we shall analyse and interpret the ways in which we may be benefited from the teachings of our educational philosophers.

Today when we stand bewildered and are not able to make up our mind as regards the course that our education should follow, it is felt that the basic teachings of the educational thinkers can contribute immensely towards the needed reforms of the existing educational system in the country and we may particularly be guided by them in relation to the following aims and aspects of our education:

A. (1) The Physical Aim,
   (2) The Religious and the Moral Aim,
   (3) The Knowledge Aim Not Supreme,
   (4) The Vocational Aim,
   (5) The Individual and the Social Aim,
   (6) The Cultural Aim,
   (7) The Aesthetic Aim, and
   (8) The Harmonious Development Aim.

B. (1) The Curriculum,
(2) The Discipline,
(3) Women's Education, and
(4) State and Education.

SECTION A

The Physical Aim

It is wrong to assume that the educational philosophers in this country being idealistic in temperament neglected the realities of life or exaggerated the value of the spirit and underestimated the importance of the body. The philosophers in India had been followers of the *Upanisads* where, it has been advocated that life eternal constitutes the well-being of the body, mind and spirit. The body is considered to be the basis for the performance of duties, and therefore, this basis must be kept in perfect order through appropriate exercises, Asans and Pranayam. In the third chapter we have noted that Swami Dayananda gives a definite place to *Asanas* and *Pranayams*[1] in the life of a student. Swami Vivekananda, Annie Besant, Tagore, Sri Aurobindo and Gandhiji, too, have likewise recognised the value of a sound mind in a sound body and they have advocated the inclusion of physical exercises, games and athletics in any scheme of education.

Swami Dayananda, Swami Vivekananda, Annie Besant and Tagore have emphasised the idea of *Brahmacharya* (celibacy) for the student. In this emphasis they[2] advocated self-control on the part of the student. By self-control they mean the mastery not only of the body but also of the mind. Swami Dayananda has attributed the downfall of India to the non-observance of the principles of self-control or *Brahmacharya*. Swami Vivekananda has endorsed this stand when he says:

> *"It is owing to want of continence that everything is on the brink of ruin in our country. By observance of strict Brahmacharya all learning can he mastered in a very short time; one acquires an unfailing memory of what one hears or knows but once. .."*[3]

In the same vein Shri Aurobindo remarks that an infinite energy—*Prakriti*, *Maya* and *Shakti*—pervades every name and form and when this infinite energy is the fullest in amount in a man, he becomes a *Siddha* or a perfect man. How to develop this energy to the highest limit? For this Sri Aurobindo too recommends the practice of *Brahmacharya*. He says:

> *"The practice of Brahmacharya is the first and most necessary condition of increasing the force within turning it to such uses as may benefit the possessor or mankind. All human energy has a physical basis. The mistake made by European materialism is to suppose the basis to everything and confuse it with the source. The source of life and energy is not material but spiritual, but the basis, the foundation on which the life and energy, stand and work, is physical. The ancient Hindus clearly recognised this distinction between Karma and Pratishtha, the north pole and the south pole of being. Earth or gross matter is Pratishtha. Brahma or spirit is the Karma. To raise up the physical to be spiritual is Brahmacharya, for by the meeting of the two, the energy which starts from one and produces the other is enhanced and fulfils itself..."*[4]

Thus according to Sri Aurobindo observance of *Brahmacharya* will lead one to the highest limit of perfection. Needless to emphasise that we will do well to inculcate this spirit of *Brahmacharya* in our modern students who very often are unaware, of its benefits.

Gandhiji, too was a staunch believer, in *Brahmacharya* (celibacy) and had himself observed this discipline during the latter half of his life. Similarly, in a letter to one of his colleagues at Shantiniketan, Tagore also had recommended the life of a *Brahmachari* for a student :

> *"Education is a 'Brahmacharya Vrata', for carrying out the vow of Brahmacharya the students will have to get used to the hardships and difficulties of life, and give up the pride of luxury and wealth. In order to remove the pride of wealth from the minds of the students, it is the duty of the teachers to crush it forthwith, if and whenever they come across even a tiny trace*

of it. The least attachment or even inclination in a student towards the things of luxury, fashion and taste should at once be discouraged. Luxury in matters of toilet or regarding dress should be extremely avoided. Poverty should not be regarded as a thing for hatred or shame by any student. Taste in matters of dress and diet should be totally tobooed..."[5]

Thus we find that Tagore places before the student the strict ideal of a *Brahmachari*. We have already noted in the chapter on Tagore that he was totally dissatisfied with the prevailing educational system in the country, therefore, he established his Shantiniketan amidst natural surroundings wherein the students would breathe in air which was not debased by the sophistications of modern society. Quite naturally then, the *Brahmacharya* ideal of the ancient system appealed to him very much and he recommended the same to his students at Shantiniketan.

We may note that the educational philosophers were very much pained at the neglect of *Brahmacharya* on the part of the students and the consequent lack of physical vigour, robust physique and a healthy outlook towards life. Therefore, we can say that they were quite alive to the problem of physical education and recommended the inculcation of the ideal of *Brahmacharya* in the student and the inclusion of suitable physical exercises, games and sports in the curriculum for body development. It is thus evident that we must try to incorporate this ideal into our present system of education in such a manner that the same is strictly followed.

The Religious and the Moral Aim

While the Indian educational philosophers regarded the physical aim as the basis of any system of education, they have upheld the religious aim as supreme which may enable the student to realise his spiritual nature, or to acquire knowledge of the self. From times immemorial India has been a land of spiritual consciousness, hence even in the ancient times the Guru or the preceptor endeavoured to impress upon the mind of the pupil that the phenomenal world is shadowy and elusive and that the Real is Eternal. Thus an attempt was always made to provide a spiritual background in the formative period of a student's life in order that the student in his later life might conquer all worldly temptations which could obstruct spiritual progress. The *Guru* himself was a reservoir of spiritual experiences which infused the spirit of piety and religiousness in the mind of the pupils.

> *"The rituals which were performed at the beginning of both the literary and professional education ... the religious observances (Vratas) which the student had to observe during the educational course, the daily prayers which he offered in morning and evening, the religious festivals, that were celebrated with eclat in the school or the preceptor's house ... all these tended to foster piety and religiousness in the mind of the young student ..."*[6]

The educational philosophers have also emphasised the importance of spiritual development of the student, as they were alive to the efficacy of spiritual strength. That is why, all of them lay major emphasis on the student's moral and religious development. We have seen the stress that Vivekananda has laid on the realisation of spiritual Brotherhood. Annie Besant, too, struggled all through her life in India to make the Indians conscious of their spiritual heritage and to live up to the ideal. Dayananda also wanted to regenerate India by making her conscious of the spiritual greatness of the *Vedas*, and hence raised the slogan of 'Back to Vedas'. The life that he recommended for a student is directed towards the creation of spiritual consciousness in him. Gandhiji, Sri Aurobindo and Tagore, too, are great spiritualists and in all their educational pronouncements and writings they have impressed upon us the necessity of creating a spiritual consciousness in the students by giving them moral and religious education.

Under the pressure of modern materialism the world appears to be drifting towards chaos. So educationists all over the world emphasise the urgent necessity of giving religious and moral education in order to make students balanced personalities. Happily, being true to their heritage, Indian educational philosophers have also endorsed this stand. But having realised the implied difficulties in giving religious education in India—a land of religions—Annie Besant, Gandhiji, Sri Aurobindo and Tagore have outlined the nature of religious and moral education to be given to children in schools.

We have already seen that by religious education they do not mean observance of rituals and study of a particular religious scripture. Very rightly, by religious education they have, meant the inculcation of the spirit of spiritual consciousness in the students, and the realisation of the essential unity of all religions. This ideal, undoubtedly is likely to develop among the students the spiritual brotherhood of Swami Vivekananda, the ideal of human unity of Sri Aurobindo, and the conception of human solidarity of Tagore and an understanding of world as a family as advocated by Gandhiji. These great thinkers never became tired of emphasising the commonness of man and they wanted to impress this idea on the minds of students in India belonging to the various religions as they were. It is hardly necessary to observe that the educational system in our country (or in any country) must imbibe this spirit and accordingly we must devise ways and means for giving the religious and moral education so that the unity or our democratic nation may remain intact.

The Knowledge Aim Not Supreme

In ancient India, education stood for illumination, whereas today to many it is becoming synonymous with book-learning and passing of examinations. In ancient days the knowledge was imparted for disciplining the mind in such a way as to help the individual in every walk of life and to enable him to reach his perfection, Appreciating this point of view Annie Besant says:

> *"The educated man differs from the uneducated not in the extent of his knowledge, but in the evolution of his faculties and his power of applying them to any case that presents itself... Your education is to open, your eyes, to train your faculties, so that they may be at your disposal in the later life, and may grow and be strengthened therein by the struggles, the successes and the failures of the life of manhood ..."*[7]

Thus to Annie Besant the real value of education lies in the mental discipline that it imparts and the mental evolution it promotes and not in the factual knowledge that may be gained.

She is against the system of education which aims at merely imparting knowledge. She says:

> *"You are not here only to pass examinations or to absorb your teachers' knowledge; you are here to develop your faculties—spiritual, intellectual, moral, physical—so that thereafter you may use them in the service of God and men, to the credit and honour of your country, your faculties and yourselves ... "*[8]

These days our curriculum has become subject-centred, and in our schools and colleges it is the subjects that are taught and not children and youths. So it will be to our great benefit if we remember the words of Annie Besant and introduce the necessary reforms in our educational machinery. Great Western educators like Dewey, Kilpatrick and others have also realised the futility of a subject centred curriculum and have advocated an activity centred educational system. Gandhiji too, in our own country, as we have already studied, stood for a craft-centred (in effect activity centred) education for our children. Thus Annie Besant's and Gandhiji's views are a timely warning against the mad race towards heavy concentration of subjects in the educational system of our country. Undoubtedly, the educational institutions in India are devoting their entire energy to the teachings of subjects and they seem hardly conscious of educating and developing students as individuals. So it is high time that we take heed, and try to benefit from the experience of our educational philosophers and endeavour to develop the wholesome personalities of individuals and not merely get engrossed in teaching various subjects.

The Vocational Aim

The educational philosophers under review have always been alive to the inadequacies of the prevailing system of education for enabling the youth to become self-supporting at the end of their student career. Swami Vivekananda remarks:

> *"What we need to study, independent of foreign control, different branches of the knowledge that is our own and with*

it the English language and Western science. We need technical education and till else that will develop industries, so that men instead of seeking for service, may earn enough to provide for themselves and have saved against a rainy day."[9]

To the Swami the education that does not prepare the common man to face the struggle of life is no education at all. To Gandhiji education must be an insurance aganist unemployment[10] and one of the major aims as foreseen in his Wardha Scheme of education was the ultimate eradication of the problem of employment from society by establishing small cottage industries run by educated persons. Similarly, Tagore emphasises the vocational aim of education, when he says:

"Our centre of culture should not only be the centre of the intellectual life of India, but tire centre of her economic life also. It must cultivate land, breed cattle to feed itself and its students; it must produce all necessaries devising the best means, using the best materials, calling science to its aid. Its very existence should depend upon the success of its industrial ventures carried out on the co-operative principle, which will unite the teachers and students in a living and active bond of necessity. This will also give us practical industrial training, whose motive power is not the greed of profit."[11]

Thus Tagore gives us the right directive for the fulfilment of the vocational aim of education.

Swami Dayananda Annie Besant, Swami Vivekananda, Sri Aurobindo and Gandhiji all believe in the age-old *Varnasrama Dharma* which implies that each individual should contribute to society his due share according to the stage of evolution he has reached. Annie Besant speaks about the *Varnasrama Dharma* in a very beautiful manner:

"As most progressive people, hypnotized by words; object to caste, because it has been abused—you can drop the word and call it vocation."[12]

Thus we find that our educators, have emphasized the need of the vocational aim of education. At present this need is not adequately fulfilled with the result that after finishing their school and college career our youths do not know how to earn their living. Most of them want some job under some employers and hundreds of applications are received for a single post. This trend has to be curbed, if our country is to progress in the present age in rapid industrialization. Evidently, we must include in our educational system some such measures which may ultimately help the educated youth to solve his problem of earning a living. In this context also we have to look towards our great educators for inspiration and guidance.

The Individual and the Social Aim

Swami Vivekananda and Tagore are the great upholders, of such education that develops individuals. It should be noted that in India, there has never been a controversy, as in some Western Countries, about the social and individual aims of education. In the West the necessity of reconciling the two aims of education has been felt and it has been rightly held that the good of the individual and that of the society are mutually inclusive. In India, such an explanation has not been considered necessary because of her spiritual conception of individuality. Swami Vivekananda says:

> *"The ideal of all education, all training, should be ... man-making. But, instead of that, we are always trying to polish up the outside. What use in polishing up the outside when there's no inside? The end and aim of all training is to make the man grow ..."*[13]

Thus he emphasises the development of individuality as the aim of education. He wants to awaken the inherent Brahman (God) in each student through faith and through education. He asserts that it is by awakening the inherent Brahman that the student will realise his true individuality.

Tagore too upholds the view that the foremost aim of education is the development of individual personality of the students. He wants to give full freedom to the individual in order to carve his own destiny. According to him individual should develop his personality so as to be capable of understanding the all pervading unity not of mankind alone but of the entire universe. He finds this unity in diversity:

> *"Due to the omnipresence of the impersonal and universal Brahman of which each one of us is a part. As parts, each of us is different from the rest and each is unique. In each of us the Brahman manifests into unique, though imperfect, manner. So we move through life as individuals trying to realise the Brahman more fully each in his own way. Again in Brahman and through Him we find unity not only amongst ourselves, human beings, but also between man and nature. Realisation of this unity prevents us from placing undue emphasis on the growth of individuality which might degenerate into a sharpening of the ego."*[14]

Thus Tagore's conception of individuality is unique and it is fundamentally Indian in nature. According to him education should be so planned as to enable one to attain this type of individuality.

To Gandhiji the individual has been the one supreme consideration.[15] He wants to see God in His Creation. He thinks to achieve this ideal by uniting all. He considers himself an integral part of the whole. It is impossible for him to find Him apart from the rest of humanity.[16] This indicates that while Gandhiji advocates the development of individual as the ideal, he is not prepared to ignore the social good, because he can think of the individual only in the context of the rest of humanity. Similarly, in Tagore's conception of seeing unity in diversity, we find that the social good is automatically implied.

Likewise Swami Dayananda and Sri Aurobindo also have the good of mankind in mind. According to them the individual should develop himself with the aim of contributing his share towards the regeneration of mankind. Swami Dayananda as a reformer wanted to eradicate evil not only in India but wherever he sensed it. Sri Aurobindo, too, believes that by the development of supramental consciousness mankind will be liberated from its miseries and troubles. Thus the educational philosophers in this country never ignored the social aim of education while advocating the individual aim. In fact, the social aim of education has always been implied in their stand for the development of individuality—because the individuality has always been spiritual in conception and nature, according to great Indian traditions.

Modern educators in India must take lessons from the teachings of our educational philosophers. Only then they can succeed in shaping out a scheme of education by which the right type of individuality, which feels at one with the whole universe, may be developed. Solution of some of our modern troubles lies in the development of this type of individuality. Then alone will India give the message of peace, truth, love and non-violence to the whole world. India has been a land of tolerance. All kinds of religions and people have found a breathing space here. What an irony that the same land today is full of intolerance! For wiping away this intolerance and for establishing Gandhiji's conception of *Ramarajya* wherein everyone will have justice in all walks of life, it is necessary to develop in man the consciousness of mature individuality. The prevailing system of education in the country must be modified in such a way as to promote the consciousness of such an individuality. In this attempt alone lies the salvation of both the individual and the society.

The Cultural Aim

The educational philosophers have been reasonably proud of the cultural heritage of India. These great personages felt greatly unhappy at the indiscriminate imitation of the Western modes of living by their countrymen. We must also note that while they were not impressed by some of the Western ways of life, they were not blind to their niceties and they endeavoured all through their lives guiding their countrymen towards a wise assimilation the same. In this endeavour they never failed to remind us of the greatness of our own cultural heritage.

Annie Besant constantly reminded students in India of the great ancient culture of their country. She says:

"Is there less to be proud of in India than in England? Have you not a history that stretches back scores of thousands of years ere England was heard of? ... Our ancestors were great ... they did noble deeds, and such deeds we also shall strive to do. They held the name of Aryavarta high; we shall endeavour to raise it and hold it higher ... You will only prove yourselves true-born if you live again as your sires lived. They are but base-born who wear their fathers' names but do not manifest their fathers' virtues. Act, then, so that future generations may see that you remember the heroes of the past ... least the Rishis, looking down on India, see that you are the descendents of their minds as well as their bodies; let them be able to say: 'These youths are worthy of their inheritance we bequeathed to them, and they will hand on enriched—the legacy, they received from us."[17]

Thus in these inspiring words Annie Besant reminds the students of India to imbibe their great cultural heritage. She wants them to be Indians first and foremost.

Swami Dayananda considered the revival of the Vedic culture as the panacea for all ills prevailing in society. Swami Vivekananda remarks:

"Teach the masses in the vernaculars. Give them ideas; they will get information, but something more will be necessary. Give them culture. Until you can give them that, there can be no permanence in the raised condition of the masses."[18]

Swami Vivekananda wanted to create self-reliance and self-confidence in the Indian youths by reminding them of the greatness or Indian culture, and he vividly explained this greatness to the Western world as well. He has rightly pointed out to us that we cannot shine in the world as a great people unless we take root in our own culture.

Sri Aurobindo, too, has been a great upholder and exponent of the Indian culture. He says:

"The ancient Indian culture attached quite as much value to

> *the soundness, growth and strength of the mind, life, and body as the old Hellenic or the modern scientific thought although for a different end and a great motive. The new India will seek the same end in new ways under the vivid impulse of fresh and large ideas and by an instrumentality suited to more complex conditions; but the scope of her effort and action, and suppleness, and variety of her mind will not be less, but greater than of old. Spirituality is not necessarily exclusive; it can be and in its fullness must be all inclusive ... But the spiritual motive will be in the future of India, as in her past, the real original and dominating strain. To realize intimately the truth of spirit and to quicken and remould life by it is the native tendency of Indian mind, and to that it must always return, in all its periods of health, greatness and vigour ...*"[19]

Sri Aurobindo wants to mould education in India so as to attain this ideal. Such was his abiding faith in the inherent strength of Indian Culture. Gandhiji and Tagore, too, were in perfect agreement with the above conviction and all their lives have been eloquent testimonies to the same.

Thus our educators have stood for the revival of our great cultural heritage in the face of the foreign influences. But it must be noted here that they did not mean to decry the Western civilization. They were alive to its many strong points and sustaining virtues for human life, and so they were not against the rational assimilation of the same. Thus, cultural exchange between the East and the West must be promoted by our educational institutions and all of us should work together for a reconciliation and reconstruction of ideals that may promote the good of mankind. But in this reconciliation and reconstruction one must not forget one's own cultural heritage, otherwise chaos rules the society.

It is a truism to state that the educational institutions in India are not fostering the Indian cultural values. Therefore, they are not able to guide our youths towards the inculcation of these values in their lives. Consequently, the average youth today is crushed under the pressure of pessimism and unhealthy outlook of life. He seldom realises that life has a purpose behind it, and so he seeks shelter under the essential purposelessness of human endeavour. Our students, today, are losing reason and getting emotional and sentimental. The growing indiscipline in them is an eloquent testimony to this. They are not able to conceive anything valuable except the physical and material. Hence they have learnt more to doubt than to admire and believe. Such a state of affairs has led to the lowering of standards, the fading away of high ideals and the absence of a worthy purpose in life. All these tendencies may be arrested if we practice the teachings of the educational philosophers and incorporate in our educational system the great Indian traditions advocated by them from time to time. Education in our country should be so re-organised as to enable the individual to develop his personality in the context of modern requirements but with a background of our great ancient cultural heritage.

The Aesthetic Aim

The aesthetic aim of education is intimately related to the moral and cultural aims. A close relationship may be seen between morals and arts. Therefore it should be the business of education to promote in the students a genuine love for beauty and art. It is after this attainment that the individual will be truly educated. It was towards the realization of this ideal amongst others that our ancient *Gurukulas* were situated in the calm and serene atmosphere of forests. Annie Besant remarks:

> *"But for a country in which a man is valued for what is, nor for what he has, in which a man's life consisteth not in the abundance of the things which he possesseth, the Indian ideal is more suitable. The essence of that ideal is not the forest as such, but the being in close touch with Nature; to let her harmonies permeate the consciousness, and her calm soothe the restlessness of the mind. Hence it was the forest which best suited the type and the object of the instruction in the days which evolved Rishis: instruction which aimed at profound rather than at swift and alert thought."*[20]

Thus to Annie Besant the forest atmosphere is most suitable for the development of pupils on the pattern which produced our

Rishis who may be regarded as an embodiment of aesthetic development. Like Annie Besant other educational philosophers in India, too, have tried to make us conscious of the ideals that characterized the natural surroundings of the forest schools of ancient India. That is why all of them draw inspiration from the ancient *Gurukul*. Swami Dayananda advocated the establishment of schools amidst natural surroundings of the *Gurukul* pattern and Tagore likewise founded his Bolpur school in the peaceful atmosphere of nature and named it Shantiniketan (the abode of peace).

One of the main objectives behind Tagore's Shantiniketan has been to foster the aesthetic development of the pupils in a calm atmosphere which is conducive to the development of their aesthetic nature. Tagore says:

> *"A most wonderful thing that we notice in India is that here the forest, not the town, is the fountain-head of all its civilization... It is the forest that has nurtured the two great Ancient Ages of India, the Vedic and the Buddhistic. As did the Vedic Rishis, Lord Buddha also showed His teachings in many woods of India. The royal palace had no room for Him, it is the forest that took Him into its lap. The current of civilization that flowed from its forests inundated the whole of India."*[21]

Quite naturally then, Tagore is a great advocate of the *Tapovana Ashrama*. His own Shantiniketan is a testimony to the same in our times.

> *"Nature occupies a very important place in Tagore's life and philosophy. Nature, like man, is the manifestation of the Brahman. Through its variegated forms, colours and rhythms Brahman reveals Himself manifold and perhaps more clearly than through man; so it is necessary for human beings to come into close contact with Nature with its purifying and vitalizing influences; Man must realise his kinship with Nature as lie must realise her kinship with human beings."*[22]

Evidently, Tagore believes that Nature is the best medium

through which the highest conception of aesthetic development may be achieved. So he is against the atmosphere of the modern schools situated near or in the heart of cities. He believes in the ancient ideal of *Tapovana* which was away from the din, bustles and turmoils of modern civilization. It was free from all outside interferences or influences. The Tapovana, in a peaceful and ennobling atmosphere, imparted the type of education which was most essential for the preservation of society. The students in it imbibed the highest ideals of life and cultivated the virtue of simple but complete living. Needless to say that under the circumstances the students were naturally inclined towards the cultivation of all that is beautiful in life. Hence the Tapovana fulfilled all the conditions that were necessary for the promotion of the aesthetic development of the inmates. It is on the pattern of ancient Tapovana that Tagore established his Shantiniketan. It is with this conception of aesthetic development in the background that he compares the growth of the child with that of a tree and places the emphasis on the long forgotten relation between nature and childhood.[23]

Tagore speaks of the modern educational system as an education factory[24] lifeless, colourless, dissociated from the context of the universe, within the bare white walls staring like the vacant eyes of the dead. Thus the modern educational system has deprived the child from the natural surroundings which could have promoted in him a real aesthetic sense. Modern education is confined mostly within the four walls of the classrooms with the results that it has become artificial and has lost its value to a great extent. So it is high time that we heed the note of warning from Tagore[25] and organise our educational institutions in such natural surroundings which may promote in students the highest aesthetic development which our ancient Tapovana was capable of doing. There can be no remedy for our present ill unless we organise our education with a motive to foster the highest aesthetic sense in the students. The right type of aesthetic development alone will save us from falling prey to the modern sophistications which are eating away the very vitality of our life. We stand indebted to Tagore for pointing out so emphatically the need of establishing a relationship between nature and childhood, and hence it is necessary that in order to give our educational system a meaning, we must incorporate in it the ideals advocated by Tagore.

The Harmonious Development Aim

The educational philosophers in India were conscious of the defect of the predominance of intellectual character in the prevailing educational system in the country at the cost of a more harmonious development of the students' personality. All of them have emphasised the need of a harmonious development of personality. Swami Vivekananda says:

> *"Education is not the amount of information that is put into your brain and runs riot there undigested all your life. We must have life-building, man-making, character-making, assimilation of ideas. If education were identical with information, the libraries would be greatest sages in the world, and encyclopaedia is the Rishi."*[26]

Thus the Swami stands for the type of education which develops all the faculties in a person in the desired manner.

Annie Besant, too, is against the over-emphasis upon intellectual development under the prevailing system of education. She remarks:

> *"Modern education in India has practically confined itself to the training of the mental and intellectual nature, and has ignored the unfolding of the spiritual nature, the evoking and training of the emotional nature ... The result has been, in the older generations, the over-strain of the nervous system, the enfeebling of the physical health, the shortening of the period of vigorous maturity ... Further, the exclusive development of the intelligence and the neglect of the emotions has once stimulated the self-regarding instincts and has largely destroyed the feeling of social and National Dharma, of duty to society and to the Nation, hence the decay of public spirit, of social service, of responsibility and of sacrifice for the common weal ."*[27]

Thus, according to her, none of the aspects of human nature should be neglected if the growth of a balanced personality is desired.

Tagore appears to be more emphatic about the growth of a balanced personality, because he views education in the context of a synthetic view of life. He insists that the different elements of man must be in complete harmony. The following ideas may illustrate this point:

"(i) *The purpose of education must be in line with the highest purpose of man, the fullest growth and freedom of soul.*
(ii) *For mental health and development it is absolutely necessary that there are schools not only for lessons, but also for inculcating a feeling of personal love towards others. The school must be an Ashrama where men have gathered for the highest purpose of life.*
(iii) *The purpose* of *education should be to give man the unity of truth.*"[28]

Thus we find that Tagore stands for the education of the whole man. He says:

"There is a close and inseparable connection between the faculties of the mind and the body. Each gains strength by cooperating with the other. We should know that the great task of our educational efforts in our institution is to provide for the education of the mind and all the senses through various activities."[29]

Annie Besant and Tagore have rendered us a great service by drawing our attention to the defects of the lopsided intellectual character of modern education and to the need of making efforts towards the harmonious development of the individual. It has been argued by various authorities that the system of education in our country attends more to the needs of the mind than of the heart and body with the result that disintegrated personalities are not uncommon in our society. We will do well to accept this pointer of the educational philosophers of our country and act accordingly so that harmonious development of the individual may be secured.

So far we have been dealing with the aims of education and have tried to understand the pointers of our educational philosophers to us as regards the aims that should guide us in our educational endeavour. Now we shall understand the curriculum which is a medium through which the efforts are made for fulfilling the purposes of education. After curriculum we shall consider the conception of Discipline. Women's Education and the relationship between State and Education as advocated by the educational philosophers.

SECTION B

The Curriculum

Swami Dayananda's "Back to the Vedas" scheme of education naturally failed to give due importance to many secular subjects that must be taught today. However, it may be remarked that the Swami was not quite unaware of the needs of the time and if he had lived longer, perhaps, he would have modified his stand with regard to the curriculum that he suggested.

Annie Besant gives us a right directive with regard to the content of education. A look at the scheme of studies[30] as given by her will convince one about the wholeness of the 3 Hs: Heart, Head and Hand as advocated by Gandhiji[31] as well. But we must note that by suggesting a course of studies the educators in our country did not mean to make the curriculum subject-centred and forget the personality of the child. It will be clear from the foregoing discussion that all through their writings they have given prominance to the personality of the individual. Through education they meant to develop the personality and not to teach certain subjects. Hence the curriculum has been accepted only as the medium through which the development of the personality might be promoted. Our educators have made the life as the centre of education and not the subjects or curriculum as such.

> *"Tagore makes 'life' the centre, not the life of this child or that, nor even a particular aspect of human life in preference to some other, but life as a whole and at its richest and best, jointly lived by teachers and students. If this remains the centre of attention, the different factors are naturally correlated, as also the different aspects of knowledge."*[32]

Thus it is the whole life of man that should make the curriculum for the school, and not this subject or that. Undoubtedly, this notion of whole life will include everything that is needed for promoting the growth of the individual. While planning our education, if we keep before us the concept of the whole life of man, there will be no trouble; and education will be just that which it should be.

In the eighth chapter of the present dissertation we have seen that Tagore has approached life as a poet with a totality of vision. In the same spirit he has approached education as well. He thinks that the pure interest in truth alone can hold together the various aspects of reality. Therefore in his system of education he has not disregarded 'the operational aspect of Truth' though he lays the major emphasis on its manifestation. Under truth he includes all that affects the life of the human race and of the individual. To him truth must be independent of utilitarian purposes so that the individual may find his richest fulfilment Therefore to him the content of education should be a representation of the Truth in all aspects of life, viz., physical, mental, moral and spiritual—both from the absolute and the pragmaic point of view. If we take the clue from this notion of Tagore, all our present day troubles with regard to the content of education will disappear.

Annie Besant appears to be in perfect agreement with the above idea when she says:

> *"As man is a spiritual being, manifesting in the external world as Intelligence, Emotion and Activity, the education of the young must help the inspiring life to unfold itself, and must train the organs of intelligence. Emotion and Activity, that is, must be religious, mental, moral and physical. Any so called education which omits any one of these four departments of human nature is imperfect and unscientific and its outcome will he a human being deficient in one or more of the groups of capacities on the balanced evolution of which the extent of his usefulness to society depends."*[33]

From the above we may infer that the curriculum must represent the four aspects of human nature—physical, mental, moral and religious. No modern educator can disagree with Annie Besant's view and we will do well to be guided by this in the organisation of our curriculum.

It is worth noting that according to Annie Besant each subject in the curriculum should fulfil two conditions, viz., first, it should help the individual to develop all his latent faculties so that he may come up in the scale of evolution: secondly, it should assist him in developing the consciousness that he is a part of the:

> *"Larger environment—the home, the school, the college, the city, the province, the State, the race, humanity, the world. There is no break in principle, the first three are preparatory stage for the second three, and this whole six for the remaining three."*[34]

The two conditions as explained by her are for the development of the two phases of man's life—firstly, spiritual—the inner life of man as an individual; and secondly, external life of man as a unit of the society which has its moral conventions and obligations to be followed by its members. If our curriculum fulfils these two conditions, we shall have the desired system of education in our country.

The Discipline

Discipline is an important aspect of any educational system. It is this aspect of our educational system at all stages, which has challenged educators to find a solution for the problem. Discipline of the authoritarian type crushes the personality of the individual and retards his growth. The educational philosophers were quite conscious of the evils of the authoritarian type of discipline as generally prevalent in schools. So they advocated the establishment of the ancient system of self-imposed discipline in place of the discipline imposed from without. Sri Aurobindo says:

> *"The method practised in the West is crude and marred by the excess of outer discipline, for which the pupils have no respect except that of fear and the exiguity of the inner assistance. The little good that is done is outweighed by much evil. The*

old Indian system of the Guru commanding by his knowledge and sanctity the implicit obedience, perfect administration, reverent emulation of the student was a far superior method of moral discipline."[35]

Thus Sri Aurobindo rightly points out that we should accept the ancient idealistic method of maintaining discipline. Towards this end both the teacher and the pupil will have to endeavour a great deal. The teacher should be competent enough to command respect by his very reverent personality, which is an embodiment of all virtues, and the pupil should lead moral and chaste life so that he may develop a sense of self-discipline from within. Upholding the conception of discipline of the ancient *Gurukul* Swami Vivekananda, Swami Dayananda and Annie Besant, also agree with this point of view. Gandhiji, too, has stood for the principle of inner discipline. Tagore endeavoured to maintain this method of discipline in his Shantiniketan which has been established on the ancient *Gurukul* pattern. Thus by reviving the conception of discipline of the ancient *Ashrama* the educators have focused our attention of the efficacy of the same, and if we endeavour to incorporate it in our modern educational set-up the problem of discipline will gradually disappear.

Women's Education

The educational philosophers have been alive to the problem of women's education. In the country and we have seen that Swami Dayananda, Swami Vivekananda and Gandhiji have spoken emphatically for the liberation of women folk in India by giving them the right type of education and by granting them equal status before men. Dayananda was prepared to grant equal status to women by permitting them to study the Vedas. He recommended that the girls should observe *Brahmacharya* and should receive education.[36] To Vivekananda "The women of India must grow and develop in the footprints of Sita and that is the only way".[37]

Vivekananda had definite ideas about the type of education that should be given to Indian women. Once he said:

"*Religion, arts, science, housekeeping, cooking, sewing,*

hygiene—the simple essential points of these subjects ought to be taught to our women. It is not good to let them touch novels and fictions ... But only teaching rites of worship won't do; their education must be an eye-opener in all matters. Ideal characters mist always he presented before the view of the girls to imbue them with a devotion for lofty ideals of selflessness. The noble examples of Sita, Savitri, Damayanti, Lilavati, Kahna and Mira should be inspired to mould their lives after them."[38]

What a pity that today many our women are drifting away from this ideal. It is high time that we take a note of warning from Vivekananda and set our women on the right track so that they may be able to attain perfect Indian womenhood capable of producing great sons like Vivekananda. Gandhiji, Sri Aurobindo, Tagore and the like.

State and Education

As regards the relation between State and Education, Annie Besant has given us a directive when she says:

"Government should assign to educational and cultural institutions the material means for their support, gifts of land, grants of money for buildings ....so that they may be able to give to the Nation the priceless assets of learned and skilled men and women of high character... Money given to Education by the Nation is not a gift, but an investment."[39]

She derives this ideal from the ancient Gurukulas of India. Speaking on the ancient system of education in India she says:

"A Monarch might enter into the convocation of a university, but no one rose to greet him and he took his seat like any other visitors; but on the entrance of its Head, the Venerable of Venerables, all rose and turned their faces towards him and in silence awaited his words. The University was the Temple of Learning, and the learned were its only Hierophants. When

Learning visited Royality ... even Shri Krishna descended from His throne and bowed at the feet of the sage."[40]

Thus Annie Besant advocates autonomy in educational matters. She does not want that the State should interfere in education because it gives grants for its support. Unless this attitude pervades the thinking of our authorities which grant money to educational institutions, there cannot be academic freedom and the right atmosphere where the free spirit of enquiry reigns, will lack. Hence the State must not control educational institutions, otherwise the pursuit of higher truths will be jeopardised and it will result into indoctrination and a consequent stunted growth of individuals.

The analysis, thus, indicates that educational philosophers under discussion have suggested to a great extent the right remedies for the eradication of many of the ills existing in the current educational system of our country. Each has suggested remedies according to his own line of thinking and what is missed by one has been supplied by another thus one complementing the others. So when we take all into consideration at the same time we find a complete picture which may assist us in the solution of our educational problems. In fact, their main contribution in the field of education has been the very philosophy of life they have endeavoured to advocate keeping in view the spirit of India—a spirit which has permeated throughout the length and breadth of the country all through the ages. In the light of the teachings of our educational philosophers, the total reorientation of our educational thought coupled with a realistic approach in the context of modern era of scientific and technological transition seems to provide us with the fundamental solutions of our educational problems and blends the oriental values with the accidental practices to a great advantage of all concerned. Let us hope that the teachings of our great philosophers will be followed in order to make education of the kind which may produce men and women with a strong moral fabric.

NOTES

1. *Supra*, 41
2. *Ibid.*, p. 44.

3. *The Complete Works*, Vol. III, p. 222.
4. Sri Aurobindo: *The Brain of India*, pp. 17-18.
5. Tagore: *Vidya Aur Vidyalaya ka Adarsha*, Translation of a Tagore's letter to his colleague at Shantiniketan published in '*Shiksha*'—July, 1952.
6. Altekar, *Education in Ancient India*, p. 9.
7. *The Besant Spirit*, Vol. 2, pp. 92-93.
8. *Ibid.*, p. 90.
9. *The Compete Works*, Vol. V, p. 284.
10 *Supra*, p. 138.
11. Rabindranath Tagore: *The Visva Bharati Quarterly Education* No. Vol. XIII, Parts 1 & II, May-Oct. 1947.
12. *The Besant Spirit*, p. 43.
13. Vivekananda, *The Powers of the Mind*, p. 10.
14. Basu, A., Tagore's Educational Philosophy in Relation to Education, *Visva Bharati Quarterly*, Education Number, Vol. XIII, Parts I & II, p. 40.
15. *Young India*, November 13,1924.
16. *Harijan*, August 29,1936.
17. Besant: *Hindu Ideals*, pp. 56-57.
18. *The Complete Works*, Vol. III, p. 291.
19. Quoted in Mitras India's *Cultural Empire and Her Future*, pp. 92-93.
20. *The Besant Spirit*, Vol. II, p. 49.
21. *Visva Bharati Quarterly*, April 1924, p. 64.
22. Basu, A. : The Visva Bharati Quarterly, Education Number, Vol. VIII, Parts I and 11, May-Oct. 1947, pp. 46-47.
23. *Supra*, pp. 198-204.
24. *Supra*, pp. 217 and 223.
25. *Ibid.*, pp. 208-209.
26. *The Complete Works*, Vol. III, p. 301.
27. *The Besant Spirit*, Vol. II, pp. 40-41.
28. Adapted from *The Visva Bharati Quarterly*, Education Number Vol. XIII, Parts I and II, May-Oct. 1947, pp. 17-18.
29. *Ibid.*, p. 48.
30. *Supra*, pp. 80-83.
31. *Supra*, pp. 145-146 and 147.
32. Sarkar, S.C.: The Central Purpose of Education, *Visva Bharati Quarterly*, Vol. XIII, Parts I & 11, May-Oct., 1947, p. 89.
33. *The Besant Spirit*, Vol. II, p. 107.
34. *Ibid.*, p. 109.
35. Sri Aurobindo : *A System of National Education*, pp. 14-17.
36. *Supra*, p. 39.
37. *The Complete Works*, Vol. III, p. 256.
38. Nirvedananda : *Our Education*, p. 124.
39. *The Besant Spirit*, Vol. II, p. 37.
40. *Ibid.*, p. 32.

10

GLOSSARY

Acharya	religious teacher
Advaita	monism, the doctrine of non-duality
Advaitin	monist
Agnihotra	offering oblations in fire
Ahimsa	non-violence
Aksara	imperishable
Anadi	without beginning
Ananda	bliss
Anatma	not-self
Anitya	transitory
Aparigraha	without possession, non-possession
Artha	wealth
Asana	posture
Asat	that which is not real
Ashrama	hermitage, a stage of life
Ashrama	dharma, duties relating to a stage of life
Asura	one who is opposed to righteous conduct, a devil
Asteya	not stealing
Atman	the self
Avatara	incarnation
Avidya	nescience
Bhakti	devotion
Bhangi	a scavenger
Bhakti Yoga	union with God through devotion
Brahma	Absolute, Supreme Being
Brahmacharini	a women observing the vow of chastity
Brahmacharya	life of celibacy, observance of continence
Brahman	the Absolute, Ultimate-Reality, Universal Soul

Brahmana	a ritualistic treatise
Cit	intelligence, consciousness
Deva	a God
Devadasi	a danseuse in a temple
Devi	mother goddess
Dharma	law, duty, righteousness, nature, the code of conduct
Dharma	*artha-kama-moksa*—a formula indicating the four goals of life—virtue, wealth, enjoyment and salvation
Dharma-Sastra	code of ethics
Dvaita	dualistic philosophy
Dvaitadvaita	dualistic monism
Gayatri	a hymn of the Yajurveda, an invocation to the Almighty God
Gitanjali	song of God, a prayer song
Guru	preceptor
Gurukula	the family of the preceptor (Guru) which consists of pupils and the Guru, generally used for the forest-school of ancient India
Harijan	a man of God, the name given by Gandhiji to the untouchable class in Hindu Society
Hatha-Yoga	a mode of meditation involving physical strain
Himsa	violence
Hind Swaraj	Indian Home Rule
Hindustani Talim Sangh	an all India organization for the spread of Basic Education
Homa	a burnt offering
Isa	Lord
Iswara	Personal God
Ji	an affix to a name denoting respect
Jnana	divine wisdom, illumination
Jnana-Yoga	Union with God through *jnana*
Karma	action
Kama	desire
Kanya	girl
Karma-Yoga	Union with God through action
Ksara	the impermanent

Ksatriya	one belonging to the warrior caste
Maharsi	a great seer
Mahatma	a great soul
Mahavidyalaya	great seat of learning, college or University
Mantra	a mystic formula
Math	a monastery
Maya	illusion, mystery, creative power of God
Moksa	liberation, emancipation, freedom from birth
Mukta	one who is liberated
Nai Talim	the new education
Naraka	hell
Nirguna	without qualities
Nirvana	beautitude
Nitya	eternal
Paramatman	Supreme Self
Pisacha	devil
Pitr	the ancestral spirit
Prakriti	nature
Pranayama	a regulated and systematized process of deep breathing which burns of all impurities and exalts the soul
Prapatti	self-surrender
Prarthana	prayer
Prem	love
Purana	an ancient legend
Pardah	veil, a custom of women being kept in seclusion
Purohit	a family priest
Purusa	God; Male
Rajas	passion, energy—one of the three qualities of nature
Raksasa	a demon
Ramarajya	beneficent rule. Godly rule
Rishi (Rsis)	seer, prophet
Sadhaka	one who undergoes a system of discipline for some definite attainment
Sadhana	a process of discipline for attaining something
Saguna	possessing qualities
Saguna-Upasana	meditation on a personal God

Samhita	collection
Samnyasa	renunciation, the fourth stage of Hindu life that of a recluse
Samskara	purificatory ceremony, residual trace left on the mind
Samnyasi	a monk
Sanatana-dharma	eternal law or religion
Sangh	organization, association, society
Sarvodaya Samaj	a co-operative social order for the benefit of all
Sastra	a scripture, a science
Sat	reality
Sat-chit-ananda	formula denoting the absolute, consisting of reality, consciousness and bliss
Sati	the Hindu ritual—widow immolating herself on her husbands funeral pyre (now obsolete)
Satya	truth
Satyagraha	firmness in the cause of truth, a formula coined by Gandhiji for his technique of fighting evil
Shantiniketan	the abode of peace, Tagore's International University
Sivam	peace and happiness
Smriti	a secondary scripture, a code of law
Stuti	praise, glorification
Sundaram	beautiful
Svarga	Heaven
Swadeshi	of one's own land
Swaraj	self-government
Tamas	dullness, ignorance, one of the three qualities of nature
Tapas (Tapasya)	austerity, penance
Taporama	hermitage
Tirth	a place of pilgrimage
Tyaga	renunciation
Upanayana	initiation ceremony among Hindus
Upanga	a supplementary work
Upanisad	a mystical treatise at the end of the Veda
Upasana	meditation (communion)
Upaveda	a class of works subordinate to the Veda

Vanaprastha	the third stage in the Hindu Scheme of asramas, involving retirement to a forest
Varna	caste
Varnasrama dharm	rules relating to Hindu castes and stages of life
Veda	sacred scripture of the Hindus
Vedic	pertaining to the Veda
Vedanga	auxiliaries to the Veda
Vedanta	a system of philosophy based on the Upanisads
Yajna	sacrifice
Yoga	a system of discipline leading to union with God

BIBLIOGRAPHY

On Swami Dayananda

Articles on Arya Samaj in the *Encyclopaedia of Religion and Ethics.*

Bawa Chhajju Singh: *The Life and Teachings of Swami Dayananda Saraswati,* Lahore, 1923.

Bawa Chhajju Singh: *The Teaching of the Arya Samaj*, Lahore, 1908.

Chamupati: *The Aryan Ideal of Education*, Gurukul Kangari Press, 1934.

Dayananda Commemoration Volume, Edited by H.B. Sarda, Vedic Pustakalaya, Ajmer, 1933.

Farquhar : *Modern Religious Moments in India*, pp. 101-129, New York, 1915.

Ganga Prasad Upadhyaya: *The Origin, Scope and Mission of the Arya Samaj*, Allahabad, 1940.

Hume, R.E.: *The Thirteen Principal Upanishads.*

Lajpat Rai: *The Arya Samaj*, London, 1915.

Pandit Vishnu Lal Sharma: *Handbook of the Arya Samaj*, Lucknow.

Sarma, D.S.: Studies in the *Renaissance of Hinduism*, Banaras Hindu University, Banaras, 1944.

Satya Prakash: A Critical Study of Philosophy of Dayananda, Vedic Pustakalaya, Ajmer, 1938.

Sri Aurobindo: *Bankim, Tilak and Dayananda*, Calcutta, 1940.

Sri Ram Sharma: *Mahatma Hansraj,* Lahore, 1941.

The Light Truth: Translation of *Satyartha Prakash* by Dr. Chiranjiva Bharadwaja, published by Arya Samaj, Madras, 1932.

Vishwa Prakash: Life and Teachings of S. Dayananda, Allahabad, 1935.

Vyas, K.C.: *The Social Renaissance in India*, Vora & Co., Publishers Private Ltd., Bombay, 1957.

On Swami Vivekananda

A Short Life of Swami Vivekananda, Almora, 1940.

The Complete Works of Swami Vivekananda in 7 Vols., Advaita Ashrama, Almora, 1947.

The Disciples of Ramakrishna, Almora, 1943.

Life of Swami Vivekananda, 2 Vols., Almora.

Sister Nivedita: *Hints on National Education in India*, Udbodhan Office, Calcutta, 1950.

Sister Nivedita: *The Master as I saw Him: An Intimate Study of Swami Vivekananda*, Fifth Edition, 1939.

Sarma, D.S.: *Studies in the Renaissance of Hinduism,* Banaras Hindu University, Banaras, 1944.

Swami Abhedananda: *Ideal of Education,* Ramkrishna Vedanta Math, Calcutta, 1945.

Swami Abhedananda: *Swami Vivekananda and His Works in America,* Advaita Ashrama, Almora, 1939.

Swami Ramakrishnananda: *For Thinkers on Education,* Sri Ram Krishna Math, Madras, 1948.

Vyas, K.C.: *The Social Renaissance in India*, Vora & Co., Publishers Private Ltd., Bombay, 1957.

On Annie Besant

Ancient Wisdom, Adyar Edition, 1939.

Arundale, Dr. G.S.: *Ideals in Education*, 1939.

Besant, Annie: An Autobiography with an Additional Survey of Her Life by G.S. Arundale, Adyar Edition, 1939.

Besant, Annie: *Essentials of Indian Education,* Dr. Besant's Speeches in the Central Hindu College, 1899-1912 (B.S.S.T.).

Besant, Annie: *Civilization, Deadlocks and the Keys*, 1924.

Besant, Annie: *Education as a National Duty,* 1903.

Besant, Annie: *Education for the New Era,* 1919.

Besant, Annie: *Education for Indian Girls,* 1905.

Besant, Annie: *Education in the Light of Theosophy,* Adyar Pamphlet No. 16.

Besant, Annie (*Mrs.) : A Sketch of Her Life and Her Service to India,* By G.A. Natesan and Co. 1908.

Besant, Annie: *Hindu Ideals*, 1904.

Besant, Annie: *Ideal in Education,* Compiled mainly from the writings of Dr. Annie Besant (*Besant Spirit Series* 11).

Besant, Annie: Indian Ideals in Education, Religion and Philosophy and Art, Being Kamal Lecturers for 1924-25, delivered at the Calcutta University by Annie Besant.

Besant, Annie: Principles of Education with a scheme applying them to National Education in India, Dedicated to Parents, Guardians and Teachers by Annie Besant.

Besant, Annie: *Problems of Reconstruction.*

Besant, Annie: *The New Civilization*, 1927.

Besterman : *Besant, Mrs. Annie, A Modern Prophet,* Kegan Paul. Trench, Trubner & Co., London, 1934.

Bhagwan Das: *Annie Besant and the Changing World*, 1934.

Brahma Vidya : *Divine Wisdom, Second Edition*, 1927.

Jinarajadasa: *The Golden Book of the Theosophical Society*, 1925.

Jinarajadasa: *A Short Biography of Dr. Annie Besant*, 1932.

Pal, B.C.: *Besant, Mrs. Annie, A Psychological Study*, 1917.

Sarma, D.S.: *Studies in the Renaissance of Hinduism*, Banaras, Hindu University, Banaras, 1944.

Sri Prakasa: *Besant, Annie, A Woman and Leader,* 1941.

The Seven Principles of Man, Theosophical Manual No. 1.

The Wisdom of the Upanisads, *Convention Lecture of 1906, Third* Edition, 1925.

Vyas, K.C.: *The Social Renaissance in India*, Vora & Co., Publishers Private Ltd., Bombay, 1957.

On Sri Aurobindo

Bhattacharya, P.K.: *A Scheme of Education,* 1952.

Indra Sen: *The Message and Mission of Indian Culture,* 1951.

Indra Sen: *Integral Education*, 1952.

Indra Sen: Sri Aurobindo as a World Philosopher, an article published in *Philosophy East and West,* pp. 131-141, October, 1957, January, 1958, University of Hawaii Press.

Maitra, S.K.: The Meeting of the *East and the West in Sri Aurobindo's Philosophy*, 1956.

Pavitra (P.B. Saint-Hillaire): *Education and The Aim of Human Life Sri Aurobindo International Centre of Education*, Pondicherry, May 1961.

Sarma D.S.: *Studies in the Renaissance of Hinduism*, Banaras Hindu University, Banaras, 1944.

Sethna, K.D. : *The Indian Spirit and the World Future*, 1953.

Sri Aurobindo: *A System of National Education*, Arya Publishing House, Calcutta, 1946.

Sri Aurobindo: *Eight Upanisads: Isha, Kena, Katha, Mundaka, Prasana, Mandukya, Taitiriya and Aitareya.*

Sri Aurobindo: *Essays on the Gita*, First Series, 1949.

Sri Aurobindo: *Essay on the Gita,* Second Series, 1949.

Sri Aurobindo: *Sri Aurobindo on Himself and on the Mother,* 1953.

Sri Aurobindo: *Foundations of Indian Culture,* The Sri Aurobindo Library, Inc., New York, 1953.

Sri Aurobindo: *Hymns of the Mystic Fire.*

Sri Aurobindo: *The Human Cycle.*

Sri Aurobindo: *On Education*, 1952.

Sri Aurobindo: *On the Veda,* 1956.

Sri Aurobindo: *On Yoga*, 1955.

Sri Aurobindo: *Physical Education in Sri Aurobindo Ashram*, 1954.

Sri Aurobindo: *The Ideal of Human Unity,* 1950.

Sri Aurobindo: *The Ideal of the Karmayogin.*

Sri Aurobindo: *The Life Divine,* 1955.

Sri Aurobindo: *The Message and Mission of Indian Culture.*

Sri Aurobindo: *The National Value of Art.*

Sri Aurobindo: *The Renaissance in India,* 1951.

Sri Aurobindo: *Savitri,* 1954.

Note : All the above books (excepting the ones indicated otherwise) are published by the Sri Aurobindo Ashram, Pondicherry (India).

On Mahatma Gandhi

Agrawal, S.N.: *Constructive Programme for Students,* Padma Publications, 1945.

Agrawal, S.N.: *The Gandhian Plan,* Padma Publications, Bombay, 1944.

Andrews, C.F.: *Mahatma Gandhi's Ideas,* Alien and Unwin, London, 1929.

Bose, N.K.: *Studies in Gandhism,* Indian Associated Publishing Co., Calcutta, 1947.

Catlin George: *In the Path of Mahatma Gandhi,* Macdonald, London, 1948.

Desai, Mahadev: *The Gospel of Selfless Action or The Gita according to Gandhi* (Chiefly a translation of Gandhi's *Anashaktiyoga*), Navajivan Publishing House, 1946.

Dewey, John: *Democracy and Education,* Macmillan, New York, 1916.

Dewey, John: *The School and Society*, University of Chicago Press, 1936.

Dhawan, Gopinath: *The Political Philosophy of Mahatma Gandhi,* Navajiyan Publishing House, 1951.

Dutta, D.M.: *The Philosophy of Mahatma Gandhi,* University of Wisconsin Press, Canada, 1953.

Fischer, Louis: *A Week with Gandhi*, Duel, Sloan and Pearce, New York, 1942.

Fischer Louis: *The Life of Mahatma Gandhi*, Hai-per, New York, 1950.

Gandhi, M.K.: *An Autobiography, The Story of My Experiments with Truth*, Volume I, translated from Gujrati by Mahadev Desai, Navjivan Press, 1927.

Gandhi, M.K.: *Basic Education,* Navajivan Publishing House, 1951.

Gandhi, M.K.: *Ethical Religion*, Translated by Ramiyer, Ganesan, Madras, 1922.

Gandhi, M.K.: *From Yervada Mandir,* translated by T.G. Desai, Navajivan Press, 1937.

Gandhi, M.K.: *Gandhi Sutras*, ed., D.S. Sarnia, The Devin Adair Co., New York, 1949.

Gandhi, M.K.: *Great Thoughts* of Mahatma Gandhi, Ganesan; Madras (No date).

Gandhi, M.K.: *Hind Swaraj,* Ganesan, Madras, 1921.

Gandhi, M.K.: *Hindu Dharma*, Navajivan Publishing House, 1950.

Gandhi, M.K.: *My Soul's Agony* (Gandhi's Statements on Removal of Untouchability), Navajivan Press, 1932.

Gandhi, M.K.: *Non-Violence in Peace and War*, Parts I & II Navajivan Publishing House, 1945,1949.

Gandhi, M.K.: *Selected Writings of Mahatma Gandhi*, Ed., Renald, Duncan, Faber and Faber, London, 1951.

Gandhi, M.K.: *Selections from Gandhi,* Ed., N.K. Bose, Navajivan Publishing House, 1948.

Gandhi, M.K.: *Towards New Education,* Navajivan Publishing House, 1953.

Gandhi, M.K.: *To the Students*, Navajivan Publishing House, 1949.

Gandhi, M.K.: *To the Women,* Ed. A.T. Hingoram, Karachi, 1941.

Gandhi, M.K.: *Young India,* 1919-22. Tagore and Co., Madras, 1922.

Gandhi, M.K.: *Young India,* Vol. I, 1919-22, Ganesan, Madras, 1922.

Gandhi, M.K.: *Young India,* Vol. II, 1924-26, Ganesan, Madras 1927.

Gandhi, M.K.: *Young India,* Vol. III, 1927-28, Ganesan, Madras, 1935.

Government of India: *The Report of the University Education Commission, 1949* (Radhakrishnan), Manager of Publications, Delhi, 1950 .

Government, Kerala State: *Towards Basic Education—* Government Press, Trivendrum, 1958.

Gregg, Richard B. : *Gandhism and Socialism,* Ganesan, Madras, 1931.

Hampton, H.V., Saiyidain, K.G. and Others: *The Educational System*, Oxford University Press, London, 1943.

Hindustani Talim Sangh, Wardha: *Basic National Education, Report of the Zakir Husain Committee and the detailed Syllabus,* 1939.

Hindustani Talim Sangh, *Wardha: Educational Reconstruction, A Collection of Gandhi's Articles on the Wardha Scheme,* the Zakir Husain Report and Syllabus, and Proceedings of the All India Education Conference at Wardha, 3rd Ed., 1939.

Hindustani Talim Sangh, Wardha: *One Step Forward,* the Report of the First Conference of Basic National Education, Poona, 1939, 1942.

Hindustani Talim Sangh, Wardha: *Two Years Work,* Report of the Second Basic Education Conference, Delhi 1941,1942.

Hindustani Talim Sangh, Wardha: *Report of the Fifth All India Basic Education Conference, 1949-50.*

Hindustani Talim Sangh, Wardha: *Report of the Sixth All India Basic Education Conference, 1950-51.*

Hindustani Talim Sangh, Wardha: *Report of the Seventh All India Basic Education Conference,* Sevagram, 1951-52.

Hindustani Talim Sangh, Wardha: *Sixth Annual Report of the Hindustani Talim Sangh, 1938-44,*1946.

Hindustani Talim Sangh, Wardha: *Seven Years of Work, Eighth Annual Report of Nai Talim, 1928-45.*

Hindustani Talim Sangh, Wardha: *The Third Annual Report, 1940-41.*

Husain, Zakir: *Post-War Education, Institute of Pacific Relations,* New York, 1942.

Jeffreys, M.V.C.: *Education Christian or Pagan,* University of London Press, London, 1946.

Jeffreys, M.V.C.: *Glaucon and Inquiry into the Aims of Education,* Pitman, London, 1950.

Jones, E, Stanley: *Mahatma Gandhi: An Interpretation*, Hodder and Stoughton, London, 1948.

Kumarappa, J.C. : *Why the Village Movement*? A.I.V.I.A. Wardha, 1936.

Kumarappa, J.C. : *Education for Life*, Hindustan Publishing Co. Rajamundary, 1937.

Kumarappa, J.C.: *Gandhian Economic Thought,* Vora & Co., Bombay, 1951.

Kripalani, J.B.: *The Latest Fad, Basic Education*, Hindustani Talim Sangh, 1939.

Mani, R.S.: *Educational Ideas and Ideals of Gandhi & Tagore*, New Book Society of India, New Delhi, Nov. 1961.

Mekee, William J.: *New Schools for Young India*, University of North Carolina Press, 1930.

Menon, T.K.N. (Editor): *A Symposium on Post War Education in India,* Padmaja Publications, Baroda, 1945.

Ministry of Education, Government of India, Delhi: *Basic and Social Education,* Delhi, 1948.

Ministry of Education, Government of India, Delhi: Progress of Education in India 1937-47, *Decennial Review*, 2 Vols. 1948.

Ministry of Education, Government of India, Delhi: *Report of the Assessment Committee on Basic Education, 1956.*

Ministry of Education, Government of India, Delhi: *Report of the Secondary Education Commission,* Ministry of Education, Delhi, 1953.

Ministry of Education, Government of India, Delhi: *Post-War Educational Development in India,* Report of Central Advisory Board of Education, Manager of Publications, Delhi, 1947.

Ministry of Education, Government of India, Delhi: *Selections from Education Records,* Vols. I & II, Government Printing, Calcutta, 1920,1922.

Patel M.S.: *The Educational Philosophy of Mahatma Gandhi,* Navajivan Publishing House, 1953.

Periodicals and Newspapers

The Asiatic Review (Quarterly), London, July, 1939.

Harijan (Weekly), 1933-40; 1946,49, Navajivan Press.

*Journal of Education and Psycology (*Quarterly), Baroda, April, 1948.

Young India (Weekly, 1919-1932), Navajivan Press.

Pillai, N.P.: *The Educational Aims of Mahatma Gandhi,* Kalyanmandir Publications.Trivandrum, 1959.

Polak, H.S.L., *Brailsford, H.N. Pethick,* Lawrence: Mahatma Gandhi, Odhams, London, 1949.

Pyarelal: *A Nation Builder at Work*, Navajivan Press, 1952.

Pyarelal: *A Pilgrimage for Peace*, Navajivan Press, 1950.

Pyarelal: *Mahatma Gandhi—The Last Phase*, Vols. I & II, Navajivan Publishing House, 1956, 1958.

Reynolds, *Reginald: India, Gandhi and World Peace*, London, 1931.

Rolland, Romain: *Mahatma Gandhi*, Allen and Unwin London, 1924.

Saiyidain, K.G.: *Education for International Understanding,* Hind Kitabs Ltd., Bombay, 1948.

Saiyidain, K.G.: *Introducing the Basic Curriculum,* 1949.

Saiyidain, K.G.: *The Message of the New Education,* The New Education Fellowship, London, 1938.

Shrimali, K.L.: *The Wardha Scheme of Education,* Vidyabhavan Society, Udaipur, 1949.

Tendulkar, D.G.: *Mahatma*, 8 Vols. Jhaveri and Tendulkar, Bombay, 1951-54.

Tendulkar, D.G. and Others (Editor): *Gandhiji; His Life and Works,* Karnatak Publishing House, Bombay, 1944.

The Indian Review (Monthly), Madras, October, 1949.
The Indian Social Reformer (Weekly), Bombay, 12.12.46.
The New Era in Home and School (Monthly), London, May 1938.
The Year Book of Education (Annual), Evans London, 1940 and 1952.
Varkey, G.J.: *The Wardha Scheme,* Oxford University Press, London, 1939.
Visva Bharat, Quarterly: Gandhi Memorial Peace Number, Shantiniketan, 1940.

On Rabindranath Tagore

Tagore: *Creative Unity,* Macmillan, 1950.
Tagore: *Crescent Moon.*
Tagore : *Gitanjali,* Translated by the author, first published by the India Society, London and in 1913, by Macmillan.
Tagore: *Nationalism,* Lectures delivered in Japan and U.S.A., The Macmillan Co., New York.
Tagore: *Personality, Essays and Lectures delivered in America in 1918.*
Tagore: *The Parrot Training, a Satire on Educational Methods,* Thacker, Spink Co. Calcutta.
Tagore: *The Religion of Man, the Hibber Lectures*, George Allen and Unwin, 1930.
Tagore: *Sadhana,* Lectures delivered at the Harvard University, U.S.A. in 1912-13.
Tagore: *Reminiscences,* Macmillan & Co. Ltd., London 1933.
Tagore: *The Garden,* Collected Poems and Plays of Rabindranath Tagore, Macmillan & Co. Ltd., London, 1939.
Tagore : *City and Village,* Bulletin No. 10, Visva Bharati, Shantiniketan, September, 1946.
Tagore: *Rabindranath Tagore: On Art and Aesthetics,* Orient Longmans, Calcutta, 1961.
Tagore: *Rabindranath Tagore: Pioneer in Education*; Essays and Exchanges between Rabindranath Tagore and L.K. Elmhirst, John Murray, London, 1961.
Andrews, C.F. (Editor): *Thoughts from Tagore.*
Aronson, Alex.: *Rabindranath's Educational Ideals and the West.*

Bhattacharya, V.: Tagore: *The Citizen of the World,* Matropolitan Book Co. Private Ltd., Delhi, May 1961.

Bose, Nandlal: The Place of Art in Education, Article in *the New Education Fellowship Bulletin,* April, 1937, Shantiniketan, Bengal.

Chattopadhyaya, J.: *Rabindranath and His Ashram School.*

Das Gupta, S.N.: *Rabi Dipika.*

Das Gupta, S.: *Tagore's Asian Outlook*, Nava Bharati, Calcutta, May, 1961.

East and West, Two Patterns by Gilbert Murray and Tagore, International Institute of Intellectual Co-operation, Paris.

Education Number, 1947 of the *Visva Bharati Quarterly.*

Education Naturalised, a Lecture Translated by Surendra Nath Tagore, Shantiniketan.

Ghose, T.: *Rabindranath's Contribution to Education.*

Gupta Rameshwar: *The Essential Tagore*, Chetnagar, Banasthali Rajasthan, India, 1961.

Louis, J.A. Mercier: *The Challenge of Humanism.*

Mani, R.S.: *Educational Ideas and Ideals of Gandhi & Tagore*, New Book Society of India, New Delhi, Nov. 1961.

Memorandum of Association, Statutes, Regulations and Rules—*Bulletin No. 5, Visva Bharati,* Shantiniketan, July, 1945.

Mahalanobis, P.C.: Rabindranath Tagore's Visit to Canada, *Bulletin No. 14, Visva Bharati,* Shantiniketan, November, 1929.

Narvane, V.S.: *Rabindranath Tagore,* Central Book Depot, Allahabad.

Pearson, W.D.: *Shantiniketan*, London, Macmillan & Co. Ltd., 1916.

Radhakrishnan, S.: *The Philosophy of Rabindranath Tagore*, Good Companions Publishers, Baroda, India, 1961.

Rasdael, H.: *Theory of Good and Evil*, Volume II.

Rhy, Ernest: Rabindranath Tagore, London, Macmillan & Co., 1916. Shantiniketan and the Educational Institution, *Bulletin No. 12, Vishva Bharati*, Shantiniketan, February, 1929.

Sinha, Saradhar: *Social Thinking of Rabindranath Tagore*, Asia Publishing House, Bombay, 1962.

Sriniketan, The Institute of Rural Reconstruction, *Bulletin No. 11, Vishva Bharati,* Shantiniketan, December, 1928.

Supur, An Experiment in Rural Reconstruction, *Bulletin No. 28, Vishva Bharati,* Shantiniketan, September, 1940.

Soara, AX (Editor): *Lectures and Addresses by Rabindranath Tagore*, London, Macmillan & Co., 1921.

Tagore, S.: *Rabindranath Tagore and Universal Humanism,* Standard Vacuum Oil Company, Bombay, 1961.

Tagore, *Centenary Souvenir*, Published by S.L. Sharma, Ring Road, New Delhi,1961.

Thompson, Edward: Rabindranath Tagore, His Life and Work, Association Press, 1928. *The Vishva Bharati,* Quarterly, Shantiniketan.

Vishva Bharati, A Brief Account of the Institution, *Bulletin No. 30, Vishva Bharati*, Shantiniketan, December, 1941.

Vishva Bharati News, Volume XIV, No. 8, February, 1946, Shantiniketan, Shantiniketan Press.

The Modern Review, Calcutta.

On What We Can Imbibe

The main works of the respective educational philosophers as mentioned above.

INDEX